GREATEST 100 MATCHES

CONTENTS

Foreword by Ricky "The Dragon" Steamboat 4

"Macho Man" Randy Savage vs.
   Ricky "The Dragon" Steamboat — March 29, 1987 6

Shawn Michaels vs. Ric Flair — March 30, 2008 8

The Rock vs. Triple H — August 30, 1998 10

Undertaker vs. Edge — August 17, 2008 12

Buddy "Nature Boy" Rogers vs.
   Bruno Sammartino — May 17, 1963 14

Jeri-Show vs. D-Generation X — December 13, 2009 16

Shawn Michaels vs. Stone Cold Steve Austin — March 29, 1998 18

John Cena vs. Randy Orton — December 15, 2013 20

Iron Sheik vs. Hulk Hogan — January 23, 1984 22

Undertaker vs. Mankind — June 28, 1998 24

CM Punk vs. John Cena — July 17, 2011 26

The Shield vs. The Wyatt Family — February 23, 2014 28

Royal Rumble 2002 — January 20, 2002 30

Hulk Hogan & Mr. T vs. Roddy Piper
   & "Mr. Wonderful" Paul Orndorff — March 31, 1985 32

Trish Status vs. Lita — September 17, 2006 34

Bob Backlund vs. Stan Hansen — April 6, 1981 36

Shawn Michaels vs. Shelton Benjamin — May 2, 2005 38

The Rock vs. "Hollywood" Hulk Hogan — March 17, 2002 40

Undertaker vs. The Rock vs. Kurt Angle — July 21, 2002 42

Daniel Bryan vs. Dolph Ziggler — October 24, 2010 44

Sgt. Slaughter vs. Pat Patterson — May 4, 1981 46

Sami Zayn vs. Cesaro — August 21, 2013 48

The Hart Foundation vs. Team Austin — July 6, 1997 50

Money in the Bank 2012 — July 15, 2012 52

Team Piper vs. Team Flair — November 27, 1991 54

The Rock vs. Mankind — January 4, 1999 56

Shawn Michaels vs. Razor Ramon — March 20, 1994 58

John Cena vs. Daniel Bryan — August 18, 2013 60

Kurt Angle vs. Brock Lesnar — September 18, 2003 62

Royal Rumble 2011 — January 30, 2011 64

Stone Cold Steve Austin vs. Chris Jericho — December 9, 2001 66

Bruno Sammartino vs.
   "Superstar" Billy Graham — April 30, 1977 68

Undertaker vs. Jeff Hardy — July 1, 2002 70

Paige vs. Emma — February 27, 2014 72

Bret "Hit Man" Hart vs. Owen Hart — August 29, 1994 74

Undertaker vs. Brock Lesnar — April 6, 2014 76

Team WWE vs. Team Alliance — November 18, 2001 78

Hulk Hogan vs. Andre the Giant — February 5, 1988 80

The Rock vs. Brock Lesnar — August 25, 2002 82

John Cena vs. Kurt Angle vs.
   Shawn Michaels — November 1, 2005 84

Triple H vs. Cactus Jack — February 27, 2000 86

The Usos vs. The Wyatt Family — July 20, 2014 88

Randy Orton vs. Ric Flair — October 19, 2004 90

The British Bulldogs vs. Nikolai Volkoff
   & Iron Sheik — May 3, 1986 92

The Dudley Boyz vs. The Hardy Boyz vs.
   Edge & Christian — April 1, 2001 94

Mr. Perfect vs. Ric Flair — January 24, 1993 96

Triple H vs. Shawn Michaels — August 25, 2002 98

Triple H vs. Batista — April 3, 2005 100

Bret "Hit Man" Hart vs. The 1-2-3 Kid — July 11, 1994 102

The Shield vs. Evolution — June 1, 2014 104

Bret "Hit Man" Hart vs.
 Stone Cold Steve Austin—March 23, 1997 106

Triple H, Mr. McMahon, & Shane McMahon vs. The Rock,
 Undertaker, & Kane—June 25, 2000 108

Brock Lesnar vs. Eddie Guerrero—February 15, 2004 110

Shawn Michaels vs. Kurt Angle—April 3, 2005 112

Sasha Banks vs. Bayley—August 22, 2015.....................114

Hulk Hogan vs. Andre the Giant—March 29, 1987 116

Triple H vs. Shawn Michaels vs. Chris Jericho vs. Kane vs.
 Booker T vs. Rob Van Dam—November 17, 2002 118

'Superstar' Billy Graham vs.
 Dusty Rhodes—October 24, 1977 120

Batista vs. Undertaker—April 1, 2007 122

Rey Mysterio vs. John Cena—July 25, 2011 124

Randy Orton vs. Batista vs. Daniel Bryan—April 6, 2014 126

Bret "Hit Man" Hart vs. Shawn Michaels—March 31, 1996..........128

Chris Benoit vs. Chris Jericho—January 21, 2001 130

John Cena vs. Kevin Owens—May 31, 2015....................132

Randy Orton vs. Cactus Jack—April 18, 2004 134

Shawn Michaels vs. Chris Jericho—March 30, 2003...................136

Bruno Sammartino vs. Larry Zbyszko—August 9, 1980.................138

Royal Rumble 2001—January 21, 2001.........................140

Edge vs. Ric Flair—January 16, 2006...........................142

John Cena vs. CM Punk—February 25, 2013 144

Bret "Hit Man" Hart vs. Bam Bam Bigelow—June 13, 1993 146

The Rock vs. Stone Cold Steve Austin—March 28, 1999.............148

Trish Stratus vs. Mickie James—April 2, 2006..................150

Team Savage vs. Team Honky Tonk—November 26, 1987...........152

John Cena vs. Rob Van Dam—June 11, 2006................154

John Cena vs. Shawn Michaels—April 23, 2007...........................158

Kurt Angle vs. Triple H vs. Rikishi vs. Undertaker vs.
 Stone Cold vs. The Rock—December 10, 2000 160

Owen Hart vs. British Bulldog—March 3, 1997............................162

Triple H vs. Randy Orton—October 7, 2007 164

"Macho Man" Randy Savage vs. Hulk Hogan—April 2, 1989 166

Triple H vs. Undertaker—April 1, 2012 168

The Rock vs. Kurt Angle—October 22, 2000 170

Charlotte vs. Bayley vs. Becky Lynch vs.
 Sasha Banks—February 11, 2015...............................172

Jeff Hardy vs. CM Punk—August 23, 2009 174

The Rock vs. Stone Cold Steve Austin—April 1, 2001 176

Mr. Perfect vs. Bret "Hit Man" Hart—August 26, 1991 178

Brock Lesnar vs. John Cena vs.
 Seth Rollins—January 25, 2015 180

Daniel Bryan vs. Cody Rhodes vs. Big Show vs. Santino Marella vs.
 The Great Khali vs. Wade Barrett—February 19, 2012 182

Undertaker vs. Shawn Michaels—October 5, 1997 184

The Two-Man Power Trip vs.
 The Brothers of Destruction—April 29, 2001.............................186

John Cena vs. The Rock—April 1, 2012.........................188

Hulk Hogan vs. Ultimate Warrior—April 1, 1990 190

CM Punk vs. Chris Jericho—April 29, 2012 192

Bret "Hit Man" Hart vs. The British Bulldog—August 29, 1992.....194

John Cena vs. Brock Lesnar—August 17, 2014....................196

Triple H vs. The Rock—August 26, 1999 198

Royal Rumble 1992—January 19, 1992.........................200

Undertaker vs. Shawn Michaels—April 5, 2009 202

Ultimate Warrior vs.
 "Macho King" Randy Savage—March 24, 1991 204

FOREWORD

by Ricky "The Dragon" Steamboat

Ricky "The Dragon" Steamboat vs. "Macho Man" Randy Savage—March 29, 1987

This match made a statement. The bar was raised and the standard blueprint for how to design a match was forever changed. This match, not knowing then but knowing now, changed my career as well as my life.

The power that one great match can have is astounding. Each match that you will read about in this book has undoubtedly left its own unique mark on the Superstars involved, as well as the course of WWE history. But since WWE has given me the honor of introducing this collection, let me tell you about the one that I will be forever tied to…

Savage and I, from the very beginning, were set on putting on a match that would be different and also take advantage of how huge this 'Mania would prove to be. Hearing the numbers coming in—50,000 tickets sold…60,000… 70,000…80,000…90,000—this event promised to be the biggest of all time. We both agreed that the story should be centered on the Championship rather than me seeking revenge. Beating Savage for the Intercontinental Championship should prove to hurt him more than I could hurt him physically. The two of us would take notes and quiz each other night after night leading up to the show. My character was making a comeback from what could have been a career-ending injury and winning the Championship would speak volumes.

I remember the roar of the crowd as I was riding down in the cart with George Steele. I had to get in the mindset and focus on the ring. It is sort of like tunnel vision—you are aware of everything around you, but then again, you are not…

Focus on the ring.

Focus on the ring.

The match kept a perfect pace—quick and fast at times, then slow and deliberate during the rest. George had a few moments: helping me back in the ring, stealing the Title from Savage, shoving Randy off the top rope. Each one of these moments was crucial in the match.

The thing that made the match so different was the number of false finishes. There were 21. That's right, 21, in a match that went 17 minutes! Savage and I covered each other every 45 seconds and took the crowd, the announcers, the people at home, and even the boys in the back on a ride that is still talked about and celebrated decades later. And it was all about two guys trying to beat each other in a match that revolved around the Championship.

After 21 false finishes, who would have thought that a simple Small Package would have received that type of reaction for the final 1-2-3? It was the match that made it happen. We didn't need a Ricky Steamboat cross body off the top rope, a Jake Roberts DDT, a Hogan Leg Drop. We didn't need a Stone Cold Stunner, a People's Elbow, or Ric Flair's Figure-Four Leg Lock. We could have used *anything* to finish that match and garnered that same reaction. What made the Small Package finish was the ride—it was *the match*.

For all its accolades, I am thrilled to see my most definitive match leading off this celebration of the greatest WWE matches of all time. I hope you enjoy it.

5

"MACHO MAN" RANDY SAVAGE

VS.

RICKY "THE DRAGON" STEAMBOAT

THE LEAD-UP

Sports-entertainment matches often fall into two major categories: competitors looking to win a Championship or competitors settling a personal grudge. The match between Ricky "The Dragon" Steamboat and "Macho Man" Randy Savage at *WrestleMania III* can easily fit into both categories. A few months earlier, when challenging Savage for the Intercontinental Championship, Steamboat found himself facing a potential career-ending injury. Draped over a guard rail outside the ring, Steamboat's larynx was driven into the rail by a Macho Man elbow off the top rope. Some may have thought it was an accident until Savage looked to finish the job by driving the ring bell into Steamboat's throat. The diagnosis was a crushed larynx and many questioned if he'd ever wrestle again. But Steamboat's will and heart were not to be denied, and The Dragon returned, looking for revenge against Savage, as well as another shot at the Intercontinental Championship.

WWE BOOKS

WRESTLEMANIA III
INTERCONTINENTAL CHAMPIONSHIP MATCH

March 29, 1987
Pontiac Silverdome
Pontiac, Michigan

6

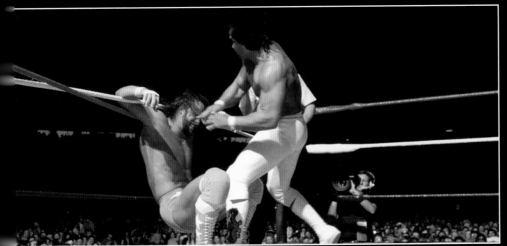

THE MATCH

Looking to neutralize Savage's manager Miss Elizabeth, Steamboat was accompanied to the ring by George "The Animal" Steele. Savage and Steamboat locked up before Steamboat took control with some powerful arm drag takedowns and a deliberate chokehold. The latter move was surprising, as The Dragon tended to follow the rules, but it may have reflected Steamboat's frustration with Macho Man's deliberate attempt to injure him in their earlier match.

Control of the match moved at a blazing speed the WWE Universe was not accustomed to seeing. The two men were evenly matched, comfortable with high-flying moves off the top turnbuckle as well as technical mat wrestling. Each man came tantalizingly close to winning again and again, as the bout was filled with a number of near pinfalls. Savage would hit Steamboat with a wrestling move and The Dragon would then counter into a different move. Savage focused some of his offense on Steamboat's throat, and Steamboat showed an uncharacteristic brutality in his offense, intensifying his attack when Savage was tied up in the ropes and the official was trying to free the Champion. Steamboat was almost counted out at one point when Savage tossed him over the guard rail, but his friend Steele picked him up and brought him back to the ring before the official could complete the 10-count.

Unfortunately, during a collision between the two Superstars, the official was knocked down. The lack of a referee definitely hurt Macho Man's chances of winning. Savage slammed Steamboat to the canvas and then hit The Dragon with his patented flying elbow off the top turnbuckle. The lack of an official to make the three-count frustrated Savage. Macho Man tried to bring the bell into the ring, perhaps looking to repeat the injury to Steamboat's throat. Luckily, George "The Animal" Steele was there to prevent Savage's plan, and when Macho Man tried to grab the bell again, Steele slammed him into the ring. The delay allowed Steamboat to recover. When Savage tried to body slam The Dragon, Steamboat was able to turn the maneuver into a small package. The official counted three, and Ricky "The Dragon" Steamboat was the new Intercontinental Champion.

Savage attempted to regain the Title from Steamboat, but he was not successful. However, The Dragon did not keep the Championship long. Just two and a half

SHAWN MICHAELS vs. RIC FLAIR

WRESTLEMANIA XXIV
CAREER THREATENING MATCH FOR RIC FLAIR

March 30, 2008

Citrus Bowl
Orlando, Florida

THE MATCH

The two competitors locked up to start the match with Flair giving Michaels a hard shove while yelling "Old Yeller!" The Nature Boy was clearly taking exception to Michaels' comments earlier that he was going to put Flair down like the cinematic dog. Michaels responded with a hard shove of his own, one that caused Flair to bleed from the mouth. Flair shook off the cut, and delivered a series of his signature knife-edge chops, and Michaels reversed their positions and countered with some chops of his own. Flair demonstrated things would not be easy for HBK with a knee drop, body slam off the top rope, and a high cross body. Michaels looked to end the match with a moonsault off the second rope onto Flair, but the Nature Boy moved out of the way and the Heartbreak Kid landed on the announcers' table with a strong enough force to break it.

Michaels was almost counted out, but he returned to the ring by eight. Flair pressed his advantage, hitting Michaels with a side suplex, a double-underhook suplex, and a standing vertical suplex, but each move only resulted in two counts. Michaels finally stemmed Flair's offense with a swinging neckbreaker and then dumped Flair out of the ring. Again Michaels tried a risky moonsault, this time from the top rope. He had a better result, knocking down the Nature Boy. Both men were down and barely responded to the official's 10-count, but each did make it back into the ring. The two traded blistering chops, and Michaels got the better of the exchange. Michaels had the Nature Boy set up for Sweet Chin Music, but HBK could not bring himself to deliver the finishing blow. While Michaels stopped, unable to hit the kick, Flair took advantage, wrapping Michaels' legs in the Figure-Four submission move. Michaels was able to flip over, putting the pressure on Flair's legs and forcing him to break the hold.

After a chop block and dodging a Michaels' enziguri, Flair locked in a second Figure-Four, putting Michaels in excruciating pain. Michaels tried desperately to reach the ropes and again attempted to flip over and transfer the pain to Flair. But this time Flair was ready and he rolled through, keeping the move on. However, the roll put Michaels closer to the ropes and he was able to force a break. Flair celebrated his moves, but that proved costly—turning his attention back to Michaels, Flair ate a Sweet Chin Music. The Nature Boy barely kicked out of the pinning combination.

Michaels tried to pick up Flair, but the Nature Boy lived up to his "Dirtiest Player in the Game" rep by hitting HBK with a low blow that the official did not see. Michaels eventually landed a second Sweet Chin Music and again set himself in the corner to tune up the band and perform the match-ending move. Again, Michaels hesitated, but Flair put up his fists and insisted Michaels give his best. After mouthing "I'm sorry…I love you," Michaels hit his third Sweet Chin Music of the match, pinning Flair and ending the Nature Boy's illustrious career.

THE AFTERMATH

Michaels, after pinning Flair, quickly left the ring, giving the spotlight to his longtime friend. Overwhelmed by the emotion of the situation, Flair broke down in the ring and then rolled out and shared a series of hugs and kisses with his family sitting at ringside. The WWE Universe was given the opportunity to see a proper sendoff for the Nature Boy the next night on *Raw*. Not only did Flair give a farewell speech, but a series of former allies and rivals came out to salute Flair's amazing four-decade career.

THE ROCK
vs.
TRIPLE H

SUMMERSLAM 1998
LADDER MATCH FOR THE INTERCONTINENTAL CHAMPIONSHIP

August 30, 1998

Madison Square Garden
New York, New York

THE LEAD-UP

In 1998, the rivalry between Triple H and The Rock was not just a personal conflict between two Superstars—it was war between two factions. Triple H and D-Generation X found themselves constantly at odds with The Rock and his Nation. A fair and balanced match seemed almost impossible, as both sides continually interfered in bouts to either help one of their teammates or screw over a member of the opposing stable. The month before, Triple H and The Rock had fought to a time-limit draw in a 2-out-of 3 Falls Match for the Intercontinental Championship, so the rematch at *SummerSlam* was set to be a Ladder Match.

THE MATCH

Both men came to the ring with backup. Triple H brought the 9th Wonder of the World, Chyna, while The Rock had the World's Strongest Man, Mark Henry, backing him up. After the Title was raised to the rafters, Triple H came out strong with a series of punches. The Rock tried to regain the momentum by whipping The Game into the ropes, but the Great One ate a knee to the face instead. Triple H went for an early Pedigree, but The Rock countered with a back body drop over the top rope that dumped the challenger out of the ring. The Rock tried to get the ladder, but Triple H caught the Brahma Bull and slammed him against the guardrails and dragged the Champion back to the ring.

Triple H continued his assault on The Rock, downing the Champion with a high knee. Thinking he was in an advantageous position, the challenger went for the ladder, but The Rock followed him out of the ring, slammed the challenger to the ground, and brought the ladder to the edge of the ring. Triple H tried to punch The Rock, but the Champion tossed The Game into the ladder. The Rock set up the ladder and began climbing it, but Triple H leapt off the top turnbuckle and knocked the Champion off the ladder. After ramming the ladder into The Rock's midsection, Triple H tried to climb up to the Title, but The Rock pulled him off the ladder. The Champion then started targeting Triple H's right leg and knee, pinning it inside the ladder and using both his legs and a chair to drive the ladder into the challenger's knee.

The Rock propped the ladder from the ring steps to the guardrail and slammed the challenger on the ladder, following it up with an elbow on Triple H. The Rock brought the ladder back into the ring and once again, began the ascent to the Title, but Triple H shoved him off. Triple H took the ladder outside the ring and tried to slam The Rock into it, but the Champion reversed the move and catapulted Triple H into the ladder. Triple H then tried to Pedigree The Rock onto the ladder, but The Great One gave him a back body drop right onto the ladder instead. Triple H kicked the ladder into The Rock, cutting the Champion's face open. The two men each climbed one side of the ladder, but both ended up knocked off. The Champion tried to hit Triple H with the ladder, but the challenger slammed the ladder into The Rock using a foreign object.

Triple H thought he had the advantage but The Rock smashed Triple H onto the ladder and then gave The Game a People's Elbow on top. Triple H climbed the ladder and attempted to jump onto The Rock, but The Great One countered and delivered a Rock Bottom. Before The Rock could take advantage, the challenger nailed him with a Pedigree. Mark Henry blinded the challenger with powder, yet Triple H still tried to climb the ladder to the Title. The Rock started climbing the other side, but Chyna gave the Champion a low blow, which caused him to fall. Triple H grabbed the Title and became Intercontinental Champion.

THE AFTERMATH

Triple H ended The Rock's eight-month reign as Intercontinental Champion, but The Game did not hold on to the Title for long. A knee injury forced Triple H to vacate the Championship, and WWE held an 8-man tournament to crown a new Champion. The Game's DX stablemate, X-Pac, made it to the finals, but he fell to the World's Most Dangerous Man, Ken Shamrock. Both Triple H and The Rock continued their rivalry over a much bigger prize, the WWE Championship. The Rock won the Title at *Survivor Series 1998*, and less than a year later, Triple H won his first WWE Championship the day after *SummerSlam 1999*.

UNDERTAKER
vs. EDGE

SUMMERSLAM 2008
HELL IN A CELL

August 17, 2008

Conseco Fieldhouse
Indianapolis, Indiana

THE LEAD-UP

Edge and Undertaker had an epic rivalry for the World Heavyweight Championship from late 2007 throughout 2008. Edge won the Title at *Armageddon 2007*, but Undertaker defeated the Rated-R Superstar for the Championship at *WrestleMania XXIV*. Edge's fiancée, Vickie Guerrero, continued to tip the odds in Edge's favor until *One Night Stand*, where after Undertaker lost to Edge, The Deadman was forced to leave WWE. Months later, when it was clear that the Rated-R Superstar was cheating on her, Vickie used her powers as *SmackDown* General Manager to both re-instate Undertaker and set up a Hell in a Cell match between Edge and Undertaker at *SummerSlam*.

THE MATCH

A maniacally grinning Edge danced around Undertaker early on, dodging The Deadman's strikes and landing some blows of his own. Undertaker finally landed some offense when he hit a big boot to Edge's face. The two ended up outside the ring, and Undertaker drove the Rated-R Superstar's back into the cell wall. Undertaker rolled Edge back into the ring, and then brought the ring steps into the ring as well. He propped them into the corner and tossed Edge into them. Undertaker tried to do it a second time, but Edge reversed the move and tossed The Deadman into the steel steps. Edge then drop kicked and Speared Undertaker into the steps.

Although new to Hell in a Cell, Edge was a veteran of TLC matches, and decided to bring their flavor to this match. He set up a two-story tower of tables and a ladder he found underneath the ring. Edge draped Undertaker across a table and then jumped off the ladder and onto The Deadman, driving him through the table. Edge attempted to pin Undertaker, but only got a two-count. The Rated-R Superstar tried to deliver a Conchairto, but Undertaker blocked the move and tossed Edge outside the ring. Aiming to punish Edge more, Undertaker followed the Rated-R Superstar, but Edge Speared The Deadman through one of the cell panels.

The two men started brawling outside of the cell. Undertaker tossed Edge into a security wall and tried to plaster Edge with a TV monitor, but Edge ducked and instead hit Undertaker with one. Putting a dazed Undertaker on top of one of the announcers' desks, Edge ran across the other announcers' table to Spear Undertaker through the table. Back in the cell, Edge found a camera under the ring and plastered The Deadman with it. He started to follow that up with a Spear, but Undertaker caught him by the throat and delivered a Chokeslam. Both men were woozy, but Edge hit an Impaler DDT for a two-count. Undertaker attempted a Last Ride on Edge, but the Rated-R Superstar reversed the move into a Spear and another almost pinfall.

Undertaker finally did hit that Last Ride, but Edge kicked out at two. Undertaker tried to Tombstone Edge from the stairs, but Edge escaped by slamming The Deadman's back onto the stairs. Edge tried to mock the Undertaker by going Old School, but Undertaker Chokeslammed Edge through the two tables Edge had set up earlier in the match. Undertaker demonstrated that he, too, could steal an opponent's move by Spearing Edge. He grabbed the TV camera Edge used earlier and hit the Rated-R Superstar with it, following it up with a Conchairto on Edge. All that was left was the Tombstone Piledriver and the three-count, giving Undertaker the victory.

THE AFTERMATH

Undertaker left the ring and started up the entrance ramp when he saw Edge stirring on the Titantron. Angry that he had not done more to incapacitate the Rated-R Superstar, The Deadman returned to the ring and tossed Edge onto a ladder. Placing a second ladder next to the first, Undertaker climbed up beside the Rated-R Superstar and delivered a Chokeslam off the ladder that sent Edge crashing through the ring itself. As flames erupted from the hole in the ring, it seemed The Deadman had sent Edge right to Hell.

BUDDY "NATURE BOY" ROGERS vs.

THE LEAD-UP

Throughout the 1950s and early 1960s, Capitol Wrestling (a precursor to today's WWE) was a member of the National Wrestling Alliance. A wrestler that Capitol promoted, Buddy Rogers, captured the NWA's World Heavyweight Championship in 1961, and lost the Title in controversial fashion in January 1963. Former NWA Champion Lou Thesz defeated Rogers in a single-fall match to capture the Title, but Capitol refused to recognize the switch because NWA World Title matches were supposed to be two out of three falls. To make their protestations even more clear, Capitol withdrew from the NWA and held a tournament to crown its own World Champion, a tournament won by Rogers, making him the first WWE Champion.

BRUNO SAMMARTINO

WWE CHAMPIONSHIP MATCH

May 17, 1963
Madison Square Garden
New York, New York

The new WWE Champion Rogers had a tall task ahead of him, as his first major Title defense would be against Bruno Sammartino. The Italian Strongman had become a bit of a sensation with his impressive weight-lifting records, and he used that strength to his advantage in the ring. People flocked to see Sammartino compete in both singles competition and in tag teams with his partner, future Hall of Famer Antonino Rocca. When he earned the #1 contender spot, fans eagerly anticipated his match against the hated Rogers.

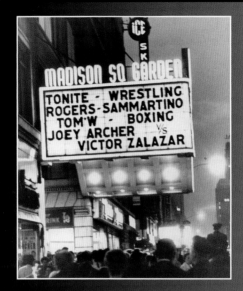

THE MATCH

The Title bout between Rogers and Sammartino was set for Madison Square Garden in May, 1963. In the days of the wrestling territories, WWE promoted matches up and down the northeast, or "Maine to Maryland" as it was known back then. Marquee events were held in Boston, Philadelphia, Washington, D.C., and other cities, but the crown jewel of the region was New York. In the city, nothing could top Madison Square Garden as the preeminent venue. The arena sold out for the highly anticipated Title match, and it was difficult to decide whether fans were more passionate about seeing Sammartino win or Rogers lose.

Rogers and Sammartino met in a match in Toronto in August 1962 when Rogers was the NWA World Champion. Rogers was injured during the bout and Sammartino won the match. However, Bruno would not accept the NWA Title because of the Champion's injury. As they prepared to meet for the WWE Championship eight months later, the fans of Bruno had to hope that he would prove a successful challenger yet again, and would accept the Title this time.

The match itself was a bit anticlimactic, as Sammartino dominated the match with three moves. Starting off with a drop kick, Sammartino then locked the Champion into a powerful bear hug. The Italian strongman then rolled Rogers into Sammartino's patented backbreaker move, and Rogers had no choice but to submit. The crowd was stunned. They hoped to see their hero win the Title, but no one guessed it would happen in less than a minute. But Bruno Sammartino was the WWE Champion, the second one in the company's history.

THE AFTERMATH

Fans eagerly anticipated a rematch between the first and second WWE Champions. It seemed likely to happen, and was even announced as a match for October 3, 1963. However, the physical ailments that plagued Rogers during his first match with Sammartino continued to linger, so Rogers announced his retirement. He made a few short comebacks, but his time in main events was largely over. However, those looking to catch a sight of Rogers can look in a number of directions. His influence continues to be felt in sports-entertainment, particularly in the ring style of a second "Nature Boy," Ric Flair. Rogers interview style, ring moves, and cocky and brash manner is emulated by a number of Superstars to this day. It is no wonder that Rogers was a member of the first full class of WWE Hall of Fame inductees in 1994.

While Rogers' reign as WWE Champion was short, his successor Sammartino had an incredibly long run with the Title. The Living Legend held on to the Championship for the rest of the decade and into the 1970s, before finally losing the Title to Ivan Koloff in 1971. Less than three years later, Sammartino captured the Championship again, becoming the first repeat Champion in WWE history. Throughout his two reigns as Champion, Sammartino was a beloved figure, selling out Madison Square Garden almost 200 times. He joined Rogers in the WWE Hall of Fame in 2013.

JERI-SHOW VS. D-GENERATION X

THE LEAD-UP

D-Generation X was one of the most popular factions in WWE history, particularly when Triple H and Shawn Michaels reformed the duo in 2006. While the two Superstars took time away from the team to pursue singles competition, they reunited in 2009 to battle Legacy. The pair then turned their attention to the Unified Tag Team Champions Chris Jericho and Big Show, known as Jeri-Show. This dominant duo won the Unified Tag Team Championship in July 2009, and at times looked unstoppable. DX was granted a Tables, Ladders, and Chairs Match for the Titles against the Champions at *TLC 2009*.

THE MATCH

In a TLC Tag Team Match, all four men fight in the ring at the same time. From the opening bell, the two pairs started brawling, with Jericho squaring off with Michaels and Big Show attempting to take out Triple H. Triple H tossed Big Show into a guardrail, and then set up a table near the time keeper. In the ring, Jericho tried to lock in The Walls of Jericho, but Michaels countered into an inverted Atomic Drop. Michaels tried to drop an elbow on Jericho from the top rope, but Y2J got his knees up to block the move. Jericho went to get a ladder, but instead sprinted up the ramp to help Big Show against Triple H. Michaels quickly followed to halt their double teaming of The Game.

Both members of DX isolated Jericho in the ring, repeatedly using a ladder as a weapon. They suplexed the ladder onto Jericho and rammed it into Big Show. Michaels tried to climb the ladder with his partner guarding it, but Big Show took out The Game and pulled HBK off the ladder. The Champions dominated both members of DX, tying Triple H up in a ladder and tossing Michaels out of the ring. Triple H stemmed the Champions' momentum by tossing Jericho into a ladder and taking out Big Show. Michaels attempted to deliver Sweet Chin Music to the Giant, but Y2J interrupted and gave HBK a Codebreaker.

Triple H gave Jericho a Facebuster and Show speared The Game. Now the only man in the ring, Big Show set up a ladder and began to slowly climb. Triple H hit Show in the back, but that only served to anger the giant, who delivered a knockout punch to Triple H. Big Show tried to climb the ladder again and it took a combined effort from Michaels and Triple H to knock it (and Big Show) over. Michaels tried to climb the ladder next, but Jericho toppled it, sending HBK crashing onto Big Show on the floor outside the ring. Jericho had his fingers on the Titles, but Triple H Power Bombed him off the ladder.

Triple H started to climb the ladder next, but he received a Chokeslam from Big Show. The giant then took on a new tactic. Perhaps sick of climbing, he mangled the ladder beyond use. After Jericho and Big Show used a second ladder to punish DX, Show tore that one in half. Big Show then put both members of DX through a table before Jericho attempted to reach the Titles by standing on Show's shoulders. DX returned and tossed both Jericho and Big Show from the ring. Triple H propped the half ladder up while Michaels climbed to grab the Titles, making the duo Unified Tag Team Champions.

THE AFTERMATH

D-Generation X held on to the Unified Tag Team Championship for less than two months. They faced Big Show with a new partner, The Miz, as well as CM Punk and Luke Gallows in a Triple Threat Elimination Match. DX pinned the Punk/Gallows team and eliminated them, but The Miz rolled up Michaels and pinned him to win the Championship for his new team. The team failed its rematch for the Titles before Michaels lost a Retirement Match against Undertaker at *WrestleMania XXVI*. Since then, DX has made occasional appearances, but the duo has not competed.

THE LEAD-UP

When Stone Cold Steve Austin won the 1998 Royal Rumble and Shawn Michaels successfully defended his Title at the same event, the main event for *WrestleMania XIV* was set. The match was going to be even more special, as Mr. McMahon had arranged for Mike Tyson to be the Special Enforcer. But Austin interrupted the announcement and started a brawl with Tyson and his entourage, angering Mr. McMahon. The WWE Universe already wondered if Tyson could be impartial, and when Tyson revealed his allegiance to D-Generation X, it seemed clear that the deck was stacked against the Texas Rattlesnake.

SHAWN MICHAELS vs. STONE COLD STEVE AUSTIN

THE MATCH

Michaels tried to frustrate Austin early on, by dancing away from Stone Cold every time he tried to lock up with the Champion. Austin let HBK know exactly how he felt about Michaels' actions by delivering a pair of middle fingers to the Champion. Twice Austin tried to lock up with Michaels, but HBK ducked the grabs and hit the Texas Rattlesnake with punches each time. Michaels then ran away from Austin, ducking outside the ring. Austin finally caught HBK and punched the Champ and rammed his head into the turnbuckle. The Texas Rattlesnake tossed Michaels over the ropes into his DX stablemates, Triple H and Chyna. When The Game attacked Austin outside the ring, the official ordered them to leave ringside.

Austin and Michaels continued to fight outside the ring, with HBK using a cymbal stand as a weapon against the challenger and then Irish Whipping Austin into a dumpster. Michaels dragged Austin back to the ring, but the Texas Rattlesnake took control of the match with some punches and a powerful wristlock. Austin dropped Michaels' neck over the ring ropes and attempted the first pin of the match, only getting a two-count. Austin knocked Michaels off the apron, driving the Champion into the announcers' table. The Texas Rattlesnake brought Michaels back into the ring and attempted several pins, but HBK kicked out each time.

The two continued to battle outside the ring, with Austin slamming Michaels' head into the guardrail several times, while HBK struck the challenger in the skull with the ring bell. Back in the ring, the Heartbreak Kid began to focus on injuring Austin's knee, slamming it into the ring post and then driving it into the mat. Michaels kept Austin down on the mat with a series of kicks to the knee. Austin rolled out of the ring to collect himself, but Michaels hit a baseball slide that drove the challenger into the announcers' table and Tyson tossed Austin back into the ring. There Michaels tried to maximize the damage with a Figure-Four Leg Lock that Austin finally countered by flipping over.

Michaels attempted to slow down Austin with a sleeper hold. Austin backed Michaels into a corner to try and break the hold, not knowing the official was behind them. By ramming Michaels into the corner, the pair knocked the official out of the match. Austin hit and stomped Michaels all over the ring, but HBK managed to knock down the Texas Rattlesnake with a flying forearm and a top-rope elbow. With Austin down, Michaels started tuning up the band, preparing to deliver Sweet Chin Music. Austin ducked under the kick and tried to grab Michaels for a Stone Cold Stunner. Michaels blocked the move and looked again to deliver a kick to Austin, but this time when Austin countered the kick, he did land a Stone Cold Stunner. With the official still down, Tyson entered the ring and made the three-count. Stone Cold Steve Austin was the new WWE Champion.

Austin tossed Tyson an Austin 3:16 shirt, and the enforcer displayed the shirt for the crowd to enjoy. This was the last straw for Michaels, who confronted the boxing Champion about his actions, thinking that Tyson would be on DX's side. Michaels got in Tyson's face and Iron Mike decked HBK with a punch, and then draped the Austin 3:16 shirt over the former Champion. Jim Ross prophetically declared that the Austin era had begun in WWE, and he was right—this was the first of six WWE Championship reigns for the Texas Rattlesnake. It was also the last time Michaels would compete for more than four years, until his triumphant return at *SummerSlam 2002*.

JOHN CENA vs. RANDY ORTON

TLC: TABLES, LADDERS, AND CHAIRS 2013
TABLES, LADDERS, AND CHAIRS MATCH TO UNIFY THE WWE
AND WORLD HEAVYWEIGHT CHAMPIONSHIPS

December 15, 2013
Toyota Center
Houston, Texas

THE MATCH

To open the match, Cena locked Orton in a side headlock and then dropped The Viper to the ground with a shoulder tackle. Leaving the ring, Cena went for a table, but Orton knocked him down. The Viper then grabbed a ladder and took it into the ring. While Orton set up the ladder, Cena re-entered the ring and used the ladder to assault Orton. Cena finally grabbed the table and propped it up in the corner. Orton responded with a series of brutal strikes inside and outside the ring. Cena returned the favor, blasting Orton repeatedly.

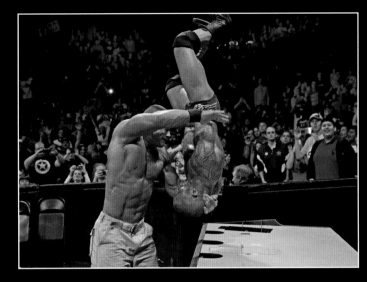

Orton set up a ladder and tried to climb to the Titles, but Cena was able to knock The Viper off. After some brawling, Cena tried to climb the ladder, but Orton was able to take him down as well. Cena then executed a Five-Knuckle Shuffle off the ladder onto Orton. Using the ladder as a weapon, Cena hit The Viper and launched him from the ring apron through a table on the floor below. Cena set up the ladder again and began to climb, but Orton was able to make it back into the ring and knock Cena off and RKO him.

Outside the ring, Cena picked up the steel steps and hit Orton with them twice. Cena then set up another table in the ring and came back for Orton. But The Viper was ready for Cena, and Orton plastered him with a series of clubbing blows with a microphone. Orton looked to punt Cena or put him through the Spanish announcers' table, but neither plan worked—Cena gave Orton an Attitude Adjustment through the table. Cena then climbed the ladder and had his hands on the Titles, but Orton knocked away the ladder. Swinging from the two Titles, Cena was exposed. Orton took advantage and whacked Cena in the midsection.

Orton tore at the mats around the ring to find a pair of handcuffs he had clearly hidden earlier. He used them to handcuff Cena to the bottom rope. Taunting Cena with the key, Orton tossed it into the crowd. Orton, thinking Cena was completely incapacitated, took his time to get one of the taller ladders and set it up. However, as Orton climbed the ladder, Cena frantically took apart a turnbuckle, freeing the rope from the corner. While he was still cuffed to the rope, Cena now had enough slack to climb the ladder opposite Orton. Cena even knocked Orton off the ladder, but while he was figuring out how to grab the Titles with just the one free hand, Orton gripped the ring ropes and used them to pull Cena off the ladder. Cena crashed into a table below, giving Orton all the time he needed to climb the ladder and obtain both Championships, becoming the first ever WWE World Heavyweight Champion.

THE AFTERMATH

Orton successfully defended the Championship at the *Royal Rumble* against Cena. Cena was in control of the match, but some well-timed interference by Bray Wyatt and the Wyatt Family helped distract Cena enough for Orton to win the match. Orton then defended the Title against five other competitors in an Elimination Chamber Match, allowing The Viper to enter *WrestleMania 30* as the WWE World Heavyweight Champion. Orton thought he was going to be facing Batista in a one-on-one match, but Daniel Bryan forced a Triple Threat Match. Bryan got Batista to tap out to the "Yes!" Lock, meaning Orton lost the Title without being involved in the decision.

21

IRON SHEIK VS. HULK HOGAN

THE LEAD-UP

After an almost six-year run as the WWE Champion, Bob Backlund saw his reign end in December of 1983, in a controversial match with Iron Sheik. Leading into the competition, Iron Sheik had injured Backlund, and during their Title match, Sheik locked Backlund in the dreaded Camel Clutch. Backlund refused to submit, but fearing injury, Backlund's manager, Arnold Skaaland, did. Unfortunately, Backlund's injury prevented him from getting a rematch, so the next top contender, Hulk Hogan, stepped in to face the Iranian Champion. The entire crowd at Madison Square Garden, already in the corner of Hogan, really wanted to see him shut down the anti-American rhetoric of the Champion and his manager, Ayatollah Freddie Blassie.

WWE CHAMPIONSHIP MATCH

January 23, 1984

Madison Square Garden
New York, New York

THE MATCH

Hulk Hogan was so pumped to start the match that he didn't even give Iron Sheik time to remove his robe. Hogan cornered the Champion with a series of punches and then knocked him down with a big elbow. To further Iron Sheik's indignity, the challenger then clotheslined Sheik with his own robe and started choking him with it. The official stepped in and took the robe away, but Hogan was relentless with his powerful attacks. Hogan eventually hit the Champion with a boot to the face and went for his first pinfall of the match. Iron Sheik would not be so easily beaten, and he managed to kick out of the attempt.

Hogan continued to press his advantage, dropping Sheik with a big elbow to the head and getting another two-count. Hogan threw the Champion into the corner, but when he went for a splash, Sheik dodged and finally gained the offensive advantage. The Champion hit the downed Hogan with several kicks to the kidney area. He then followed with a painful Backbreaker, but Sheik could only keep the challenger down for a two-count.

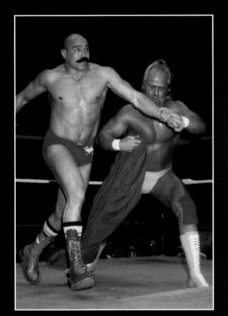

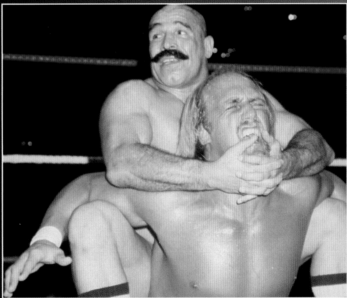

Sheik continued his onslaught with additional kicks to the midsection. He even loaded up his boot to do additional damage before putting Hogan in a Boston Crab, but Hogan used his strength to power out of the move. Iron Sheik looked to further soften Hogan with a suplex before putting the challenger into Sheik's Camel Clutch—it was a move no one had managed to escape. When Iron Sheik locked his fingers together and pulled back to maximize the pressure on Hulk's back, the end seemed inevitable.

Hogan used his amazing power to get to his knees, which lessened the pressure on his back. Hogan was then able to stand and slam Iron Sheik into the turnbuckles. The force of the blow dropped Sheik to the canvas, allowing Hogan to employ his famous Leg Drop. A three-count later, Hulk Hogan was the new WWE Champion. An indignant Sheik tried to interrupt Hogan's post-match celebration by attacking him and then throwing a steel chair into the ring, but Hogan defended both attacks and continued to celebrate with the jubilant Madison Square Garden crowd.

THE AFTERMATH

Announcer Gorilla Monsoon correctly predicted the next era of WWE when he stated, "Hulkamania is here!" Hulk Hogan would go on to hold the WWE Championship for the next four years, only losing it in February 1988 due to a crooked official. No one has had as long a reign since, and only Bruno Sammartino and Bob Backlund had longer Championship reigns. While Iron Sheik never held the WWE Championship again, he would go on to win the World Tag Team Title with Nikolai Volkoff at the first *WrestleMania*. Both Hogan and Iron Sheik would be inducted into the WWE Hall of Fame in 2005.

UNDERTAKER vs. MANKIND

1998 KING OF THE KING
HELL IN A CELL

June 28, 1998
Pittsburgh Civic Arena
Pittsburgh, Pennsylvania

THE LEAD-UP

Mr. McMahon was desperate to take the WWE Championship from Stone Cold Steve Austin, so he turned to any Superstar who could help dethrone the Texas Rattlesnake. When Dude Love could not get the job done, Mr. McMahon arranged for a #1 Contenders Match between Undertaker and his brother Kane. Mick Foley shed his Dude Love identity, changed into his Mankind persona, and helped Kane win the #1 Contenders Match, angering Undertaker. The two agreed to extend their historic rivalry by competing in the second-ever Hell in a Cell Match.

Mankind decided to start the match outside the demonic structure. He threw a chair on top of the cell and climbed up after it. As Undertaker approached the ring, Mankind dared The Phenom to join him on top of the structure. It was the first of a few tactical errors Mankind made that night. Undertaker scaled the cell and the two men began exchanging blows. The carnage quickly began as Undertaker tossed Mankind off the cell and he fell over fifteen feet to the floor, landing on and breaking the Spanish announcers' desk. In response to Mankind's fall, announcer Jim Ross exclaimed, "As God as my witness, he is broken in half!"

A hush fell over the crowd as ringside and backstage officials came to check on Mankind. The announcers speculated that the match was over while the cage was raised (with Undertaker still on the roof) for medics to bring a stretcher for Mankind. But the deranged Mankind was not done—he rolled off the stretcher and started to climb the structure a second time. Again, this was not a wise decision, as Undertaker then chokeslammed Mankind through the roof of the cell into the ring below. The force was so great it knocked a tooth out of Mankind's mouth and up through his nose. Undertaker dropped into the cell, a drop so high that he damaged his ankle coming down. Again officials tried to stop the match, but both Undertaker and Mankind would not end things without a decisive conclusion.

Undertaker continued his assault on Mankind, but Mankind finally got the advantage when Undertaker launched himself at Mankind and missed, instead hitting the unforgiving steel. Mankind used a leg drop to drive a foreign object into the face of Undertaker, cutting The Phenom open. With both men bloody messes, Mankind made his third tactical error. Mankind went under the ring and grabbed a bag filled with thousands of thumbtacks. He spread them on the mat and then attempted to drive Undertaker onto the thumbtacks. At first, both men were able to avoid the thumbtacks, so Mankind changed tactics, locking his Mandible Claw submission maneuver on Undertaker. Before he succumbed to the move, however, Undertaker stood up and drove Mankind to the mat, planting him into the pile of thumbtacks. Writhing in agony, Mankind then found himself on the receiving end of a Tombstone Piledriver. The Phenom had defeated Mankind in one of the most brutal encounters in WWE history, one Jim Ross speculated both men would never completely recover from.

THE AFTERMATH

It's rare for the loser of a match to receive a standing ovation, but the crowd recognized the incredible effort Mankind put into the bout. Again, officials tried to place Mankind on a stretcher, but he refused, looking to walk out on his own two feet. Mankind and Undertaker would continue their rivalry in the weeks that followed as Mankind and Kane became World Tag Team Champions and they faced the unlikely team of Undertaker and Stone Cold Steve Austin for the Titles. While Undertaker and Austin won the Titles, Kane and Mankind would eventually win them back and hold them until Kane betrayed Mankind in order to side with his brother Undertaker in their quest to win the WWE Championship.

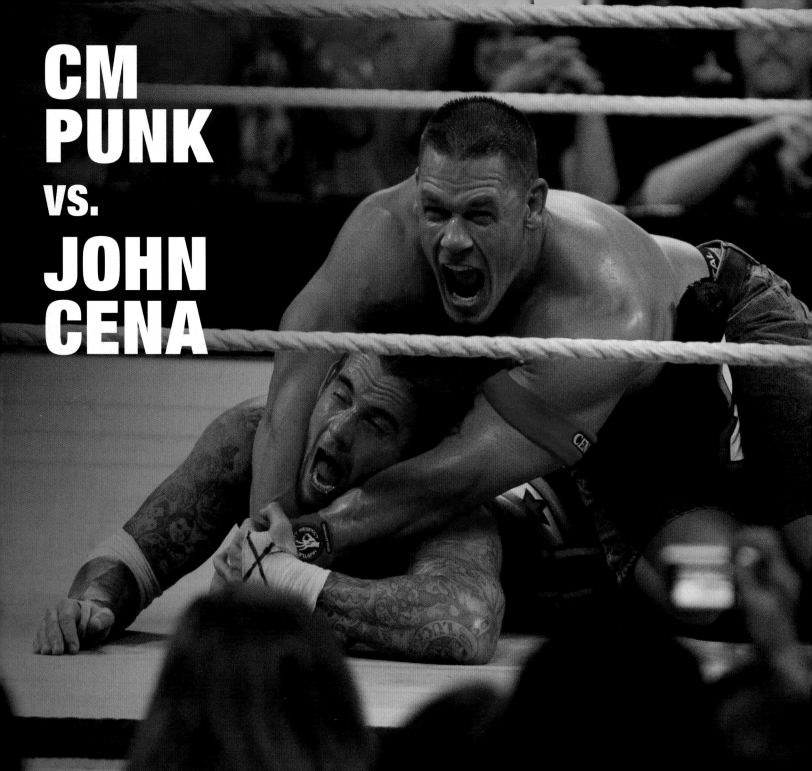

CM PUNK VS. JOHN CENA

THE LEAD-UP

In the summer of 2011, CM Punk pulled back the curtain on behind-the-scenes drama at WWE. The Straight Edge Superstar's contract was ending the night of *Money in the Bank*, and he was thinking of leaving WWE. However, he'd earned an opportunity at the Title against WWE Champion John Cena and the event was slated to be in his hometown of Chicago. In his infamous "pipe-bomb promo" on *Raw*, Punk ripped the WWE and how Vince McMahon ran it. While Mr. McMahon wanted to suspend Punk and be done with him, John Cena insisted Punk be reinstated so they could have their match, despite Punk's claims that he would not re-sign and take the WWE Championship with him after winning the match.

MONEY IN THE BANK 2011
WWE CHAMPIONSHIP MATCH

July 17, 2011

Allstate Arena
Rosemont, Illinois

The Chicago crowd practically shook the building cheering the entrance of their local hero. John Cena is typically accustomed to a crowd that is split in his support, but on this night, an overwhelming majority booed his every move. From the look on Cena's face, it was one of the few times in his incredible career the crowd got to him. The match started with some exchanges of holds and maneuvers. John Cena used his power to try and keep Punk down, while the Straight Edge Superstar used his kicks and martial art moves to wear out the Champion.

Several times, John Cena had Punk set up for the Attitude Adjustment, but Punk managed to fight his way out of the move before Cena could finish him off. Along the same lines, Cena fought his way out of the Go To Sleep on several occasions. Cena had Punk locked into an STF for two extended periods and the announcers speculated Punk would have to tap out, but Punk was able to reach the ropes the first time and power out and reverse the move a second time.

Cena finally hit Punk with an Attitude Adjustment, but Punk kicked out at the two-count. At this point, both Cena and Punk had to wonder what it was going to take to win. Both men started taking unusual chances. Cena went to the top rope for some high-risk, high-impact moves. Punk was able to reverse one into a Hurricanrana and a Go To Sleep, but Cena rolled out of the ring, preventing Punk from attempting an immediate pin.

Mr. McMahon and John Laurinaitis came to the ring just as Cena locked Punk into the STF again. McMahon saw an opportunity to end the match and ordered Laurinaitis to ring the bell (in a move reminiscent of the "Montreal Screwjob"). But Cena, seeing Laurinaitis heading for the ring area, broke the hold, jumped out of the ring, and decked him. He then confronted Mr. McMahon, effectively telling him to stay out of the match. Cena reentered the ring, but Punk had recovered enough to hit Cena with the Go To Sleep. One three-count later, and CM Punk had won his first WWE Championship. McMahon was distraught and he ordered Alberto Del Rio to come down and cash in his opportunity. But before Del Rio could, Punk nailed him with a kick to the head. Punk was going to end the night as WWE Champion.

THE AFTERMATH

Punk kept true to his word, leaving the arena with the WWE Championship, but not before blowing Mr. McMahon a kiss. Without a WWE Title or titleholder, an eight-man tournament was held to crown a new Champion. Rey Mysterio won the Title, but his first Title defense, against John Cena, was unsuccessful. As Cena held the Title high over his head, CM Punk made his shocking return, holding his Title high. The two would meet at *SummerSlam* in order to unify the fractured Title, and Punk beat Cena again to become the undisputed WWE Champion. That distinction would last less than five minutes, as Alberto Del Rio cashed in his Money in the Bank opportunity to defeat a worn-out CM Punk.

THE SHIELD
(DEAN AMBROSE, ROMAN REIGNS, AND SETH ROLLINS)

VS.

THE WYATT FAMILY
(BRAY WYATT, LUKE HARPER, AND ERICK ROWAN)

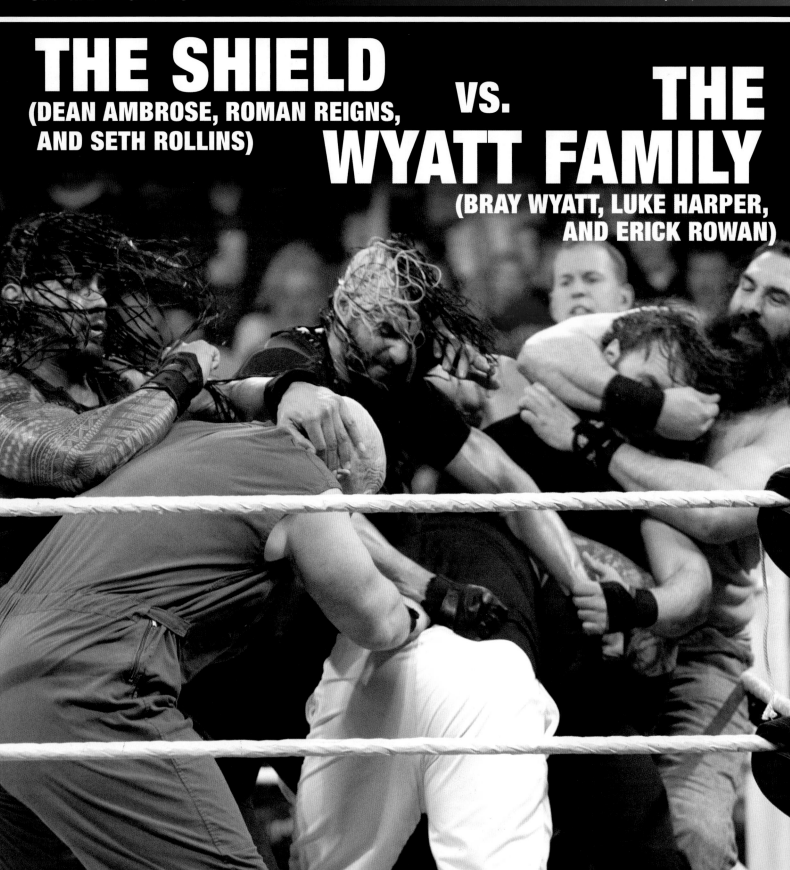

THE LEAD-UP

In late 2012, the WWE Universe was introduced to The Shield, the three Hounds of Justice that became one of the most successful factions in WWE history by running roughshod over the entire WWE. Less than a year later in the summer of 2013, The Wyatt Family followed The Shield's blueprint. Led by the charismatically unhinged Bray Wyatt, The Wyatt Family also caused chaos throughout WWE. It seemed like it was only a matter of time before the two factions would meet. After The Wyatt Family cost The Shield three spots in an Elimination Chamber Match for the WWE World Heavyweight Championship, the two groups were set to clash at *Elimination Chamber 2014.*

THE MATCH

In addition to being incredible in-ring performers, both factions had wildly popular ring entrances. Roman Reigns, Seth Rollins, and Dean Ambrose made their way to the ring from the crowd. The Wyatt Family's entrance involved a darkened arena with the only light coming from an old-style lantern. Fan anticipation was so high a "This is Awesome!" chant started before there was any action. The six men stared at each other with no one making the first move until Ambrose sprinted at Wyatt and began attacking him.

Fans were split down the middle, as dueling chants of "Let's go Wyatts!" and "Let's go Shield!" filled the arena. Both sides worked as effective teams with quick tags when they had the offensive advantage. The Wyatt Family was able to isolate Dean Ambrose and hit him with a series of high-impact moves. Ambrose was eventually able to reach his corner and tag in Seth Rollins, who amazed the crowd with some incredible moves, including foiling a Superplex attempt by Luke Harper by landing on his feet. He then dumped Harper out of the ring and nailed him with a dive through the ropes to the floor below. But Wyatt was able to slam Rollins outside of the ring and turn the advantage back to his team's side.

Controlling all six men was an impossible task for the official as the action spilled in and out of the ring. Wyatt and Harper looked to put Seth Rollins through the Spanish announcers' table, but Ambrose saved his teammate and Dean and Bray Wyatt brawled into the stands. Eventually only Wyatt returned to the ringside area, and under his direction, Harper and Rowan together slammed Rollins, breaking the Spanish announcers' table.

Thanks to the **carnage outside the ring,** Reigns found **himself the only member of** The Shield still **standing.** After Reigns and his cohorts had **systematically dismantled** individual Superstars **for the better part of a** year, it was ironic **that Reigns found himself** surrounded by the **three members of the** Wyatt Family. After **being beaten on by Harper** and Rowan, Wyatt **set Reigns for Sister** Abigail's Kiss, but **Reigns stunned Wyatt by** powering out of **the move.** Reigns fought back valiantly, **hitting both Rowan and Wyatt** with his signature **Superman Punch,** but the numbers game **proved overwhelming and** Reigns was pinned **after Bray Wyatt's second** attempt at the **Sister Abigail was successful.**

Fans were clamoring for more confrontations between the two squads, but each moved on to other issues. Bray Wyatt began a high-profile rivalry with John Cena

throwing The Bizarre One out of the ring. But Goldust held on to the top rope. The duo was eventually joined by Big Boss Man, Bradshaw, Lance Storm, Al Snow, and Billy. While Big Boss Man, Storm, and Bradshaw were the first three eliminations, it was the eighth entrant, Undertaker, that made the first significant impact, eliminating every other competitor. Matt Hardy and Jeff Hardy followed, and while they worked together against The Deadman, he still eliminated both of them.

What followed was perhaps the most shocking elimination in *Royal Rumble* history. *Tough Enough* Season One Champion Maven entered the Rumble. While Undertaker was still fighting with the already eliminated Hardys, Maven drop kicked The Deadman out of the ring. Maven did not have long to celebrate though, as Undertaker decimated the young man for having the gall to eliminate him. Undertaker continued to beat Maven deep into the crowd, making it impossible for him to return to the match. The team of Christian and Chuck worked together and eliminated two competitors, until the 19th entrant, Stone Cold Steve Austin, entered and eliminated both of them. Stone Cold also eliminated Perry Saturn and the two competitors that came after him, Val Venis and Test. Austin was alone in the ring until the 22nd entrant appeared, a returning Triple H.

The two former WWE Champions attacked each other with intensity, each looking to win the match and ultimately the main event at *WrestleMania*. Austin and Triple H worked together to eliminate The Hurricane and Faarooq. Then a returning Mr. Perfect and Kurt Angle entered the match. The four competitors were then overwhelmed by the massive Big Show, who chokeslammed all the remaining Superstars. But Kane, the next entrant, body slammed Big Show out of the match before he was then eliminated by Angle. After RVD and Booker T entered and were quickly knocked out of the match, the Rumble was down to four men—Angle, Triple H, Stone Cold, and Mr. Perfect.

Angle managed to eliminate crowd favorite Stone Cold, but the Texas Rattlesnake did not take his elimination well, returning with a foreign object to plaster the three remaining competitors. Perfect and Angle tried to double team Triple H, but their alliance did not last long and Triple H took out Perfect, leaving just him and Kurt Angle. The Olympic Hero was sure he'd won the match when he tossed The Game over the top rope, but Triple H's feet never touched the floor. The Game flipped himself back into the ring and tossed Angle out to win the match and the Title opportunity at *WrestleMania X8*.

THE AFTERMATH

Mr. McMahon forced Triple H to defend his Title opportunity at *No Way Out* against The Olympic Hero, Kurt Angle. He won that match, and went on to face the Undisputed Champion at *WrestleMania X8*. Another match at *No Way Out* between Champion Chris Jericho and Stone Cold Steve Austin was set to determine the next Champion, and Jericho successfully defended his Title against the Texas Rattlesnake. Triple H's ex-wife Stephanie McMahon aligned herself with Jericho for the *WrestleMania* bout, but even with the long odds, The Game managed to complete his comeback from an almost career-ending injury and win the Undisputed Championship at *WrestleMania X8*.

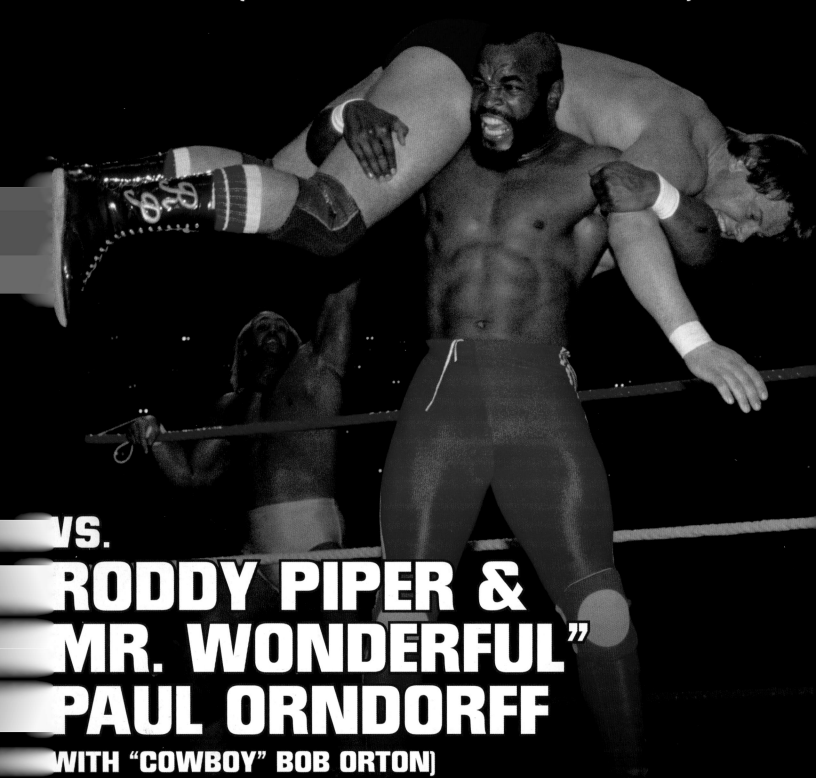

HULK HOGAN & MR. T
(WITH "SUPERFLY" JIMMY SNUKA)

VS.
RODDY PIPER &
MR. WONDERFUL"
PAUL ORNDORFF
WITH "COWBOY" BOB ORTON)

WRESTLEMANIA
TAG TEAM MATCH

March 31, 1985

Madison Square Garden
New York, New York

THE LEAD-UP

1984 and 1985 saw the worlds of professional wrestling and Rock 'n' Roll intersect. WWE aired a pair of specials on MTV, and the second one, "The War to Settle the Score" saw Hulk Hogan defend the WWE Title against "Rowdy" Roddy Piper. The match ended in a disqualification when Paul Orndorff and Bob Orton interfered on Piper's behalf. *The A-Team* star Mr. T was sitting at ringside in support of his friend Hulk Hogan and he (and Cyndi Lauper) tried to help even the odds. The brawl led to a tag team match set for the main event of the first *WrestleMania*—Hogan would team with Mr. T to face Piper and Orndorff.

THE MATCH

While it originally appeared that Hulk Hogan and Paul Orndorff would start the match, Piper tagged in for his team, which led to Mr. T demanding to be tagged in as well. Piper and Mr. T went nose-to-nose. Piper then tried to get under Mr. T's skin by slapping him across the face, but Mr. T responded with a slap of his own. *The A-Team* star then surprised Piper by taking him down with a Fireman's Carry. The enraged Piper pushed Mr. T back into Piper's corner, and Piper and Orndorff started brawling with Mr. T until Hogan came across the ring to even the odds. With in-ring official Pat Patterson unable to keep control, outside official Muhammed Ali joined the fray. Ali first prevented Bob Orton from joining the brawl and he then punched Roddy Piper.

Piper, stinging from Ali's jab, gathered his team outside the ring, where they decided they needed to take a break. The trio headed back to the dressing room, so official Pat Patterson started the 10-count to award a count-out victory to Hogan and Mr. T. Hogan, however, stopped Patterson—he didn't want that type of win. Piper's team was escorted back to the ring, and the match continued. Once things settled down again, Hogan and Mr. T showed smooth teamwork, double clotheslining Piper. Mr. T then continued to astonish all with his wrestling moves, slamming Piper and taking down Orton with a Hip Block Takedown. Hogan then reentered the match and booted Piper out of the ring.

While Hogan was focused on Piper, Orndorff snuck up on Hogan and dumped the WWE Champion outside the ring. Piper hit Hogan with a foreign object, and then Piper and Orndorff got Hogan back in the ring and managed to double team him with a variety of moves. When Hogan was finally able to counter a high-risk top-rope move by Orndorff and tag in his partner, Piper's team then started to double team Mr. T. Eventually, Mr. T escaped and tagged Hogan back in.

The match broke down once again with all four participants and each team's corner man in the ring. As Hogan and Orndorff were the legal men in the match, Patterson was attempting to get Piper and Mr. T out of the ring. Orton tried to take advantage of the chaos and looked to hit Hogan with the cast on his arm. However, the WWE Champion moved and Orton accidentally hit Orndorff instead. The Hulkster was able to pin Orndorff and win the main event of the first *WrestleMania*.

THE AFTERMATH

The match's ending eventually led to a split between Piper and Orndorff, as Piper blamed Orndorff for the loss—even though it was Orton's interference that backfired. Orndorff became a fan favorite when he faced both Piper and Orton in matches around the country and when he teamed with Hulk Hogan to face both men together.

The first *WrestleMania* was an unqualified success, with more than one million fans viewing the event in closed circuit around the country. WWE turned the event into an annual pop culture extravaganza. The enmity between "Rowdy" Roddy Piper and Mr. T spilled over into the second *WrestleMania* when the two competed in a boxing match.

TRISH STRATUS
vs.
LITA

THE LEAD-UP

For more than six years, Trish Stratus was one of the most successful Divas in WWE history. Starting as a manager, Stratus went on to hold the WWE Women's Championship six times, tying her with the Fabulous Moolah for the most Title reigns ever. Her longest rivalry was with Lita, and when Lita heard that Stratus was planning to retire after *Unforgiven*, Lita told wwe.com before Trish could break the news. Trish decided that the best way to get revenge was to challenge Lita, the current WWE Women's Champion, to a Title match at *Unforgiven 2006*. Lita, looking to send her long-time adversary out with a loss, agreed to the match.

UNFORGIVEN
WWE WOMEN'S CHAMPIONSHIP MATCH

September 17, 2006
Air Canada Centre
Toronto, Ontario, Canada

THE MATCH

Stratus came out to a thunderous ovation in her hometown of Toronto. The crowd then erupted into **a** "Thank You, Trish!" chant. After a lockup, Lita shoved Trish several times until Stratus exploded out of a **ring** corner with a clothesline, knocking Lita down. After getting a two-count, Trish then put the Champion **into** a head scissors, spinning Lita around and taking her to the mat once again. Lita rolled out of the ring to collect herself, so Trish launched herself out of the **ring** with an Air Canada, and then followed that move with another head scissors, taking Lita off the steel steps onto the floor outside the ring.

Back in the ring, Lita had the official keep Trish away until she recovered and then began punching and kneeing Trish. She took the challenger down with a snap mare takedown, and then wore her down further with a sleeper hold. After Trish fought back, she tried to perform a third head scissors, this time from the **top** turnbuckle. But the Champion fought back and, after trading blows, the two Divas fell to the floor below. As both recovered, they each climbed the turnbuckle again, raining blows on each other. Lita got the upper hand, and tossed Trish onto the mat. She looked to finish off the challenger with a moonsault, but Trish rolled out of the way.

After getting a near fall on the Champion, Trish intended to end Lita with her Stratusfaction maneuver. But Lita knew what was coming, and countered the move by dumping Trish out of the ring. After bringing her back to the mat, Lita became angrier when Trish managed to kick out before a three-count. Lita began punching the downed Trish repeatedly and then dropped her with a suplex. She once again only got **a** two-count on Trish. However, thinking that it was **only** a matter of time, Lita began to taunt Trish, which led to some punches from Trish connecting with Lita. **Lita** retook the advantage with a Russian Leg Sweep, but Trish landed a neckbreaker to get back into the match.

Trish followed with another leg scissors and a Chick Kick, but Lita still had some fight in her. She was set to hit a Twist of Fate on Trish, but the challenger countered the move into a rollup. It seemed like Trish would get the three-count, but she instead turned **the** move into a Sharpshooter. Lita had to tap out, handing the WWE Women's Championship to Trish Stratus **one** more time.

BOB BACKLUND VS. STAN HANSEN

THE LEAD-UP

Bob Backlund captured the WWE Championship in early 1978 from "Superstar" Billy Graham. In addition to defending the Title against the former Champion, Backlund took on all comers, including the Champions of the AWA and NWA. In the early 1980s, Backlund faced a particularly ominous threat, Stan Hansen. Hansen attempted to win the WWE Championship from Bruno Sammartino in 1976 and the big Texan broke Sammartino's neck. Bruno eventually turned back Hansen's Title chase, but now Hansen was back to challenge a new Champion. The two competitors agreed to settle matters inside a steel cage.

STEEL CAGE MATCH
FOR THE WWE CHAMPIONSHIP

April 6, 1981

Madison Square Garden
New York, New York

THE MATCH

Backlund was initially leery of the cage as Hansen stalked the entrance, yelling at the Champion. As soon as Backlund started to enter the structure, Hansen struck, clubbing Backlund on the back. However, once he cleared the ropes, the Champion reversed a whip into the cage wall, driving Hansen's head into the steel. Backlund rammed the challenger twice more into the cage wall and then raked his opponent's face across the harsh metal. Hansen tried to climb out of the cage, but Backlund pulled him back in. Backlund landed a shot to Hansen's midsection, but the big Texan countered with a kick to the gut and a knee to the Champion's chest.

Hansen started to dish out the punishment, tossing the Champion into the cage and working his body with a double axe-handle and a shot to Backlund's midsection. But the Champion's resiliency was clear as he elbowed his challenger and reversed an Irish whip to send Hansen crashing into the steel wall. Backlund followed that up with a Piledriver. Thinking his challenger was down enough for him to escape, the Champion started climbing the cage. But Hansen got to his feet and brought Backlund to the mat with a low blow. Despite his pain, Backlund was able to move out of the path of a big Hansen elbow.

Again Backlund raked Hansen's skull against the steel cage, and it opened a cut on the challenger's face, blood pouring out of the wound. The two traded blows in the center of the ring until the Champion evened one score by hitting Hansen with a low blow. Backlund tried to leave via the cage's door, but Hansen pulled him back in and dropped him to the canvas with a vicious elbow. Hansen attempted to drop another elbow on the Champion, but again Backlund rolled out of the way. Backlund delighted the crowd by raining punches on a downed Hansen, and then landed a back body drop on his opponent. Hansen demonstrated that he was still in the match by catching Backlund with a series of rights to his midsection and a bodyslam, as well as dropping a knee on the Champion.

Hansen started to leave the ring but Backlund grabbed the challenger's leg and reeled him back. Backlund also tried to leave, but the challenger pulled him back into the cage. Both Hansen and Backlund climbed to the top rope as they each tried to escape the cage. The two competitors hammered each other with rights and Backlund added a headbutt for good measure to drop the challenger back to the canvas. Hansen tried to climb the opposite corner, but Backlund pulled him down, and Hansen's head hit the top turnbuckle. Seeing his opponent down for the count, Backlund exited through the cage door to win the match and retain the WWE Championship.

THE AFTERMATH

Bob Backlund continued to defend the WWE Championship throughout the rest of 1981, as well as 1982 and most of 1983. In December 1983, an injured Backlund attempted to defend his Title against Iron Sheik. When Sheik had Backlund in his Camel Clutch, the Champion refused to submit, but Backlund's manager Arnold Skaaland threw in the towel to prevent further injury to his client. All told, Backlund's reign lasted more than 2,100 days, second only to Bruno Sammartino's first Title run. Like Sammartino, Backlund regained the Title, but his second reign (in 1994) only lasted three days. In 2013, Bob Backlund was inducted into the WWE Hall of Fame.

SHAWN MICHAELS vs. SHELTON BENJAMIN

THE LEAD-UP

Batista won the World Heavyweight Championship from Triple H at *WrestleMania 21* and defended the Title in a rematch with The Game at *Backlash*. In order to decide the next challenger for The Animal, *Raw* General Manager Eric Bischoff set up a Gold Rush Tournament to take place over three weeks of the show. Eight men competed in a single elimination tournament. Edge, Kane, and Chris Benoit all won their opening bouts, so the last spot would be filled by a quarterfinal match between the reigning Intercontinental Champion Shelton Benjamin and "The Heartbreak Kid," Shawn Michaels.

THE MATCH

Benjamin probably assumed he had the technical advantage heading into the match due to his amateur background competing at the University of Minnesota. But Michaels surprised Benjamin with a few moves of his own, particularly a pair of wristlock takedowns and two hammerlocks. Twice Benjamin countered Michaels' move, but the Heartbreak Kid reached the ropes and forced a break. Michaels executed a hip toss takedown to put Benjamin back on the mat, but Benjamin used a kick to HBK's head and a pair of arm drag takedowns to grab an offensive advantage, frustrating Michaels.

Michaels got Benjamin on the top rope and attempted to deliver a superplex. In the air, Benjamin was able to twist his body and counter the move into a high cross body. The move took something out of both men, and they were almost counted out by the official. Michaels then delivered a pair of knife-edge chops, but Benjamin performed a Samoan Drop on the Heartbreak Kid. Benjamin kept the momentum with some punches, clotheslines, and an Inverted Backbreaker. Michaels barely managed to kick out before the official could count three. The two men continued to battle and Michaels hit a desperation flying forearm, and again both men were down in the ring prompting the official to start another 10-count. Michaels kipped up at eight, but was startled to see Benjamin kip up as well.

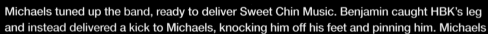

Benjamin went for a kick, but Michaels countered the move into an attempted suplex. Benjamin skinned the cat and turned the move into a victory roll and pin attempt. Michaels countered the move into his own pinning attempt, but Benjamin countered Michaels' counter. Both came close to gaining a pinfall, but the match continued. Michaels delivered additional knife-edge chops and tried to toss Benjamin into a corner, but Benjamin reversed the Irish Whip and hit a big splash on HBK in the corner. Benjamin attempted his T-Bone Suplex, but Michaels blocked the move and countered with a back body drop. Benjamin deposited the Heartbreak Kid on the top rope, but Michaels pushed Benjamin off the top rope and landed a flying elbow on his opponent.

Michaels tuned up the band, ready to deliver Sweet Chin Music. Benjamin caught HBK's leg and instead delivered a kick to Michaels, knocking him off his feet and pinning him. Michaels barely managed to kick out before the three-count. Benjamin showed off his insane athleticism by jumping from the mat to the top turnbuckle to deliver a high cross body. Again, Michaels kicked out. Looking to create some breathing room, Michaels attempted to toss Benjamin out of the ring, but Shelton landed on the apron and leapt to the top rope and launched himself at Michaels. Unfortunately for Benjamin, Michaels connected with Sweet Chin Music, taking out the Champion and gaining the Heartbreak Kid a three-count for the victory.

THE AFTERMATH

Michaels advanced to the semifinals of the tournament, but a week later he lost to Edge. After losing his opportunity at the World Heavyweight Championship, the Heartbreak Kid focused instead on a rematch with Kurt Angle, who defeated Michaels at *WrestleMania 21*. Michaels faced Angle at *Vengeance 2005* and evened their series at one match a piece. Benjamin continued to successfully defend his Intercontinental Championship until June 2005 when a debuting Carlito, drafted from *SmackDown*, defeated Benjamin for the Title. Edge, who eliminated Michaels from the Gold Rush Tournament, lost in the finals to Kane, who then unsuccessfully challenged Batista for the World Heavyweight Championship.

THE ROCK vs. "HOLLYWOOD" HULK HOGAN

THE LEAD-UP

In his war with Ric Flair for control of WWE, WWE Chairman Mr. McMahon decided to kill his own creation by introducing the poison of the New World Order to WWE. "Hollywood" Hulk Hogan berated the WWE fans, claiming they had turned on him and forced him to leave. The Rock disputed Hogan's version of events and challenged the Hulkster to face the People's Champion on the grand stage of *WrestleMania*. Hogan accepted, and then he and his nWo partners did everything they could to take The Rock out in the weeks leading up to the match. But The Rock was ready for *WrestleMania* and the WWE Universe was ready to see two icons battle.

WRESTLEMANIA X8

SINGLES MATCH

March 17, 2002

SkyDome
Toronto, Ontario, Canada

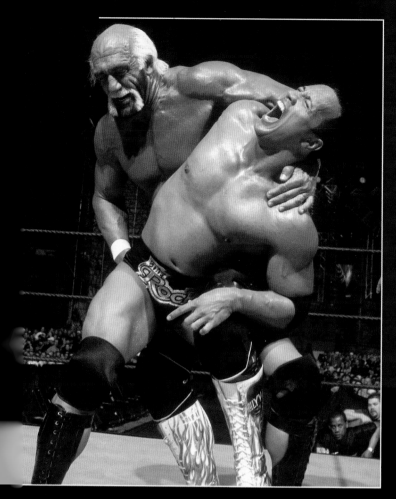

THE MATCH

As the two Superstars faced off at the start of the match, Hogan was clearly overwhelmed by the positive reaction from the Toronto crowd. The competitors finally locked up and Hogan used his strength to toss The Rock into the corner. Hogan's power surprised The Rock, but "Hollywood" using The Rock's "bring it" gesture surprised him even more. Hogan continued to press his offensive advantage until The Rock nailed a flying forearm on the Hulkster. The Great One then gestured Hogan to "just bring it," a move that drew a surprising amount of boos from the SkyDome crowd. The Rock then nailed Hogan with a series of open-palmed strikes, leading Hogan to roll out of the ring to collect himself.

The Rock went to catch Hulk with a Rock Bottom, but Hogan blocked the move with an elbow to The Rock's head. Hogan regained the offensive advantage with a series of elbows, Irish Whips, and clotheslines. Hogan put The Rock to the mat with a suplex and went for the cover, only getting a two-count. Hogan used some underhanded moves, including raking The Rock's back and even biting The Great One, but the SkyDome crowd stayed firmly in his corner. The Rock battered the Hulkster with a series of rights, but Hulk then tossed The Rock over the top rope and onto the floor outside the ring.

The two men fought outside, pushing the bounds of what's sanctioned in a match. The Rock slammed the Hulkster repeatedly on the announcers' table and tried to use a foreign object, but the official took the weapon away from The Rock, distracting him enough to let Hogan clothesline The Great One. Hogan rolled The Rock back into the ring and whipped The Rock into the official, knocking the official down and out. The Rock put the Hulkster into the Sharpshooter, but the official was not able to see Hogan tap. Hogan used the lack of an official to deliver a low blow and a Rock Bottom, but The Great One kicked out at two. The crowd loved it when Hogan whipped The Rock with his weight belt, but booed lustily when The Rock did the same to the Hulkster.

The Rock finally landed a Rock Bottom, but was stunned that Hulk kicked out of the pinfall attempt at two. Hogan began "hulking up" and hit The Rock with the big boot and a leg drop, but now Hulk was stunned when The Rock kicked out at two. Hogan tried a second leg drop, but The Rock rolled out of the way. The Great One then delivered two Rock Bottoms and a People's Elbow to pin the Hulkster and win the match between these two generational icons.

THE AFTERMATH

Hulk Hogan found himself on the outs with his nWo running mates after *WrestleMania*. Hall and Nash were frustrated that he accepted The Rock's challenge and lost the match. After he was kicked out of the group, Hogan delighted the WWE Universe by ditching the black and white of the New World Order for his traditional colors of red and yellow. The Hulkster became the #1 contender for the Undisputed Championship and at *Backlash 2002* defeated Triple H for his 6th WWE Title, tying him with Stone Cold and The Rock for most Title reigns. The Rock broke the tie later that year when he won the Championship at *Vengeance 2002*.

UNDERTAKER
vs. THE ROCK
vs. KURT ANGLE

THE LEAD-UP

Undertaker was defending his Undisputed Championship against Triple H at *King of the Ring* when The Rock inserted himself into the match and almost cost the Champion his Title. An enraged Deadman demanded a match with Rock at *Vengeance*. Before he could get there though, he had to defend the Title against Kurt Angle on *SmackDown*. The match ended controversially, as Angle was pinned at the same time that Undertaker tapped out. The officials decided to rule the match a draw, keeping the Title with Undertaker. In the interest of fairness, Mr. McMahon added Angle to the *King of the Ring* match, making it a Triple Threat contest for the Title.

THE MATCH

The three men eyed each other warily, but soon Undertaker focused on The Rock, and The Great One responded in kind. Furious that they were ignoring him, Kurt Angle made the mistake of striking both men. Undertaker and The Rock responded by double-teaming the Olympic Champion, tossing him out of the ring. The two traded blows until The Rock clotheslined the Champion out of the ring, where Angle tossed him into the steel ring steps. Back in the ring, Angle hit The Rock with a pair of overhead belly-to-belly suplexes, but Rock countered with a DDT.

All three men ended up outside the ring, and Angle slammed The Rock and then found himself taken down by The Deadman. The Champion brought The Rock back into the ring for some additional punishment, but was surprised when The Great One hit him with his own move, a Chokeslam. Angle broke up the pinfall attempt. Rock then used Kurt Angle's own Ankle Lock on the Olympic Champion, but Angle countered the move and hit a Rock Bottom on The Great One. An Undertaker leg drop prevented Angle from securing a three-count. Angle tried to give Undertaker an Olympic Slam, but Undertaker stopped the move and gave Angle an Olympic Slam instead. The Rock prevented The Deadman from getting the three-count.

Rock then hit the Champion with a Spinebuster and the People's Elbow, but Angle pulled The Great One from the ring before he could pin the Champion. The pattern continued where each man got one of his fellow competitors down, but the third prevented a pinfall. Angle tried to bring in a foreign object, but Undertaker struck him first before the Olympic Hero was pinballed between The Rock and Undertaker. Undertaker tried to deliver a Chokeslam, but The Rock blocked it with a low blow that briefly knocked down the official. Angle dropped Undertaker with a shot and The Rock with an Angle Slam, but could only get two-counts from each man.

The Rock almost got Angle to submit to a Sharpshooter, but Undertaker broke up the move. Angle got Undertaker in an Ankle Lock, but Undertaker fought out of it. He attempted to deliver a Last Ride to Angle, but the Olympic Hero countered it into a Triangle Chokehold. Twice, Undertaker slammed Angle to the mat, but Angle would not release the hold. The Rock prevented the submission, so Angle put The Great One in an Ankle Lock. Angle landed another Angle Slam on Undertaker, but he turned into a Rock Bottom from The Rock. Finally, The Great One kept Angle down for a three-count to win his first Undisputed Championship.

THE AFTERMATH

The Rock's reign as Undisputed Champion did not last long. The following month at *SummerSlam*, The Great One defended his Championship against 2002 *King of the Ring* winner Brock Lesnar. The Beast took the Title from the People's Champion. He then successfully defended the Title versus both Undertaker and Kurt Angle until *Survivor Series 2002* when Big Show won the Title. The Rock left WWE for six months after his *SummerSlam* defeat and the WWE Universe did not see him again until February 2003.

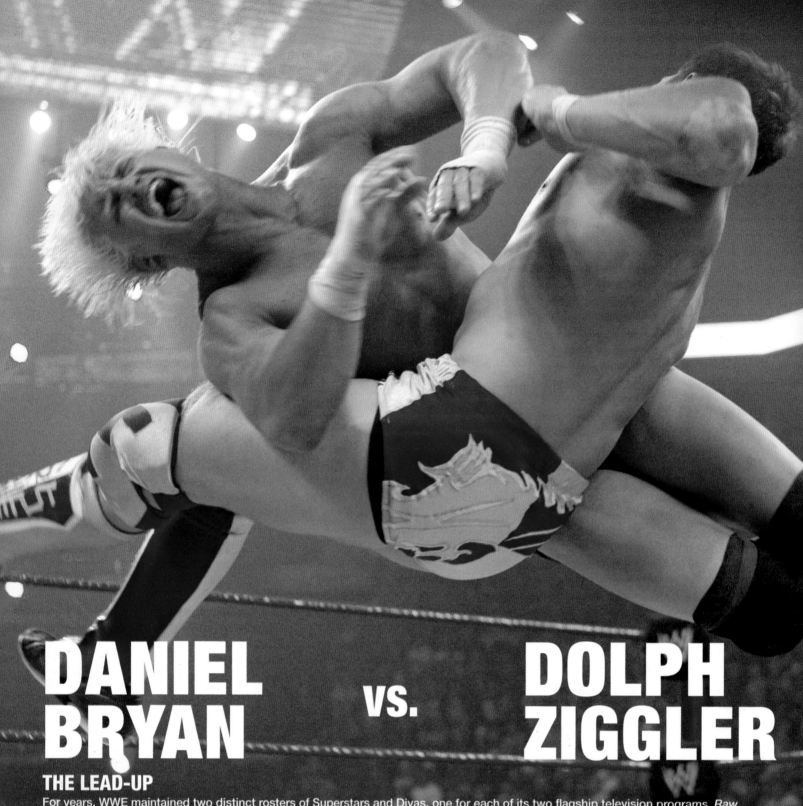

DANIEL BRYAN VS. DOLPH ZIGGLER

THE LEAD-UP

For years, WWE maintained two distinct rosters of Superstars and Divas, one for each of its two flagship television programs, *Raw* and *SmackDown*. The two groups consistently debated which show was better, and there were often challenge matches between representatives of the two groups. However, for two years (2009 and 2010), a specific pay-per-view was designed around brand supremacy. In 2010, one of the opening matches of *Bragging Rights* pitted *SmackDown's* Intercontinental Champion Dolph Ziggler against *Raw's* United States Champion Daniel Bryan. Neither championship was on the line—just the pride of representing the brand.

BRAGGING RIGHTS 2010
CHAMPION VS. CHAMPION MATCH

October 24, 2010

Target Center
Minneapolis, Minnesota

THE MATCH

Bryan and Ziggler both attempted to exchange wrestling holds to begin the match, but in each case Bryan got the better of the exchange and quickly looked to put Ziggler in the LaBell Lock, Bryan's devastating finishing maneuver. Ziggler rolled out of the ring and looked to strategize with his cougar girlfriend, *SmackDown* consultant Vickie Guerrero. When Bryan followed Ziggler out of the ring, Ziggler put Guerrero between him and Bryan in order to protect himself. Bryan solved the problem by leaping on the ring apron, diving over Vickie, and splashing Ziggler.

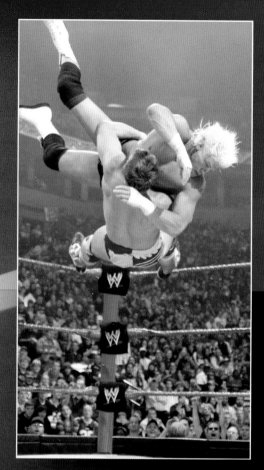

Ziggler got in a cheap shot on Bryan, and took control of the match. He looked to wear down the United States Champion with submission holds and headlocks. He tried to nail Bryan with a neckbreaker, but Bryan countered the move into a backslide and a pinning attempt. Ziggler continued to dominate, until Bryan, feeding off the cheers of the crowd, escaped a headlock and tossed Ziggler into a corner. Bryan looked to connect with his high knee, but Ziggler got out of the way in time and Bryan came crashing to the mat.

Both men continued to wow the crowd with their incredible moves and counters, as well as a series of near falls. Ziggler tried to slap the sleeper hold on Bryan, but the United States Champion countered the move. Ziggler impressed the crowd as well, twisting his body on a Superplex attempt by Bryan and turning it into a pinning combination. Even more impressive though, was that Bryan rolled through the attempt and turned it into a pinfall attempt of his own. The breathtaking back-and-forth between the two Superstars prompted the WWE Universe to start a "This is awesome!" chant.

The second time Ziggler put Bryan in the sleeper hold it looked like Bryan would fade away. But Bryan demonstrated his tenacity and resiliency and made the ring ropes, forcing a break of the hold. Ziggler, thinking that Bryan had submitted, started angrily arguing with the official. The break in concentration was the opening Bryan needed, and he got the Intercontinental Champion in the LaBell Lock. Ziggler tapped out, and Bryan had the win for his brand, *Raw*, and his own résumé as well. Both Guerrero and Ziggler continued to argue with the officials and they were ejected from the building as a result. Ziggler slunk out of the arena to the crowd chanting, "You tapped out!"

THE AFTERMATH

Bryan's victory got *Raw* off to a promising start at *Bragging Rights 2010*, but it was not an omen for the 14-man Elimination Tag Match. Although *Raw* had a 6-3 lead at one point, the team of Edge and Rey Mysterio were able to eliminate the last three members of team *Raw* and win the match for *SmackDown*. Ziggler would hold the Intercontinental Championship until January, when he lost the Title to Kofi Kingston. Bryan held the United States Championship for 176 days, until March 2013, when he lost the Title to Sheamus. Both men would go on to bigger and better things, with each having a World Heavyweight Championship reign in his future.

SGT. SLAUGHTER

THE LEAD-UP
Throughout 1981, Sgt. Slaughter ran the Cobra
Clutch Challenge, where he gave $5,000 to
any competitor that broke his hold. The Black
Demon was set to take the challenge when
Slaughter said something to him. The Demon
decided to forego the challenge and left. Color
commentator Pat Patterson interviewed Slaughter,
asking what happened and Slaughter called the
Demon and Patterson yellow. Patterson offered
to take the challenge then and there, but for
$10,000 instead of $5,000. Patterson almost
broke the hold, so Slaughter brutally
attacked him, leaving Patterson bleeding.
To settle their rivalry, an Alley Fight
match was set between the two.

vs. PAT PATTERSON

The ring announcer explained the rules of the Alley Fight. There would be no official in the ring, and no holds were barred. Each man came ready to brawl, with Patterson dressed in jeans and cowboy boots and Slaughter in his fatigues. As Slaughter entered the ring, Patterson went right after him, connecting with a series of punches and kicks. He then slammed Slaughter's head into the top turnbuckle and dropped Slaughter down to the canvas with a series of kicks to his legs. Patterson started choking Slaughter, but the sergeant was able to break the choke by pulling Patterson's hair back. Slaughter tried to then punch Patterson, but Pat ducked away, and the sergeant ended up punching the ring post.

Patterson took off his belt and whipped Slaughter's back with it. He then wrapped the belt around Slaughter's neck and began choking his opponent. At the ropes, Slaughter managed to save himself temporarily by dumping Patterson out of the ring. Before Slaughter could completely recover, Patterson retrieved the belt and began whipping him again, this time on the back and chest. Patterson again choked Slaughter, but the sergeant raked Pat's eyes to send Patterson reeling. Slaughter took control of the belt, which he used to clothesline Patterson after an Irish Whip. Slaughter also tried to choke Patterson, but he only managed to wrap the belt around Pat's face and head. Slaughter ripped Patterson's shirt off and used that to choke his opponent. Patterson staggered to the ring ropes, and his momentum sent Slaughter crashing out of the ring.

Slaughter took to the top rope, looking to re-enter the ring with a high-risk maneuver. However, Patterson dodged Slaughter's kick and both men were on the rope. Patterson was first to regain an offensive advantage, with a kick to the midsection, a scoop slam, and a knee off the second turnbuckle. To further the damage, Patterson repeated the scoop slam, knee off the second rope combo, and then bit Slaughter. Slaughter finally grabbed the offensive advantage with a series of kicks and stomps. The sergeant tossed Patterson out of the ring and onto the hard concrete floor. Patterson recovered and catapulted Slaughter over the turnbuckle and into the ring post, opening a massive cut on Slaughter's face.

Patterson connected with a series of rights, taking advantage of Slaughter's blood-streaked face. Slaughter hit Patterson with a low blow and then put some brass knuckles on his right fist. He used them to clock Patterson. Slaughter tried to use them again, but Patterson blocked him twice before hitting the sergeant on the top of the head and then the face with one of his cowboy boots. Patterson rammed Slaughter's head into the ring post again, causing Slaughter to fall out of the ring. Slaughter tried to re-enter the ring, but Patterson hit him repeatedly with the boot. Slaughter's manager, the Grand Wizard, had seen enough. Looking to protect his client, the Wizard grabbed a white towel and threw it into the ring, ending the match and giving the victory to Pat Patterson.

THE AFTERMATH

While Sgt. Slaughter tasted defeat that night, almost one decade later, he achieved the greatest victory of his career, pinning the Ultimate Warrior to win the WWE Championship. He held the Title for around two months, as Hulk Hogan wrested it from him in the main event of *WrestleMania VII*. Slaughter and Patterson reunited in 1998 as they helped Mr. McMahon in his efforts to rid the WWE of Stone Cold Steve Austin. They stand together now in the WWE Hall of Fame, with Patterson being inducted in 1994 and Slaughter a member of the 2004 class.

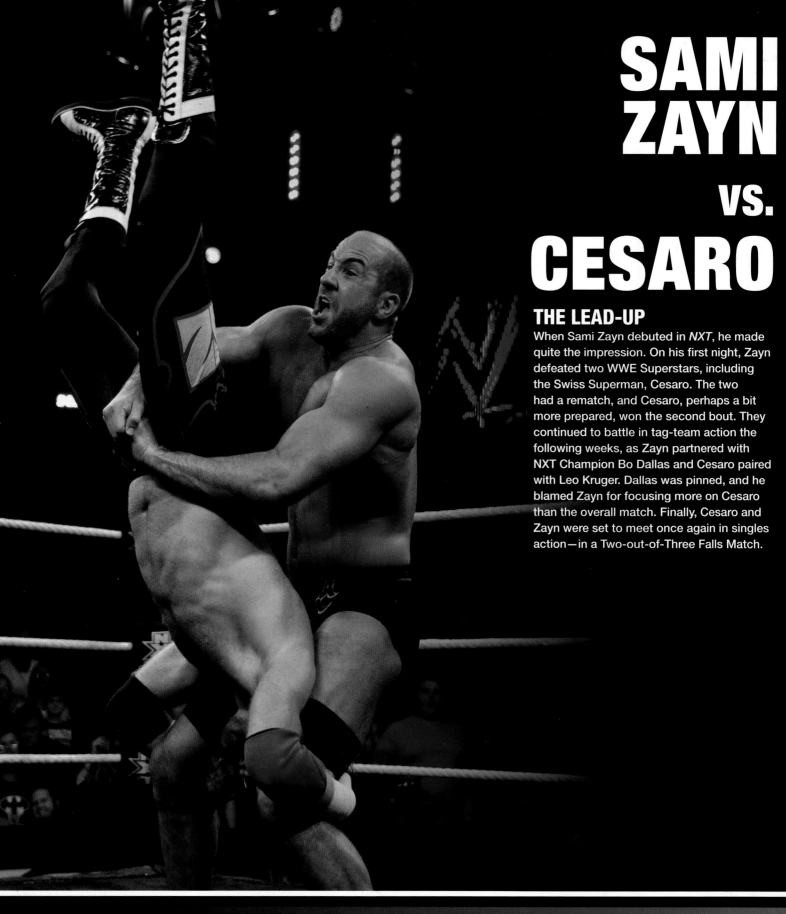

SAMI ZAYN

VS.

CESARO

THE LEAD-UP

When Sami Zayn debuted in *NXT*, he made quite the impression. On his first night, Zayn defeated two WWE Superstars, including the Swiss Superman, Cesaro. The two had a rematch, and Cesaro, perhaps a bit more prepared, won the second bout. They continued to battle in tag-team action the following weeks, as Zayn partnered with NXT Champion Bo Dallas and Cesaro paired with Leo Kruger. Dallas was pinned, and he blamed Zayn for focusing more on Cesaro than the overall match. Finally, Cesaro and Zayn were set to meet once again in singles action—in a Two-out-of-Three Falls Match.

NXT

TWO-OUT-OF-THREE FALLS MATCH

August 21, 2013

Full Sail University
Winter Park, Florida

THE MATCH

Zayn did not even wait for Cesaro to reach the ring. As Cesaro made his way down the ramp, Zayn flipped over the top rope down onto his opponent. After punching Cesaro several times, Zayn rolled him into the ring, and the bell finally rang to begin the match. With Cesaro in a corner, Zayn ran into him and hit the Swiss Superman with a boot to the face. Zayn rolled up Cesaro and got the shocking early three-count, putting Cesaro in a 1-0 hole less than a minute into the match. Cesaro tried to get in some offense with a big punch to Zayn, but Sami blocked the move and punched and clotheslined Cesaro out of the ring.

The two men briefly brawled outside of the ring before Zayn pushed Cesaro back in. Cesaro grabbed the offensive advantage until Zayn landed a risky maneuver—a high-cross body off the top rope that earned him a near fall. Cesaro then dropped Zayn's face onto the top turnbuckle for a two-count. Cesaro wore his opponent down with a series of extended chinlocks and sent Zayn crashing to the canvas with a Powerbomb. Zayn tried to work his way back into the match with a series of punches, but the arrogant Swiss Superman kept encouraging Zayn to hit him, implying the blows had no effect. Perhaps Cesaro had had enough, as he picked up Zayn and slammed him into the mat. Cesaro lifted Zayn and attempted to slam him again, but Zayn countered it into a roll-up and a two-count. Cesaro locked in another chinlock and spun Zayn around, tightening the grip. Zayn had no choice but to tap out and even the match at one fall apiece.

The tap out forced Cesaro to break the hold. While the official checked on the status of Zayn, Cesaro tensed his body, ready to pounce. The official got out of the way and the Swiss Superman performed a running uppercut and got another near fall. Cesaro demonstrated his incredible strength by climbing to the second rope and deadlifting Zayn up and over the ropes for a brutal suplex. Somehow, Zayn managed to kick out of the pinfall attempt. Zayn then managed to get a few pinfall attempts of his own by countering Cesaro power moves into roll-ups. Cesaro attempted to Powerbomb Zayn, but Zayn managed to flip over Cesaro and deliver a Powerbomb of his own. Before Zayn could attempt a pinfall, Cesaro rolled out of the ring

With Cesaro outside of the ring, trying to collect himself, Zayn rolled out of the ring on the opposite side. He challenged Cesaro to come to him, but then decided not to wait. Zayn dove through the ropes at Cesaro and delivered a tornado DDT onto the floor. Zayn headed back into the ring, but Cesaro was almost counted out; the Swiss Superman made it back in as the official counted nine. Zayn tried to pin Cesaro, but it was only a two-count. Zayn grabbed his opponent's hand, and leapt to the top turnbuckle to execute another tornado DDT, but Cesaro blocked the move and lifted Zayn over his head. Cesaro tossed Zayn straight up and blasted him with a European uppercut. He then grabbed his opponent, executed the Neutralizer, and gained the pin for a 2-1 victory.

THE AFTERMATH

While Cesaro returned to competition in WWE rings, Zayn looked to make a name for himself in NXT. Because their tag-team partnership fizzled, Zayn had a natural rivalry with Bo Dallas. However, Zayn was not able to defeat his former partner. Zayn and Adrian Neville developed a rivalry that became even more intense when Neville became the NXT Champion. After more than a year since his epic Two-Out-Of-Three Falls Match against Cesaro, Zayn defeated Neville and became the next NXT Champion.

THE HART FOUNDATION vs. TEAM AUSTIN

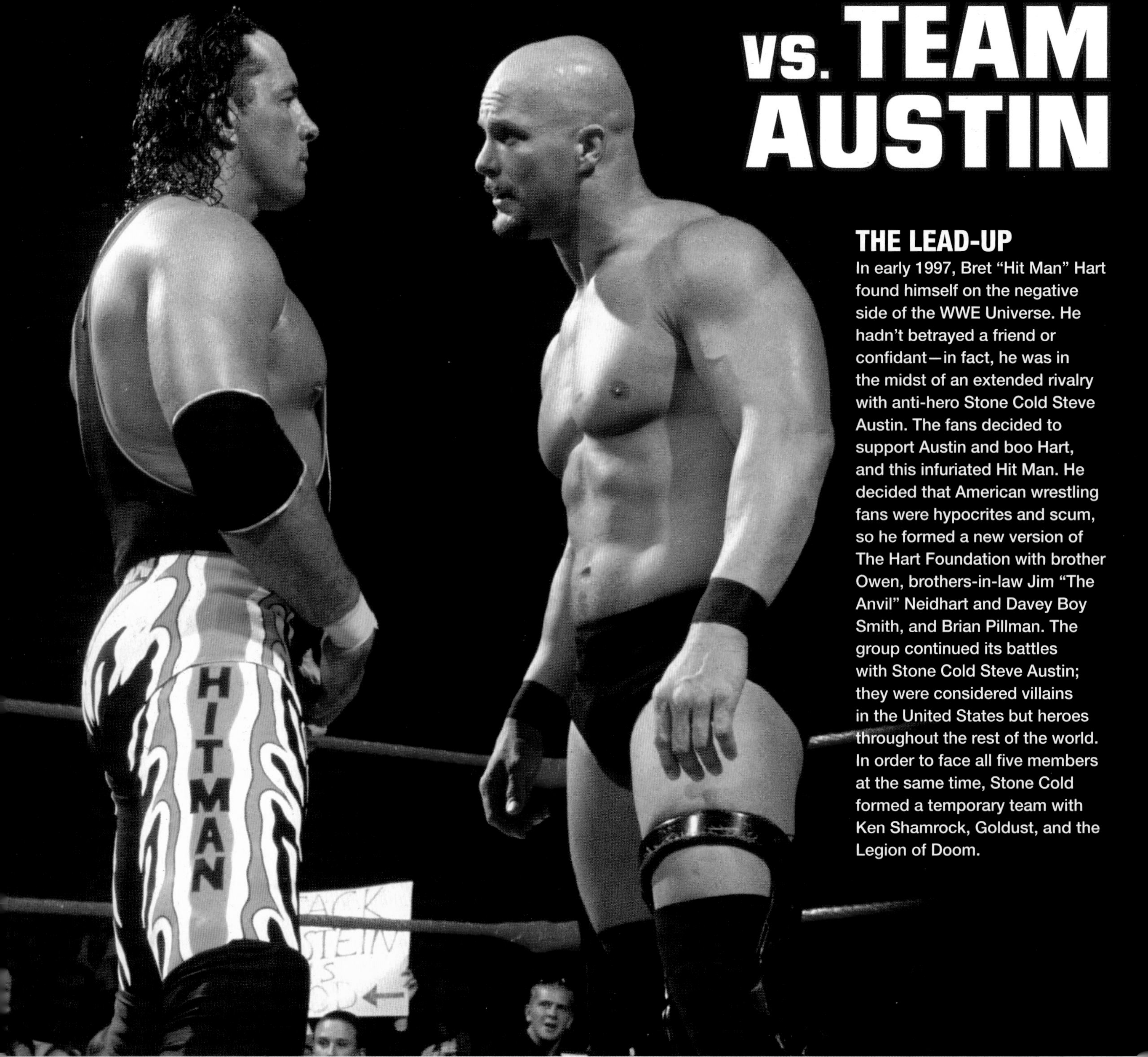

THE LEAD-UP

In early 1997, Bret "Hit Man" Hart found himself on the negative side of the WWE Universe. He hadn't betrayed a friend or confidant—in fact, he was in the midst of an extended rivalry with anti-hero Stone Cold Steve Austin. The fans decided to support Austin and boo Hart, and this infuriated Hit Man. He decided that American wrestling fans were hypocrites and scum, so he formed a new version of The Hart Foundation with brother Owen, brothers-in-law Jim "The Anvil" Neidhart and Davey Boy Smith, and Brian Pillman. The group continued its battles with Stone Cold Steve Austin; they were considered villains in the United States but heroes throughout the rest of the world. In order to face all five members at the same time, Stone Cold formed a temporary team with Ken Shamrock, Goldust, and the Legion of Doom.

IN YOUR HOUSE: CANADIAN STAMPEDE

TEN-MAN TAG TEAM MATCH

July 6, 1997

Saddledome
Calgary, Alberta, Canada

50

THE MATCH

If the pay-per-view was in any city in the United States, The Hart Foundation would have come out to loud boos. But in Calgary, home of the Hart family, the building shook with excitement and approval with the introduction of each member of The Hart Foundation. To further support the group, Bret's parents Stu and Helen Hart were at ringside, along with many of his brothers, sisters, and other family members.

With the Hart/Austin rivalry at the heart of the issue, it was fitting that the two men started off the match. The crowd roared with excitement for every successful Hart move, and boos rained down when Austin hit Hart with a low blow. Stone Cold then looked to take Owen Hart out of the match by repeatedly ramming Owen's knee against the ring post, and then hitting it with a foreign object. The plan seemed to work as medical officials had to help Owen to the back. Bret got revenge for his brother, slamming Austin's knee against the ring post, then hitting it with a fire extinguisher, and putting Austin in a Figure Four hold around the post. Austin also headed back for medical attention, so both teams were down a man.

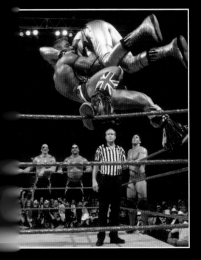

As the action continued, Stone Cold returned to the ring and reinserted himself into the action. Bret Hart put Austin into the Sharpshooter, but Animal broke up the move and knocked Austin down. Austin then attempted to beat the Hit Man with his own move as he locked Hart in the Sharpshooter. But Owen Hart appeared and saved his brother from the move. Once again, the match disintegrated as all ten men started fighting at the same time. Battling with The Hart Foundation was not enough, so Stone Cold started fighting with the Hart family members at ringside. Bret's brothers jumped the guard rail and inserted themselves into the match. During this chaos, Austin was rolled back into the ring and Owen Hart pinned him for The Hart Foundation victory.

As The Hart Foundation and their family celebrated in the ring, Shamrock, Goldust, and the Legion of Doom headed to the back. Austin, however, decided he still wanted to fight, so he entered the ring with a foreign object and blasted Hit Man on the back. It wasn't the smartest decision, as the numbers quickly overwhelmed the Texas Rattlesnake and the Harts beat him down until security handcuffed Austin and led him from the ring. Austin still had enough venom for the crowd to flip them off on the way out of the arena.

Austin's war with The Hart Foundation continued into *SummerSlam 1997*, as he successfully challenged Owen Hart for the Intercontinental Championship. It was almost the ultimate Pyrrhic victory, as an Owen Hart piledriver almost permanently ended Austin's career. For a brief moment Austin could not move, and while he managed to pin Hart for the Title, Austin had to forfeit the Title as he was out of action until *Survivor Series*, where he defeated Hart for the Title a second time. Also at *SummerSlam 1997*, Bret Hart faced Undertaker for the WWE Championship, with Hart's longtime rival Shawn Michaels serving as the Special Guest Referee. Hart was able to beat Undertaker for the Title and would eventually face Michaels at the highly controversial 1997 *Survivor Series*. That match would go down in history as the "Montreal Screwjob."

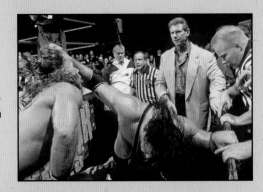

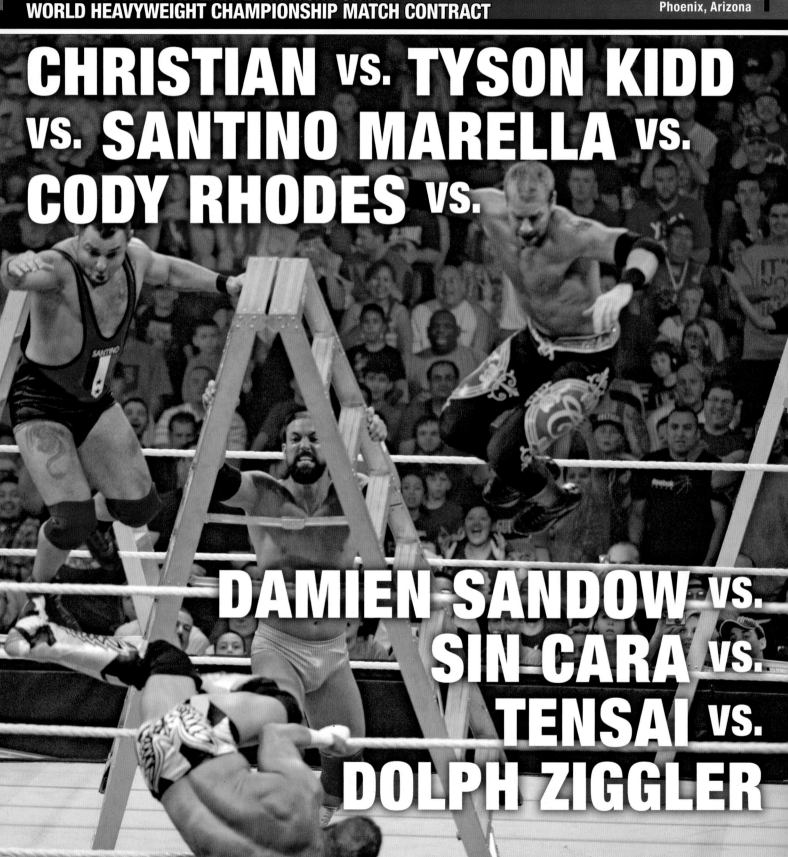

WWE MONEY IN THE BANK 2012

July 15, 2012

MONEY IN THE BANK LADDER MATCH FOR A
WORLD HEAVYWEIGHT CHAMPIONSHIP MATCH CONTRACT

US Airways Center
Phoenix, Arizona

CHRISTIAN vs. TYSON KIDD vs. SANTINO MARELLA vs. CODY RHODES vs. DAMIEN SANDOW vs. SIN CARA vs. TENSAI vs. DOLPH ZIGGLER

THE LEAD-UP

The Money in the Bank Ladder Match began at *WrestleMania 21* and, after six years, became a pay-per-view event on its own, featuring two Money in the Bank Matches. Heading into 2012, all 10 winners of Money in the Bank Matches had successfully used their Title opportunities to win World Championships, so it was understandable why the Superstars of *Raw* and *SmackDown* put such emphasis on competing in this event. For the eight men in each match, it was a way to advance careers and elevate them into the main event mix.

THE MATCH

When the bell rang, all eight men started brawling and the fights spilled out of the ring. Tensai took early advantage of his power and brought two ladders into the ring that he used as weapons against both Christian and Kidd. While Tensai was focused on Christian, Kidd tossed the ladder into his back, and then worked together with Christian to knock Tensai out of the ring. Christian attacked Kidd and then started climbing toward the briefcase when Santino joined him on the ladder, followed by Kidd. All three men reached for the briefcase, and Sandow took advantage of their focus to knock the ladder down, taking all three men out.

Sandow climbed the ladder, but Ziggler dropkicked him off. Rhodes re-entered the ring and he and Ziggler fought one-on-one until Sin Cara joined them with a missile drop kick over Rhodes and onto Ziggler. With Ziggler, Rhodes, and Sandow out of the ring, Sin Cara headed up the ladder, only to be brought back to the mat by Tensai, who also slammed Santino off the ladder as well. Kidd and Tensai got tangled up and both went over the top rope. With the ring cleared, Sandow tried to climb the ladder. Christian managed to climb over him, but Sandow took him out before he could reach the top.

Christian tried to ascend again, but Ziggler and Cody stopped him. The two Superstars climbed the ladder, but Tensai took both of them out and started to rise toward his goal. Christian and Santino worked together to halt Tensai. Without Christian in the ring, Santino delivered The Cobra to Dolph Ziggler and tried to climb, but Marella developed a fear of heights. Cody dealt with Santino and tried to climb for the Title. Vickie Guerrero distracted Rhodes until her boyfriend Ziggler hit a Zig Zag off the ladder.

Outside the ring, Tensai used a ladder as a bridge across the announcers' table and the ring. Sin Cara tried to hit Tensai with a flying cross body, but Tensai caught the masked Superstar and gave him an ugly case of déjà vu, as Sin Cara was slammed onto the ladder for the second straight year. Santino and Christian were alone on the ladder and Christian slammed Marella into the ladder and knocked him down. Now all alone, it seemed just a matter of time before Christian grabbed the briefcase. But Ziggler leapt into the ring and raced up the ladder, tossing Christian into a second ladder and knocking him down. With no one else on the ladder, the Showoff was able to retrieve the briefcase and win his first Money in the Bank match.

THE AFTERMATH

Ziggler was forced to defend his Money in the Bank contract in two matches in 2012. The first time was against Chris Jericho, in which Y2J had to wager his career against the briefcase. Ziggler won that match on *Raw* the night after *SummerSlam*, so Jericho left WWE. In December, Ziggler was forced to again defend the briefcase, this time against John Cena in a Ladder Match. With the help of AJ Lee, Ziggler kept his Title opportunity. He held onto it until the day after *WrestleMania 29*, when he defeated Alberto Del Rio to become the new World Heavyweight Champion.

TEAM PIPER vs. TEAM FLAIR

THE LEAD-UP

In late summer 1991, Ric Flair joined WWE, bringing with him a gold Championship Title. Claiming to be the "Real World's Champion," Flair and his financial advisor Bobby "The Brain" Heenan denigrated WWE Champion Hulk Hogan. Flair didn't just run afoul of Hogan, he also found himself in an extended rivalry with "Rowdy" Roddy Piper, who claimed, "I scare Flair." To settle their differences, each man captained a team of Superstars at *Survivor Series 1991*. Flair was joined by "Million Dollar Man" Ted DiBiase, the Warlord, and The Mountie. Piper's team included Bret "Hit Man" Hart, Virgil, and the British Bulldog.

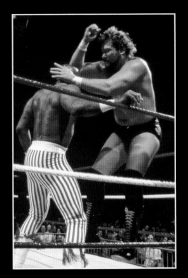

THE MATCH

Piper wanted to get his hands on Flair to start the match, but DiBiase started out for his team. Managers were supposed to be barred from ringside, but Sherri managed to stick around and even interfere in the match until Piper planted a kiss on her and the official ejected her to the back. Perhaps distracted by the loss of his manager, DiBiase found himself trapped in the corner of Piper's team, who demonstrated excellent teamwork with all four men tagging in and out to work on the Million Dollar Man.

DiBiase finally offered some offense on Bret "Hit Man" Hart and then tagged in Flair in order to get a breather. Flair went to drop an elbow on Hart, but the Hit Man rolled out of the way and gave the British Bulldog a chance to work over Flair. The Bulldog delivered a Press Slam and then gave the fans what they wanted to see—Piper versus Flair. The two men traded chops until Piper launched a barrage of punches and chops in and out of the ring. When Flair re-entered the ring, he tagged in the Warlord.

A series of quick tags eventually ended with the Bulldog being the legal man for his team. Confusion in the ring led to Flair coming off the top rope and hitting the Bulldog. He secured the three-count, and his team developed a four-on-three advantage. Piper looked like he could be the next man eliminated as Flair's team isolated Hot Rod, but Roddy managed to slap a Figure-Four on the Nature Boy. While the official was distracted, DiBiase kicked Piper to break the hold. But Piper tagged out, and then re-entered the match where he evened matters by pinning the Warlord. Piper then fought DiBiase in the ring before getting a hold of Flair once again.

Piper tossed Flair into the corner, causing the Nature Boy to flip over the top turnbuckle and down to the floor below. Back in the ring, all the remaining Superstars began brawling, ignoring the official's demand that they leave the ring and head to their respective corners. After warning the five men, the official decided he had no choice but to disqualify all of them. The only man not involved in the brawl was Flair, who was still recovering out on the floor. As a result, Flair was the sole survivor of the match, winning the bout for his team.

Ric Flair was not done making waves. The Nature Boy inserted himself into the WWE Championship Match, helping Undertaker win the Title from Hulk Hogan. He would try and do it again a week later in Hulk Hogan's rematch at *This Tuesday in Texas*. But Hogan managed to regain the Title by throwing ash in Undertaker's face. The fact that both matches had controversial finishes led WWE President Jack Tunney to vacate the Championship and make the Royal Rumble Match for the WWE Championship. Flair entered that event at number three and managed to go wire-to-wire to win the match and the WWE Championship.

THE ROCK vs. MANKIND

WWE RAW

NO DISQUALIFICATION MATCH FOR THE WWE CHAMPIONSHIP

January 4, 1999

Worcester Centrum
Worcester, Massachusetts

THE LEAD-UP

Mankind's dream was to become WWE Champion, and he was willing to work with Mr. McMahon and the Corporation to make it happen. In the finals of the WWE Championship tournament at *Survivor Series 1998*, Mankind thought he had the backing of Mr. McMahon, but The Chairman screwed over Mankind and supported The Rock instead. The deranged Mankind wanted a Title match at the *Royal Rumble*, but he changed his mind when Shane McMahon unfairly called a pin on him in a Royal Rumble qualification match. Mankind grabbed the younger McMahon and threatened to break his shoulder unless Mr. McMahon granted Mankind a no-DQ Title match later that night on *Raw*.

THE MATCH

It almost seemed like a Lumberjack Match at the start, as D-Generation X came to the ring in support of Mankind, and the Corporation accompanied The Rock. Mankind found himself arguing with Mr. McMahon, and The Rock used the distraction to his advantage, attacking the challenger to open the match. The Rock dumped Mankind out of the ring and among the Corporation, but called off the members from attacking Mankind, claiming he had things under control. The Rock backed up his confident assertion by using the steel ring stairs as a weapon against Mankind.

The Rock continued his vicious streak by suplexing Mankind onto the ring floor. The Corporate Champ tried to humiliate the challenger by taking the match announcer's headset and stating for the TV crowd The Great One's ability and talent. Mankind used the distraction to attack The Rock, but The Rock regained the momentum by hitting Mankind with the ring bell. The Rock continued to push the allowable limits by choking Mankind with an electrical cable and then delivering a Rock Bottom that sent Mankind crashing through the announcers' table.

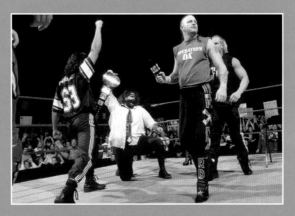

Back in the ring, The Rock kicked Mankind repeatedly and managed a two-count. The Great One draped his challenger across the ropes and then argued with the official, allowing Shane McMahon to get a bit of revenge from earlier in the night by striking Mankind in the face. The Rock got another near fall with a Russian Leg Sweep. He then dropped Mankind to the mat with a scoop slam. The Rock thought he had the match won when he delivered the Corporate Elbow, but Mankind annoyed the Great One by kicking out. The Champion sent Mankind into the ropes to give him a back body drop, but the challenger stopped short and dropped The Rock with a swinging neckbreaker. As Mankind tried to hit the Champ with another move, the Big Boss Man interfered, drawing an admonition from the official. This distracted the referee so he did not see The Rock hit Mankind with the Championship Title. However, Mankind kicked out of the pinning attempt again.

The Champion tried to hit Mankind with the Title once more, but the challenger ducked and instead delivered a chicken-wing DDT onto the Title. Rock kicked out, so Mankind pulled Mr. Socko out of his tights and locked the Mandible Claw onto the Champion. Ken Shamrock entered the ring and nailed Mankind across the back. Billy Gunn jumped in to take out Shamrock, leading to an all-out brawl between the Corporation and DX outside the ring. At this point, Stone Cold Steve Austin's music played and Austin came to the ring, laid out Rock, and placed Mankind on top of him. The official counted three, and Mankind was the new WWE Champion.

Mankind's dream of being WWE Champion lasted most of January until The Rock won the Title back at the *Royal Rumble* in an "I Quit" Match, although Mankind never said the words aloud. The two met again in an empty arena during halftime of *Super Bowl XXXIII*, where Mankind took the Title back from The Great One by pinning him with a forklift. They agreed to a Last Man Standing match at *St. Valentine's Massacre*, one last bout to decide who would enter *WrestleMania XV*. However, when that match was declared a draw, they followed it with a Ladder Match on *Raw*, which The Rock won with the help of new WWE Superstar, Big Show.

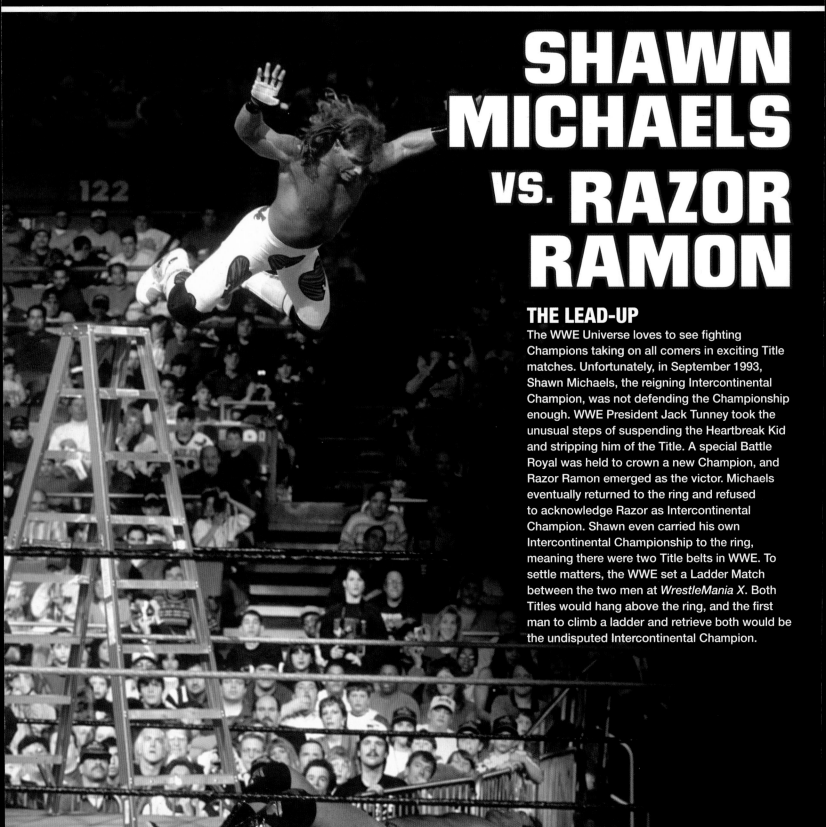

WRESTLEMANIA X
LADDER MATCH FOR THE INTERCONTINENTAL CHAMPIONSHIP

March 20, 1994
Madison Square Garden
New York, New York

SHAWN MICHAELS VS. RAZOR RAMON

THE LEAD-UP

The WWE Universe loves to see fighting Champions taking on all comers in exciting Title matches. Unfortunately, in September 1993, Shawn Michaels, the reigning Intercontinental Champion, was not defending the Championship enough. WWE President Jack Tunney took the unusual steps of suspending the Heartbreak Kid and stripping him of the Title. A special Battle Royal was held to crown a new Champion, and Razor Ramon emerged as the victor. Michaels eventually returned to the ring and refused to acknowledge Razor as Intercontinental Champion. Shawn even carried his own Intercontinental Championship to the ring, meaning there were two Title belts in WWE. To settle matters, the WWE set a Ladder Match between the two men at *WrestleMania X*. Both Titles would hang above the ring, and the first man to climb a ladder and retrieve both would be the undisputed Intercontinental Champion.

THE MATCH

Michaels came to the ring first, accompanied by his bodyguard, Diesel. Fans probably worried that Ramon would face unfair odds, as Diesel had inserted himself into a number of Michaels' previous matches. At the start, it looked like this match would be no different—early in the contest, Michaels dumped Razor out of the ring, and Diesel took advantage, dropping Razor with a clubbing blow. The official quickly pieced things together and ejected Diesel from the match, ensuring a more even pairing.

At first, both men seemed to have the same idea—wear down his opponent enough to make scaling the ladder a bit easier. Razor even peeled back some of the mats around the ring in order to slam Michaels on the unforgiving concrete. This plan completely backfired when Michaels tossed Ramon over the ropes onto the exposed spot. This painful experience gave the Heartbreak Kid the opportunity to retrieve a ladder, but Razor recovered as Michaels dragged the eight-foot ladder to the ring. Michaels turned toward the ring, only to be popped by the Bad Guy. But when Ramon tried to bring the ladder into the ring, Michaels hit a baseball slide, knocking the ladder into Ramon.

This opening led to Michaels using the ladder in innovative offensive moves. He hammered Ramon with the ladder as a battering ram, leapt off the ladder to make his splash even more effective, and dropped the ladder on top of the Bad Guy. When Razor was able to take control of the match, he also used the ladder creatively, battering Michaels with it repeatedly. The announcer began to wonder if the ladder was too bent and damaged to support the weight of the Superstars, but the ladder's condition did not prevent either man from making attempts to climb it and grab the two Championships. But each time

one competitor climbed, the other would eventually knock the ladder over or toss his opponent off the ladder (and in many cases, do both!). Razor threw Michaels off the ladder, and the Heartbreak Kid got tangled in the ring ropes. While Michaels tried frantically to free himself from the ropes, an exhausted Ramon climbed the ladder and grabbed both Championships, clutching them to his chest as he fell to the canvas. The Bad Guy had staked a singular claim to the Intercontinental Championship, and both men had participated in one of the greatest bouts in *WrestleMania* history.

THE AFTERMATH

Michaels and Ramon set an incredibly high bar for WWE's first *WrestleMania* Ladder Match. A little more than a year later, the two men would compete at *SummerSlam 1995* in a second Ladder Match, again for the Intercontinental Championship. Michaels would even the score, as he successfully defended his Title that night. It was part of Michaels' third reign as Intercontinental Champion, while Razor would hold the Title on four occasions. The Ladder Match has become an ingrained specialty match in WWE, but most competitors and fans look to this *WrestleMania X* encounter as the best-ever.

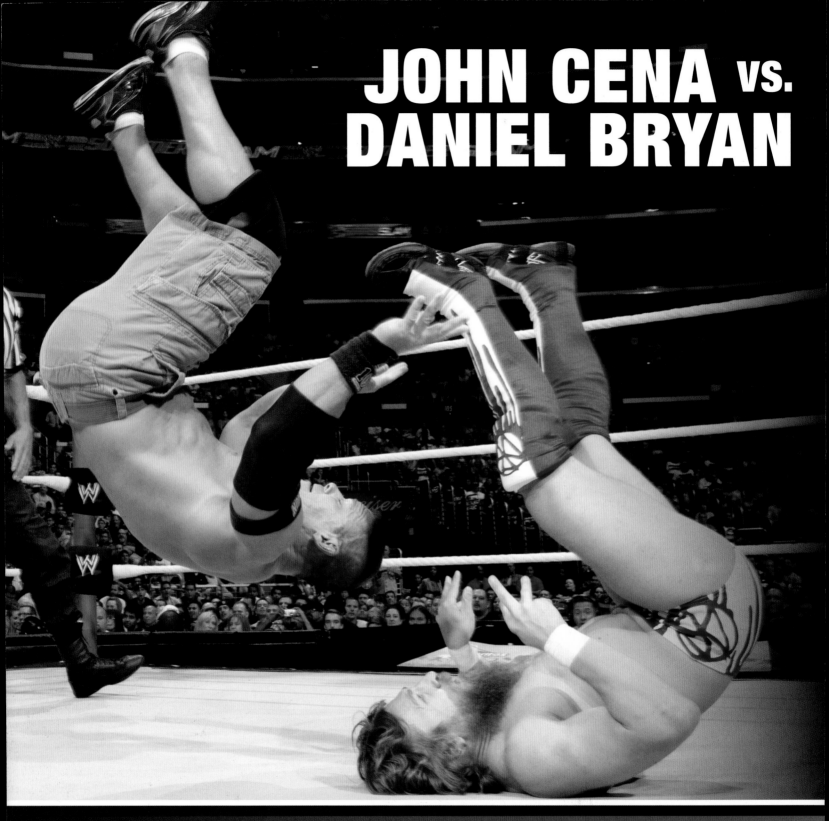

JOHN CENA vs. DANIEL BRYAN

SUMMERSLAM 2013
WWE CHAMPIONSHIP MATCH

August 18, 2013
Staples Center
Los Angeles, California

THE LEAD-UP

After *Money in the Bank 2013*, *Raw* General Manager Brad Maddox allowed the WWE Champion to choose his next challenger at *SummerSlam*. Cena listened to the WWE Universe and granted the Title opportunity to Daniel Bryan. Mr. McMahon was infuriated by the choice—while he didn't want John Cena to be Champion, he wanted Bryan even less. Looking to stack the deck against Bryan, McMahon lobbied for Maddox to be the Guest Official, but Triple H stepped in to be a fair and impartial official in the match. Bryan asserted the match would be between "Cena the Entertainer" and "Bryan the Wrestler."

THE MATCH

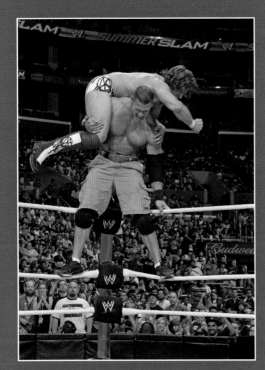

Cena tried to use his power advantage to take early control of the match. But Bryan surprised the Champion by demonstrating some of his own power and countering Cena's moves with technical ability. Perhaps bothered by the challenger's "Cena the Entertainer" claim, Cena showcased some dazzling move combinations, while Bryan tried to force a submission. After Cena knocked Bryan out of the ring and into the announcers' table, Bryan flung Cena into the steel ring steps. Bryan then tried to suplex Cena off the steps, but Cena reversed the move and sent Bryan crashing to the floor.

Back in the ring, Cena continued to press his power advantage, delivering a wicked Power Bomb. Bryan demonstrated his tenacity by kicking out at the two-count. Bryan then changed the momentum, delivering a series of punches and kicks in the corner, accompanied by "Yes!" chants from the crowd. The crowd continued to punctuate Bryan's kicks as he delivered more punishment to Cena in the middle of the ring. Cena then went on the offense, until he was halted by a Missile Dropkick from the top rope. Bryan, however, could only hold Cena down for a two-count. Cena then tried to put his challenger in the STF, but Bryan countered and turned it into an STF of his own. When Cena refused to submit, Bryan attempted a pair of German Suplexes, in which each got two-counts. Bryan followed with the "Yes!" Lock, but Cena used his incredible power to escape.

Cena nailed Bryan with an Attitude Adjustment and went for the pin. Bryan, however, stunned the Champion by kicking out. Cena then went to the top rope, but Bryan kept leaping into the corner to hit Cena. Bryan then hooked his feet under the middle ropes and flung Cena from the top turnbuckle in a blistering Superplex, sending Cena to the mat while Bryan dangled upside down from the ring's corner. Even after the Superplex and a follow-up flying headbutt, Bryan could only get a two-count. Cena finally managed to lock Bryan into the STF submission move, but Bryan reversed it into a "Yes!" Lock. Cena reached the ropes to break the hold, and stopped Bryan's momentum with an explosive clothesline out of the corner. The two continued to trade punches, kicks, and even slaps.

Cena attempted another Attitude Adjustment, but Bryan turned it into a DDT. Bryan then climbed to the top rope, but Cena caught him mid-air and again tried to finish the challenger off with an Attitude Adjustment. Again, Bryan countered the move, this time into a small package and a two-count. Bryan then delivered a kick to the head and a knee to the face. He finally kept the Champion down for the three-count, completing his assent to the top of the sports-entertainment world by winning the WWE Championship.

THE AFTERMATH

Daniel Bryan did not have long to celebrate his hard-won Championship. Bryan had not even left the ring when Randy Orton appeared with his Money in the Bank briefcase. Orton teased entering the ring, but backed off. Triple H, who had stayed in the ring with the Champion, decimated Bryan with a Pedigree. This allowed Orton to cash in his Title opportunity and win the WWE Championship. Bryan then had to deal with the re-introduction of Triple H and Stephanie McMahon as "The Authority," who supported Randy Orton as Champion and did all they could to prevent Daniel Bryan from winning the Title. But Bryan clawed his way to the top and won his WWE World Heavyweight Championship at *WrestleMania 30*.

KURT ANGLE
VS.
BROCK LESNAR

THE LEAD-UP

Kurt Angle and Brock Lesnar are two of the most gifted athletes in WWE history. Both entered WWE having won NCAA Heavyweight Wrestling Championships, and Angle won a gold medal in the 1996 Olympics. In 2003, the two had three high profile one-on-one matches for the WWE Championship. Lesnar won the first at *WrestleMania XIX*, and Angle won the rematch at *SummerSlam*. To break the tie, the two would meet in a 60-minute Iron Man Match on *SmackDown* with the competitor that scored the most decisions in the one-hour timeframe declared the winner.

SMACKDOWN
60-MINUTE IRON MAN MATCH FOR THE WWE CHAMPIONSHIP

September 18, 2003
RBC Center
Raleigh, North Carolina

THE MATCH

Both men began the hour-long match with conservative offenses, mostly punching and kicking. Angle seemed to be getting the best of the early exchanges, so Lesnar kept bailing out of the ring, frustrating both the Champion and the Raleigh crowd. Lesnar would never stay out long enough to lose a count-out decision, but his continual exiting of the ring slowed the initial pace. About nine minutes into the match, Lesnar grabbed a foreign object and hit Angle with it several times. The referee disqualified Lesnar and awarded the first fall to Angle, giving him a 1-0 lead.

The announcers were baffled as to why Lesnar would give up the first fall in such a manner, but Lesnar's plan soon became apparent. The Beast picked up the downed Champion, delivered an F-5, and pinned Angle, tying the bout at one fall each. After the mandatory 15-second break, Lesnar went right back to work on the Olympic Hero, softening him up with additional kicks until Lesnar used Angle's own Ankle Lock against him. Angle had no choice but to tap out. Twelve minutes into the match, Lesnar now had a 2-1 advantage. Lesnar tried to further humiliate Angle by also using his Angle Slam, but the Champion managed to kick out of two pinfall attempts.

The two men continued to brawl outside the ring with Lesnar delivering a punishing F-5 onto the floor. Lesnar rolled back into the ring, but Angle could not recover before the 10-count. Lesnar now had a 3-1 lead 20 minutes into the match. Angle fought his way back into the match, nailing two belly-to-belly overhead suplexes, but Lesnar used his size advantage to reassert his dominance. The Champion demonstrated his resilience, surprising the challenger with an Angle Slam to score a pinfall decision and cut the lead to 3-2 with 34 minutes remaining. Angle hit another Angle Slam that should have tied the match, but the official was "accidentally" knocked out by Lesnar. With no official to disqualify him, Lesnar hit Angle with a low blow and a shot with the Championship belt. Lesnar then pinned Angle to take a 4-2 lead with less than 30 minutes remaining.

Angle hit a dizzying array of moves over the next 15 minutes, but he could not get a pinfall decision to narrow the gap. To make matters worse, Lesnar delivered a top-rope Superplex and pinned Angle, taking a 5-2 lead with less than 15 minutes to go. But Angle would start to mount an incredible comeback. Angle pinned Lesnar after a belly-to-belly Superplex, making the score 5-3 with less than 10 minutes remaining. With four minutes left, Angle made Lesnar submit to an Ankle Lock and the Champion had cut the deficit to one, 5-4. After more jockeying for position, Angle put Lesnar in the Ankle Lock once again with 10 seconds to go, but Lesnar hung on and the time expired, giving Lesnar the win.

THE AFTERMATH

While Undertaker was Lesnar's next challenger for the WWE Championship, Angle and Lesnar continued their rivalry at the 2003 *Survivor Series*. Each captained teams of five in a 10-Man Elimination Tag Match. Lesnar eliminated Angle from the match, but Angle's team ultimately won. Lesnar continued to reign as WWE Champion until February 2004, when he lost the Title to Eddie Guerrero at *No Way Out*. Angle challenged Guerrero for the Title at *WrestleMania XX*, but Guerrero retained the Championship.

THE LEAD-UP

Every year, the WWE Universe eagerly anticipates the Royal Rumble Match. Not only is it the kickoff of the Road to *WrestleMania* with the winner getting a shot at the Title of their choice, but the match often has surprise entrants and exciting ring returns. The Rumble in 2011 was going to be even grander, as for the first time in history, there would be 40 entrants, making it the biggest Royal Rumble Match ever.

THE MATCH

CM Punk drew the unenviable position of #1 in the match—already a tall order in other years, having to go through 29 competitors, but this year he had to outlast 39 others. Before the match could even start, the four members of The Corre surrounded the ring to attack Punk, leading his New Nexus to charge the ring and begin an all-out brawl. The Anonymous *Raw* General Manager chimed in with a note stating that they all had to go back to the dressing room and await their number or they would be disqualified from the match. This allowed things to start with the announcement of #2, Daniel Bryan. The #7 entrant, John Morrison, astounded the crowd when William Regal knocked him off the apron. Instead of falling to the floor, Morrison reached the ring barrier, keeping his feet off the floor. He then used his parkour background to leap from the barrier to the ring steps and back into the ring, keeping him in the match.

Most of the first eight entrants targeted CM Punk, but things got better for the Straight Edge Superstar with the ninth entrant, Husky Harris. As part of Punk's Nexus, Harris's goal was to do everything he could to help Punk win the match. The burly Superstar blocked others from attacking Punk, and he attacked anyone that went after Punk. The numbers got even better with Michael McGillicutty's entrance at #13. The Nexus had strength in numbers. Punk's underlings removed Ted DiBiase and Punk eliminated Daniel Bryan and Chris Masters. The Nexus added David Otunga at #15 and now the quartet cleared the ring. The group then eliminated the next four entrants. The Great Khali eliminated Husky Harris to cut their number to three, but Mason Ryan gave them four again, and they took out Khali and the next entrant, Booker T.

The WWE Universe began to wonder if anyone could withstand the New Nexus, but the question was quickly answered at #22 with the appearance of John Cena. The former Champ lived up to a pre-match promise and eliminated the remaining members of the New Nexus, including Punk. Cena and Hornswoggle formed a team that eliminated several other entrants. Hornswoggle was then eliminated by Sheamus, drawing the ire of the crowd. The crowd exploded at the return of Diesel, who entered the match at #32. The ring continued to fill with Superstars and when Big Show entered, it looked like he might clear out the ring, but Ezekiel Jackson took out the World's Largest Superstar.

Rey Mysterio disposed of Kane, and Wade Barrett eliminated Mysterio. John Cena had to feel good about his chances, but Alex Riley returned to the ring and distracted Cena, allowing WWE Champion The Miz to eliminate the Champ. The final four came down to Wade Barrett, Alberto Del Rio, Randy Orton, and Santino Marella, although no one knew Marella was still in the match as he was down and out on the ring floor. Orton took out Barrett and Del Rio dumped Orton. Del Rio's music played, and the Mexican Aristocrat celebrated, thinking he had won the match. But Marella finally re-entered the match and gave the Cobra to Del Rio. He tried to toss Del Rio from the ring, but Del Rio reversed the move and took out Santino, winning the biggest Royal Rumble in history.

Del Rio had his choice of matches at *WrestleMania*; he chose to face the World Heavyweight Champion. Edge was the current Title holder, but the Rated-R Superstar had to defend his Title against five other men in an Elimination Chamber Match in order to ensure his spot on the grand stage of *WrestleMania*. Not only did Edge retain his Title in the Chamber, he also defeated Del Rio at *WrestleMania XXVII*, Edge's final match as a competitor. That *WrestleMania* also featured The Miz successfully defending the WWE Championship against John Cena, partially due to the actions of The Rock, setting in motion a year-long buildup to a match between the Great One and John Cena.

WWE VENGEANCE

MATCH TO UNIFY THE WCW CHAMPIONSHIP AND WWE CHAMPIONSHIP INTO THE UNDISPUTED CHAMPIONSHIP

December 9, 2001

San Diego Sports Arena
San Diego, California

STONE COLD STEVE AUSTIN vs. CHRIS JERICHO

THE LEAD-UP

After WWE finally defeated The Alliance and removed the threat of WCW and ECW, it was decided that only one World Champion was needed. Stone Cold Steve Austin was the WWE Champion, and The Rock held the WCW Championship. For *Vengeance*, both men would defend their Titles against #1 contenders, and then the winners of those matches would face each other to unify the Titles into a single, Undisputed Championship. On the night of *Vengeance*, The Rock was defeated by Chris Jericho, while Stone Cold Steve Austin successfully defended his Title against Kurt Angle. This meant Jericho and Austin would face each other to decide a single World Champion.

THE MATCH

Chris Jericho had just pinned The Rock and heard his name announced as the new WWE Champion, when the sound of breaking glass indicated Stone Cold was already heading to the ring. Austin backed Y2J into a corner and was set to unleash hell on Jericho when Kurt Angle, still angry about his loss to Austin, came into the ring and blindsided the Texas Rattlesnake. Before Y2J could do anything to Austin, The Rock also re-entered the ring and hit Jericho with a Rock Bottom. After all the extra-curricular activity, the match finally started.

Jericho tried to take immediate advantage of Angle's damage to Austin and went for the pin, but the Bionic Redneck kicked out. Jericho pressed his lead with kicks, chops, and whips into the corner. But Austin exploded out of the corner with a tackle and shifted the offensive advantage to his side. He went for an early Stone Cold Stunner, but Jericho blocked the move, so Austin knocked him off the apron to the floor below. Austin followed Jericho and beat Y2J into the crowd and threw him into the ring post. Austin then ripped up the padding outside the ring to expose the concrete below it. The Texas Rattlesnake suplexed Jericho onto the exposed concrete. He then rolled Jericho into the ring and attempted to spear Y2J. Jericho dodged and Austin's shoulder rammed into the ring post.

Jericho tried to force an Austin submission with an arm bar, and he furthered his leverage by putting his feet on the ropes. The official noticed the cheating and kicked Jericho's feet off the ropes, forcing Y2J to break the hold. Jericho, angry with the official's actions, suplexed Austin. He tried to further soften up the Texas Rattlesnake with a double axe-handle off the top rope, but Austin countered with a stinging punch to Jericho's midsection. Jericho fought back and put Austin in the Walls of Jericho, but Austin managed to reach the ropes. Jericho attempted to hit Austin with a flying forearm, but the Texas Rattlesnake ducked and Jericho hit the official with the move instead.

With the official down, Mr. McMahon appeared and signaled for his crooked official Nick Patrick. Before Patrick could do anything, Ric Flair came to the ring and knocked Patrick out. An enraged Mr. McMahon tossed Flair into the ring post, but Austin left the ring and dealt with the Chairman himself. With both officials incapacitated, no one was there to signal the end of the match when Jericho tapped out to Austin's application of the Walls of Jericho. In addition, no official saw Booker T enter the ring and knock Austin out with the Championship. Mr. McMahon finally revived the official who counted Jericho's pin of Austin, allowing Y2J to become the first Undisputed Champion in WWE History.

THE AFTERMATH

Both The Rock and Stone Cold wanted another shot at Chris Jericho, and each would get the opportunity to wrest the Undisputed Championship from Y2J. The Rock was up first, challenging the Undisputed Champion at the 2002 *Royal Rumble*. The resourceful Jericho managed to retain the Title, only to turn around and defend the Title against Stone Cold at *No Way Out* the following month. Jericho also won the match versus Austin, meaning he would be heading to *WrestleMania X8* as the Undisputed Champion. Jericho's luck would end that night, as Triple H defeated Y2J to become the second Undisputed Champion in WWE History. Triple H took Jericho's Title, but not the bragging right he earned by beating The Rock and Stone Cold on the same night, a right that Y2J still takes advantage of to this day.

BRUNO SAMMARTINO
vs.
"SUPERSTAR" BILLY GRAHAM

THE LEAD-UP

In 1973, Bruno Sammartino won the WWE Championship for a second time, and again he held on to the Title for years, defeating all comers and challengers.

In 1976, Stan Hansen broke Sammartino's neck in a match, but the WWE Champion got his revenge at the second *Showdown at Shea* in June, 1976. But the injury lingered over the next year and, in 1977, Sammartino was slated to face a new challenger, perhaps the most unique Superstar he'd ever faced.

"Superstar" Billy Graham started off as a bodybuilder, but truly found his calling in the wrestling ring. The flamboyant Graham brought a distinctive style to both his wardrobe and interviews, and in the spring of 1977 he was the #1 contender.

WWE CHAMPIONSHIP MATCH

April 30, 1977

Baltimore Civic Center
Baltimore, Maryland

THE MATCH

The two men locked up in the center of the ring, and Graham demonstrated his considerable power by tossing the Champion into the corner. To punctuate his point, the arrogant Graham flexed his muscles after the move, drawing boos from the crowd. Sammartino attempted to lock up again, but Graham grabbed the upper hand once more. The third time was the charm for the Champ, as he tossed Graham into a corner and then brought the challenger down with an arm-drag takedown. Sammartino tried to keep Superstar on the mat by wrenching Graham's arm, until Superstar got a leg on the rope, forcing a break of the move.

Graham rolled out of the ring, trying to halt the Champion's momentum. Back in the ring, Graham and Sammartino locked up in a test of strength, and initially the challenger had the advantage. He forced Bruno down to a knee, and while the Champion fought back to a vertical base, Graham forced him down to the canvas, even getting the first near fall of the match. Feeding off the energy of the crowd, Sammartino regained his footing and pressured Graham down to the mat. The Champion had a two-count, but Superstar again got his foot on the ropes, stopping the pinfall and forcing a break of the hold. Yet another test of strength looked to be going Graham's way, but Bruno forced the challenger down with an arm bar.

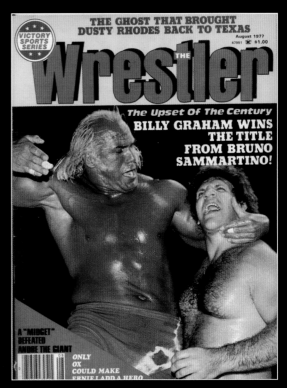

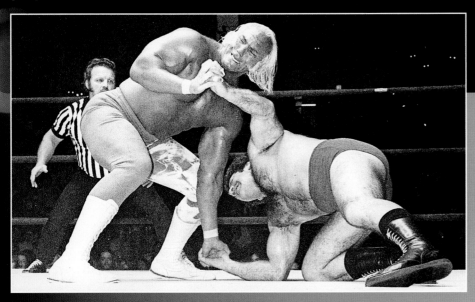

With the two back on their feet, Graham whipped the Champion into the ropes and drove a knee into his midsection. Superstar tried to keep Sammartino down with a series of stomps, a chop, and a headlock. Graham started to choke Bruno with the second ring rope but the official broke up the illegal move. The challenger whipped Sammartino into the turnbuckles, but Bruno dodged a high knee and Graham went crashing to the canvas. The Champion kicked Superstar in the leg, causing the challenger to get tied up in the ring ropes. Now it was Sammartino that used kicks and stomps to wear out his opponent, and he drove Graham's head into the top turnbuckle for good measure.

Back in the ring, the challenger begged for mercy from Sammartino's clubbing blows. However, it seemed that Superstar was playing possum and he whipped Bruno into the corner and locked in a bear hug. Reeling from the power of the move, the Champion still fought his way out of the submission maneuver. He then captured Graham in a bear hug of his own, but for the third time, Graham was close enough to the ropes to force a break. Bruno moved in to further punish Superstar, but the challenger took down the Champion and pinned Sammartino with the help of both feet being on the ropes. The official did not see the illegal move and made the three-count, crowning Superstar Billy Graham as the new WWE Champion.

THE AFTERMATH

An irate crowd booed the official decision, but it could not be changed. While the former Champion Sammartino and his manager Arnold Skaaland angrily stalked the ring, the new Champion quickly made his way back to the dressing room. Sammartino gained a series of rematches, but did not retake the Title. While his second Championship reign was half the length of the first, in total Sammartino held the Championship for more than 4,000 days—over a decade. Superstar Billy Graham was WWE Champion for almost a year, until February 1978 when he lost the Title to Bob Backlund.

UNDERTAKER vs. JEFF HARDY

THE LEAD-UP

For years, Jeff Hardy delighted the WWE Universe in tag-team competition. With his brother Matt, the Hardy Boyz won multiple Tag Team Championships and helped to pioneer the TLC Match. But Jeff had not been given much of a chance to prove himself as a singles competitor. That changed in the summer of 2002, when the enigmatic superstar ran afoul of the WWE Undisputed Champion, Undertaker. Both Matt and Jeff had history with Undertaker, particularly at that year's *Royal Rumble*. Jeff challenged The Deadman to a Championship Ladder Match and Undertaker accepted. Jeff entered the match a massive underdog, with his one ace in the hole: Undertaker had never competed in a Ladder Match.

WWE RAW

LADDER MATCH FOR THE UNDISPUTED CHAMPIONSHIP

July 1, 2002

Verizon Wireless Arena
Manchester, New Hampshire

When first introduced to the crowd, Hardy did not immediately enter the ring, instead mounting Undertaker's motorcycle. This drew the Champion out of the ring and Hardy took advantage, kicking a ladder onto The Deadman. He then hit a cross body over the ring ropes to Undertaker on the floor below. He followed with a shot from a foreign object before the Champion asserted his offense, slamming Hardy into the steps and dropping him over the ring barrier. He intended to then slam Hardy into the ladder, but the challenger moved out of the way, leading to The Deadman hurting himself.

Jeff then draped the ladder over Undertaker and drove it into the Champion with a leg drop from the ring to the floor below. Hardy was about to drag a ladder into the ring, but The Deadman used the opportunity to drive the ladder into Hardy's face and then kick it into the challenger's midsection. A wounded Hardy was slammed to the floor with a third ladder shot from the Champion, making it appear as though the match would be over as soon as Undertaker climbed the ladder. However, the Champion decided instead to inflict more punishment on Hardy. He lifted Hardy and then dropped him on the announcers' table before tossing him into the ring announcer's station.

Bringing Hardy back into the ring, Undertaker continued to systematically punish his challenger, although Jeff did manage a brief flurry of offense. Undertaker used the ladder in demonically innovative ways, sandwiching Hardy in the middle of the ring and then dropping a leg on him. Undertaker attempted to toss Hardy in the corner, but Hardy surprised the Champion by hitting a top-rope corkscrew on him. He then leapt off the ladder onto Undertaker on the ring below.

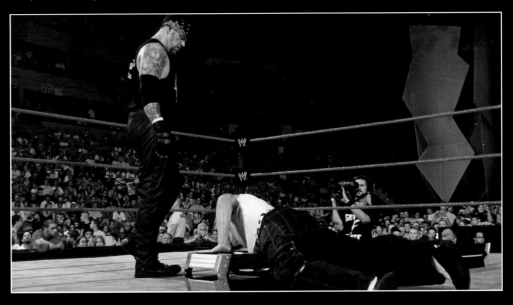

Hardy tried to make the task of climbing the ladder even easier by bringing a taller ladder into the ring, and he began to climb toward the Undisputed Championship. Undertaker pulled Hardy off the ladder and tried to perform a Last Ride, but Hardy turned it into a Hurricanrana. For a second time, Hardy started up the ladder, but again Undertaker halted his progress. Undertaker then tried to deliver a Last Ride, but Hardy grabbed one of the match's eponymous objects and blasted Undertaker with it two times. Jeff Hardy started up the ladder a third time, but Undertaker, climbing the other side, Chokeslammed Hardy off the ladder, allowing The Deadman to retrieve the Title and retain the Championship.

THE AFTERMATH

Undertaker started to leave the ring, but saw Jeff Hardy trying to stand. To prove a point, Undertaker returned to the ring and administered a Last Ride to put Hardy down. But before Undertaker could ride out of the arena, Hardy got a mic and told Undertaker he wasn't broken yet. Undertaker returned to the ring to put Hardy down again, but looking into his challenger's eyes, Undertaker instead raised Hardy's arm in a show of respect. Perhaps that seal of approval helped propel Hardy, as just one week later, he defeated William Regal for the European Championship, the first singles Title in Hardy's WWE career.

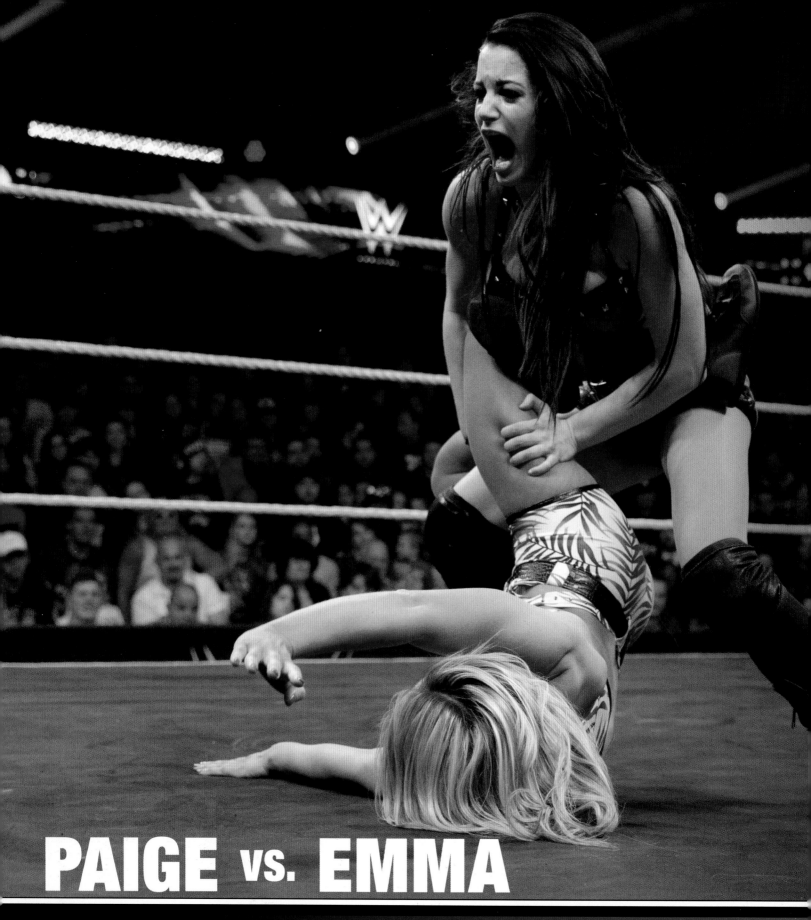

PAIGE vs. EMMA

THE LEAD-UP

In early June 2013, Stephanie McMahon announced a tournament to crown the first NXT Women's Champion. Paige took down Tamina Snuka and Alicia Fox to advance to the finals where she was set to meet Emma, who defeated Aksana and Summer Rae. In the last match of the tournament, Paige pinned her rival to become the inaugural Champion. Emma won a Dance Off to gain another shot at the Title and after she had defended her #1 contender position, it was announced that the two would meet at NXT's first WWE Network special, *NXT Arrival*, for the Women's Championship.

THE MATCH

Paige tried to intimidate Emma right from the opening bell by getting in her face and shoving the challenger. Emma did not back down, pushing the Champion back and then taking her down after Paige slapped her face. Paige went for the Paige Turner early, but Emma countered it into a backslide and a two-count. Emma also tried for an early signature move as well, but Paige had scouted her slingshot, and dropped it into a pinning combination, but Emma was able to kick out. Paige then grounded Emma with an extended headlock.

Paige went for a scoop slam, but Emma blocked the slam and tried to drive Paige into a turnbuckle. Paige countered the move and instead hammered Emma into the corner. She then drove a leg into Emma's throat, but Emma grabbed Paige's leg and dropped her face first to the mat. Emma attempted the Emma Sandwich, but Paige blocked the move. However, Emma hit her slingshot, normally the precursor to the Emma Lock. Again though, Paige's knowledge of her competitor allowed her to block the move. Paige then unleashed a series of knees to Emma's midsection.

Emma regained the offensive advantage, wrapping Paige in a tarantula and then executing the Emma Sandwich. But the challenger could only get a two-count from her pin attempt. She then tried to wear Paige down with a submission move by pulling back the Champion's arms while driving her knees and feet into Paige's back. Emma impressed the Full Sail crowd by demonstrating the strength to elevate Paige's entire body while keeping her locked in the move.

The two competitors battled on the second and top turnbuckle, with Paige looking to execute a superplex and Emma blocking the move. Emma flipped over the Champion and hit a power bomb. Paige just barely managed to kick out before the three-count. Emma hit a running dropkick, but again Paige kicked out before a three-count. Emma implored Paige to give up, but that just energized the Champion, who hit Emma with a wicked slap, a clothesline, and a kick to the midsection. Paige then finally landed her Paige Turner signature move, but Emma kicked out at two. Paige then debuted a new submission move, a Scorpion Crosslock. Emma had no choice but to submit to the painful hold, allowing Paige to retain her Championship.

THE AFTERMATH

Shortly after *NXT Arrival*, Paige made a surprise appearance on *Monday Night Raw*, where the WWE Divas Champion AJ Lee belittled her and challenged her to a match. Paige shocked the Champion and the WWE Universe by winning the match and the Divas Championship in her first WWE match. For almost a month, Paige held both the NXT Women's Championship and the WWE Divas Championship simultaneously, until she was forced to relinquish the former, ending her reign in NXT. Emma participated in the tournament to crown a new Champion, but she lost in the first round to eventual Champion, Charlotte.

THE LEAD-UP

Sibling rivalries often occur, but it's rare for them to unfold in front of millions of people. For almost a year, WWE Superstars Bret and Owen Hart had been battling. Owen even defeated Bret at *WrestleMania X*, the same night Hit Man went on to become the WWE Champion. Once Owen won the 1994 *King of the Ring* tournament and proclaimed himself the "King of Harts," it was inevitable the brothers would clash again. With many other members of the Hart family, particularly their brother-in-law Jim "The Anvil" Neidhart, inserting themselves into the confrontations, the match would take place in a steel cage, designed to keep the competitors in and everyone else out. In this particular cage match, a pinfall or submission would not secure the win—the only way to emerge victorious was to escape the cage, either over the top and to the mat below or through the cage door.

BRET "HIT MAN" HART
vs.
OWEN HART

SUMMERSLAM 1994
STEEL CAGE MATCH FOR THE WWE CHAMPIONSHIP

August 29, 1994

United Center
Chicago, Illinois

THE MATCH

Several members of the Hart family sat ringside. Most of the family, while hoping neither man would get hurt, sided with Bret because they could not understand Owen's actions. Helen and Stu Hart, the family matriarch and patriarch, in particular hoped Owen would come to his senses. The one family member squarely in Owen's court was Bret's former tag team partner, brother-in-law Jim "The Anvil" Neidhart. He wanted Owen to show that he, not Bret, was the classy one in the Hart family.

Owen did not show much class at the start of the bout. The younger Hart brother attacked his older sibling immediately. Owen pressed his initial advantage with punches to Bret's face and body, as well as slamming Hit Man against the mat and turnbuckle. Bret finally landed some offense with an inverted Atomic Drop and a clothesline, but Owen fought back. Bret finally knocked Owen to the mat and looked to escape the cage by climbing over the top. Owen managed to catch Bret and send him crashing to the ring. Owen also tried to climb out of the cage, but Bret suplexed him from the top rope.

Both Bret and Owen made several attempts to exit through the cage door, but the brothers kept pulling each other back into the ring. After pounding the Champion, Owen actually managed to make it over the top of the cage and halfway down the other side. But Bret held on to Owen's head and pulled his brother back into the ring. Bret also managed to get up and over the top, but Owen also pulled him back into the ring.

Again, Owen climbed the cage and swung his body over the cage. This time, Bret held on to Owen's hair and pulled him back in, but it was clear Owen was getting dangerously close to winning the match and the WWE Title. To try and soften up the challenger, Hit Man repeatedly rammed Owen against the cage walls. Both men continued to get closer and closer to escaping the cage, whipping the crowd into a frenzy. Owen tried to incapacitate the Champion by locking him into a Sharpshooter, but Bret reversed the hold into a Sharpshooter of his own. Both men climbed the cage and made it over the top, but Owen's legs got tangled, allowing Bret to drop to the floor and retain the WWE Championship.

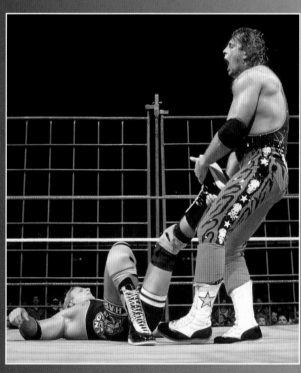

THE AFTERMATH

Many thought the heated rivalry between the two brothers would end with the cage match, but when Owen and Jim Neidhart attacked Bret in and out of the cage immediately after the match, it was apparent the issues between the two brothers were far from settled. Owen even managed to cost Bret the WWE Title at *Survivor Series 1994* when he convinced his mother to throw in the towel for Bret in a Submission Match, allowing Bob Backlund to become the Champion. It would take years for the Hart brothers to finally get back on the same page.

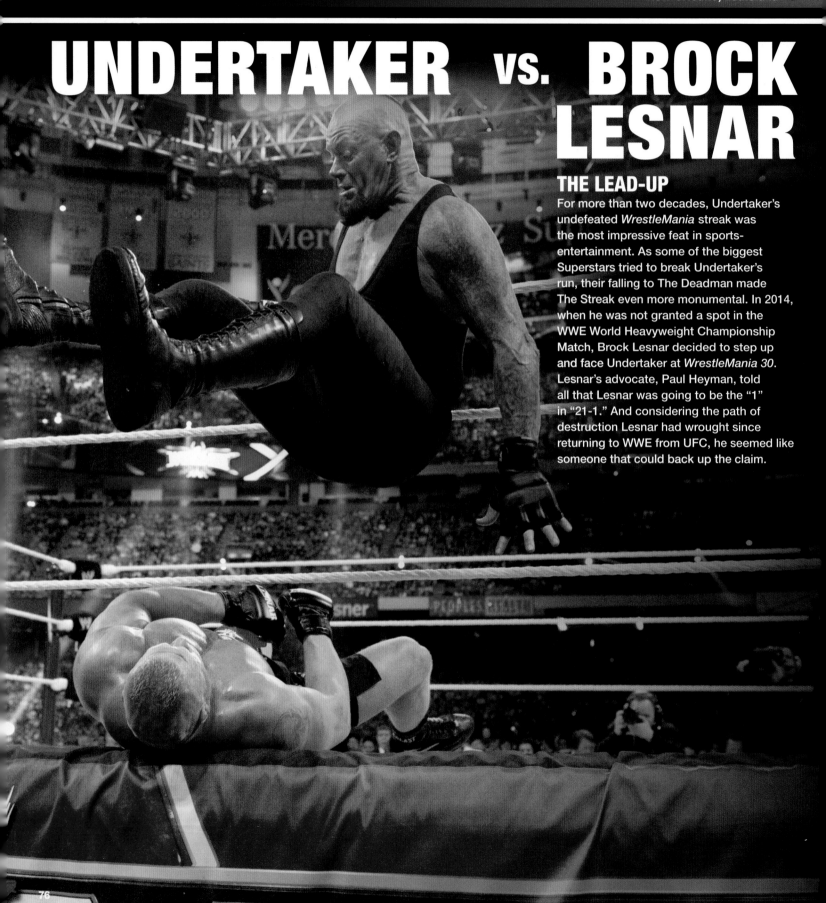

UNDERTAKER vs. BROCK LESNAR

THE LEAD-UP

For more than two decades, Undertaker's undefeated *WrestleMania* streak was the most impressive feat in sports-entertainment. As some of the biggest Superstars tried to break Undertaker's run, their falling to The Deadman made The Streak even more monumental. In 2014, when he was not granted a spot in the WWE World Heavyweight Championship Match, Brock Lesnar decided to step up and face Undertaker at *WrestleMania 30*. Lesnar's advocate, Paul Heyman, told all that Lesnar was going to be the "1" in "21-1." And considering the path of destruction Lesnar had wrought since returning to WWE from UFC, he seemed like someone that could back up the claim.

THE MATCH

Part of the mystique of Undertaker at *WrestleMania* is his entrance. Whether accompanied by druids or walking on his own, the combination of music, graphics, and darkness can psych out his opponent before he even steps into the ring. According to the announcers,

Lesnar was showing no signs of intimidation. The competitors went directly at each other, with Undertaker landing a series of body blows on Lesnar before The Beast tossed The Deadman with a belly-to-belly overhead suplex.

Both men attempted signature moves early in the match. Undertaker executed a Snake Eyes and then looked to Chokeslam his opponent. But Lesnar countered the move and unsuccessfully attempted the F-5. Each man continued to trade power moves, but it became apparent that Lesnar's game plan was to target Undertaker's left leg—to sap the power of Undertaker's Chokeslam and Tombstone. In retaliation, Undertaker performed another Snake Eyes, put a big boot to Lesnar's face, and followed with a Chokeslam. After Lesnar kicked out of a pinfall attempt, The Deadman tried to deliver a Tombstone. Lesnar countered the move into an F-5, and Undertaker kicked out after a two-count.

Lesnar started pacing the ring, planning his next move. As Lesnar bent down to pick up a prone Undertaker, The Phenom grabbed Lesnar and locked him in the Hell's Gate Submission maneuver. Lesnar countered by lifting Undertaker off the canvas and slamming him to the mat, forcing a break of the hold. Undertaker tried the maneuver again, but for a second time, Lesnar lifted The Deadman off the canvas and slammed him down. Lesnar then tried a submission move of his own, the dreaded Kimura Lock. Undertaker may have come close to submitting, but instead The Deadman countered into a painful armbar submission move.

Undertaker went for his Old School Top Rope Walk, but Lesnar grabbed The Deadman and delivered the match's second F-5. Again Undertaker kicked out at the two-count. Lesnar looked to soften up his opponent more with a pair of German Suplexes. As Lesnar was pounding The Deadman in a corner, Undertaker had one last burst of offense left in him.

Undertaker delivered a Last Ride to Lesnar and then set The Beast up for a Tombstone Piledriver. The Deadman assumed he had finished off his challenger, but Lesnar kicked out at two. With a throat-slash gesture, Undertaker indicated to the crowd that the match was about to be over. The Phenom lifted Lesnar to deliver a second Tombstone, but Lesnar countered into a third F-5. To the shock of the WWE Universe, Lesnar kept The Deadman down for the three-count to win the match and end The Streak.

THE AFTERMATH

The crowd in the SuperDome was stunned. Although they respected the power and ability of Lesnar, most expected Undertaker to eventually come through and extend The Streak. Lesnar would reach even greater heights in 2014, when he delivered one of the most dominant performances in a Title match, beating John Cena for the WWE World Heavyweight Championship at *SummerSlam 2014*. Lesnar held the Title until *WrestleMania 31*, the same event that saw Undertaker return to the ring, beating Bray Wyatt. Lesnar and Undertaker would meet again at *SummerSlam 2015*, when The Deadman would obtain a controversial victory over The Beast.

TEAM WWE

vs.

TEAM ALLIANCE

THE LEAD-UP

WWE had won its greatest rivalry of all when Mr. McMahon announced he was buying WCW. However, while a McMahon did buy WCW, it was Mr. McMahon's son, Shane. Shane combined his WCW purchase with his sister Stephanie's purchase of ECW to form an alliance looking to take over WWE. The infighting between the WWE and the Alliance dominated *Raw*, *SmackDown*, and pay-per-view events throughout the summer and fall of 2001, until Mr. McMahon proposed a single winner-take-all match at *Survivor Series*. The contest involved two five-man teams, with the winning side's company staying in business and the losing side's team disbanded.

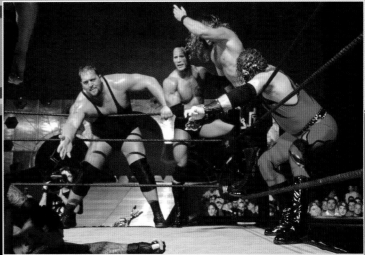

THE MATCH

The Alliance was represented by owner Shane McMahon, WCW's Booker T, ECW's Rob Van Dam, and WWE turncoats Stone Cold Steve Austin and Kurt Angle. Mr. McMahon chose a monstrous lineup of Kane, Undertaker, Big Show, Chris Jericho, and The Rock. Mr. McMahon tried to further the WWE's chances by sowing dissension in the Alliance's ranks, claiming one member of their team would defect to WWE during the match. WWE's team was not free of controversy, as Chris Jericho and The Rock were not getting along, thanks to their battles over the WCW Championship.

Strife in Team WWE was not present in the beginning. The team tagged in and out easily and had several early opportunities to pin a member of Team Alliance and grab a man advantage. But each time, Shane McMahon jumped in the ring to break up the pinfall attempt. Although it seemed like only a matter of time until Team WWE would break through, the Alliance grabbed the first advantage when they managed to hit Big Show with three finishing moves and pin him. Shane McMahon may have enjoyed the glory of eliminating Big Show, but the glory was short-lived, as Shane was eliminated next, evening the teams to four men each.

While the Brothers of Destruction lived up to their moniker with powerful in-ring moves—including Undertaker using his Old School ring-rope walk on Stone Cold Steve Austin—Kane and Undertaker were the next two Superstars to be eliminated. This stunned the crowd, as the Alliance now had a daunting four-on-two advantage. To make matters worse, Team WWE was down to Jericho and The Rock, and the announcers openly wondered whether they'd be able to get along. However, things seemed fine—The Rock took out Booker T, and Jericho pinned RVD, once again evening the odds. The Rock then managed to force a submission when he put Kurt Angle in a Sharpshooter. For the first time in the match, Team WWE had the numbers advantage, as only Stone Cold remained for the Alliance.

The Texas Rattlesnake would not go down easily, as he eliminated Jericho with a Small Package. A frustrated Jericho attacked The Rock, leaving the Most Electrifying Man in Sports-Entertainment vulnerable to Austin. But Rock demonstrated amazing resilience and the two men battled back and forth. Austin thought he had the match won, but the referee was out and could not make the call. At this point, Mr. McMahon's prediction of a traitor in the Alliance finally came true. Kurt Angle returned and hit Austin with the WWE Championship, allowing The Rock to finish Austin with a Rock Bottom, pinning him for a Team WWE victory.

Mr. McMahon was able to gloat about his victory at the next night's *Raw*, taking great pleasure in firing a number of key Alliance members, including Paul Heyman, and Mr. McMahon's son Shane and daughter Stephanie. He also planned to reward Kurt Angle by firing Stone Cold Steve Austin and awarding Angle the WWE Championship. But not everything worked out for Mr. McMahon. To finance their purchases of WCW and ECW, his children had sold their shares of WWE to Ric Flair. Making his first appearance in a WWE ring in almost a decade, Flair decided to keep Austin around, and as McMahon's new business partner, the Nature Boy had every right to do so.

THE LEAD-UP

Claiming he pinned Hulk Hogan early in their *WrestleMania III* encounter, Andre the Giant was looking for another shot at the Title. However, he no longer had Bobby "The Brain" Heenan in his corner. Andre now had the support of "Million Dollar Man" Ted DiBiase and his manservant Virgil. DiBiase tried to purchase the WWE Championship from Hulk Hogan, and when that failed, he tried to beat him for the Title. DiBiase's newest plan was to back Andre's attempt to win the Title, and then purchase the Championship from Andre. After a contentious contract signing at the inaugural *Royal Rumble*, Hogan and Andre were ready to meet at *The Main Event*.

HULK HOGAN
VS. ANDRE THE GIANT

THE MAIN EVENT
WWE CHAMPIONSHIP MATCH

February 5, 1988

Market Square Arena
Indianapolis, Indiana

THE MATCH

To the crowd's delight, Hulk Hogan came sprinting to the ring. He made a slamming gesture toward Andre, perhaps trying to remind the Giant he had slammed him at *WrestleMania III* and he was prepared to do it again. Andre did not react, standing stoically until he turned to DiBiase and Virgil for one last strategy session. Hogan had enough and charged the trio, pulling both Virgil and Million Dollar Man into the ring before dispatching each with big boots.

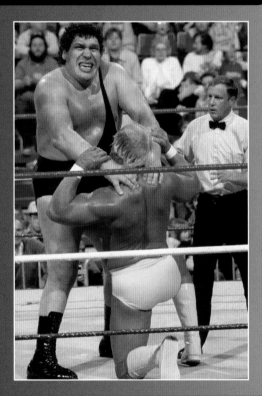

The match then began in earnest. Hogan started off strong, wailing on the Giant with a number of clubbing blows. While Hogan had Andre reeling, he could not knock Andre down. The Hulkster decided to go to the top rope, but that was a mistake—Andre grabbed Hogan off the turnbuckle and slammed him to the canvas. Andre tried to follow with a headbutt, but Hogan moved, causing Andre to crash to the mat. Hogan went for the pin, but Andre reached up and choked the Champion, breaking the pin.

Andre took control of the match, using body slams, punches, chops, and a series of illegal chokes. The official would warn the Giant and give him a count of five to break the hold. Each time, Andre would release the move before the official reached five—after all, Andre could not win the Title if he was disqualified. Hulk finally made an incredible comeback, hammering the Giant with chops and punches. He again went to the second turnbuckle; this time, taking Andre off his feet. But Virgil argued with the official, so he did not see Hulk drop the leg on the Giant and cover Andre for the victory. Hulk got up to deal with Virgil, but the distraction gave Andre time to recover.

Andre slammed the Champion to the mat and covered him for the pin. Although the Hulkster clearly lifted his shoulder, the referee continued to count the pin. He indicated a three-count and handed the Title to Andre while the ring announcer delivered the bad news to the fans. Andre promptly announced he was relinquishing the Championship to DiBiase and put the Title around Million Dollar Man's waist, further enraging the crowd. Hogan was baffled by the referee's decision. He began complaining to ringside officials when suddenly another official—one that looked exactly like match referee Dave Hebner—appeared. The twin referees argued and came to blows, and Hogan attacked the crooked referee.

THE AFTERMATH

While Jack Tunney decided he couldn't reverse the official's decision, he noted that Andre's decision to surrender the Title to DiBiase was invalid. As a result, Tunney held up the Title and announced that there would be a 14-man tournament to crown a new WWE Champion, with all matches happening at *WrestleMania IV*. Hogan and Andre would receive byes into the second round, but they would face each other. Their match ended in a double disqualification, clearing the path for a new WWE Champion. "Macho Man" Randy Savage won four matches to become the 11th WWE Champion in the history of the company.

THE ROCK VS. BROCK LESNAR

THE LEAD-UP

In 2002, Brock Lesnar was known as "The Next Big Thing," and he certainly earned the moniker. Just a few short months after his WWE debut, Lesnar entered the *King of the Ring* tournament and won it all, earning a Title opportunity at *SummerSlam*. The man defending the Championship was determined at *Vengeance* 2002, when Kurt Angle and The Rock both challenged Champion Undertaker in a Triple Threat Match for the Undisputed WWE Championship. The Rock won the Title, setting up an interesting dynamic at *SummerSlam*. Brock Lesnar was looking to become the youngest man to ever win the WWE Championship. To accomplish this feat, Lesnar would have to defeat The Rock, who himself was the youngest man to hold the WWE Championship when he first won the Title in November 1998.

SUMMERSLAM 2002
UNDISPUTED WWE CHAMPIONSHIP MATCH

August 25, 2002
Nassau Veterans Memorial Coliseum
Uniondale, New York

THE MATCH

The Rock sprinted to the ring, ready to start the action before the bell even rang. Lesnar and The Rock traded blows at first, but then Lesnar threw The Rock to the mat with a belly-to-belly suplex and delivered a pair of backbreakers. The action spilled outside the ring, where Lesnar's Advocate, Paul Heyman, kicked The Rock while the official was distracted. Lesnar continued his assault by throwing The Rock over and then on a ring barricade.

As The Rock attempted to put Lesnar into the Sharpshooter, Paul Heyman started distracting the official. For this interference, Heyman received a right hand from The Rock. The second time Heyman tried to interfere, The Rock pulled him into the ring. While The Rock was setting Heyman up for a Rock Bottom, Lesnar attacked, regaining control of the match. The Next Big Thing tried to wear down The Rock with a Bear Hug. The Rock managed to break the hold with a series of punches, and Heyman tried to distract the official again. His interference backfired, as The Rock used the opportunity to hit the challenger with a low blow. The announcers marveled at how split the crowd was, as many fans cheered Lesnar and booed The Rock, particularly when he dumped Lesnar out of the ring.

The Rock pulled the monitors out of the Spanish announcers' table, leading to speculation that he had plans for Lesnar and the table. But once again, Heyman put himself into the middle of the action. If it was designed to give his client the upper hand, it did not work. The Rock launched Lesnar into the ring post and then put Heyman through the announcers' table with a vicious Rock Bottom.

Back in the ring, The Rock gave Lesnar another Rock Bottom and covered him for the victory. But The Rock was stunned when Lesnar kicked out of the pin attempt and then gave The Great One a Rock Bottom of his own. The Rock managed to kick out of the resulting pin attempt. The Rock then hit a Spinebuster and prepared to deliver the People's Elbow, but Lesnar popped up and leveled The Rock with a brutal clothesline. Lesnar looked to deliver his patented F-5, but The Rock countered. He twice tried to deliver another Rock Bottom, but Lesnar blocked them both and finally hit the F-5. Lesnar pinned The Rock and won the Undisputed WWE Championship.

THE AFTERMATH

Before *SummerSlam*, the Undisputed WWE Championship was defended on both *Raw* and *SmackDown*. To the dismay of *Raw* General Manager Eric Bischoff, Stephanie McMahon announced that Lesnar and the Championship would be exclusive to the *SmackDown* brand. As a result, Bischoff announced the creation of the World Heavyweight Championship. The two World Championships would remain split until they were reunited again in December 2013. Lesnar's first challenger to the WWE Title would be Undertaker, while The Rock would not challenge for the WWE Championship again until January 2013.

JOHN CENA vs. KURT ANGLE vs. SHAWN MICHAELS

THE LEAD-UP

Throughout the second half of John Cena's first year as WWE Champion, *Raw* General Manager Eric Bischoff did all he could to end Cena's reign. At *Unforgiven 2005*, Bischoff chose Kurt Angle as the #1 contender. Angle won the match by disqualification, meaning Cena retained the WWE Title. Bischoff decided to make Cena's life even harder by setting up a Triple Threat Match at *Taboo Tuesday*. Angle would get one of the spots in the match with the second challenger determined by the WWE Universe. Fans could pick among Shawn Michaels, Kane, and Big Show. With 46% of the vote, Shawn Michaels was chosen for the third spot in the match.

THE MATCH

The three Superstars warily eyed each other as the crowd wondered who would make the first move. Angle started things off by knocking Michaels out of the ring and then going after the WWE Champion. Cena fought back, but the match soon became chaotic—any time one competitor would gain any momentum against another, the third competitor would inevitably break things up. All three men attempted early pinfalls, but no competitor could be kept down.

Michaels and Angle decided to work together to take John Cena out of the match. The two combined their efforts to pummel Cena in the ring, and then they tossed Cena into a ring post and out of the ring. The two then drove the Champion through the announcers' table. Once it seemed that Cena was out of commission, Michaels and Angle went at each other. Michaels hit a powerslam on Angle for a near fall, but Angle then performed a few suplexes and a submission hold to wear down the Heartbreak Kid. Angle tried to set Michaels up for a top-rope belly-to-belly suplex, but Michaels countered and tossed the Olympic Champion off the turnbuckle. However, as Michaels attempted to leap off the tope rope, Angle demonstrated his quickness, catching Michaels for a second-turnbuckle Angle Slam. Somehow, Michaels kicked out of the resulting pinfall attempt.

Angle decided to put Michaels in the Ankle Lock, but Cena finally made his way back into the ring. Cena tossed Angle out of the ring and set Michaels up for the Five-Knuckle Shuffle. Angle interrupted and pulled the Champion outside the ring. Michaels then launched himself out of the ring and onto Angle. Back in the ring, Michaels continued his momentum, hitting Angle with a flying forearm, an inverted atomic drop, and two clotheslines. Cena re-entered the ring, only to receive a series of knife-edge chops and another flying forearm. But the Heartbreak Kid's focus on Cena allowed Angle to recover and he tossed Michaels out of the ring with a belly-to-belly suplex. With just Cena and Angle in the ring, the Champion nailed Angle with a Five-Knuckle Shuffle.

Cena looked to finish Angle off with the Attitude Adjustment, but Angle countered into his Ankle Lock submission. Cena was not able to reach the ropes, and twice he flipped over, but each time Angle held on. It seemed inevitable that Cena would be forced to tap out, but Michaels recovered and delivered a flying elbow to Angle. Michaels then hit Sweet Chin Music on The Olympic Hero. Before HBK could pin Angle, Cena grabbed Michaels, executed the Attitude Adjustment, and pinned him. Once again, Cena had overcome difficult odds to remain WWE Champion.

THE AFTERMATH

Kurt Angle received one more Title opportunity at *Survivor Series*, and even had his manager Daivari as the Special Guest Referee. Despite the added advantage, Cena still retained his Championship. Cena held onto the Title until *New Year's Revolution 2006*, when after successfully defending the Title against five challengers in an Elimination Chamber Match, Cena then had to face Edge, who was cashing in his Money in the Bank Title opportunity. Edge won the Title that night, although Cena would regain it at the *Royal Rumble* and successfully defend it at *WrestleMania 22*.

TRIPLE H vs. CACTUS JACK

THE LEAD-UP

Mick Foley had a lifelong dream—to headline *WrestleMania*. The easiest way to realize his dream would be as the WWE Champion. Foley had the chance to become Champion at the *2000 Royal Rumble* when, in his Cactus Jack persona, he faced Triple H for the WWE Championship in a Street Fight. Triple H won the match, but the next night on *Raw*, he granted Cactus one last Championship opportunity and even told him he could pick the type of match. The only condition was that Foley had to put his career on the line. Foley agreed and picked Hell in a Cell as the match type. He promised to leap from the cage onto Triple H, while The Game promised to end Mick Foley's career.

THE MATCH

After both men were introduced and the cell was lowered, Cactus Jack went to the door and found that instead of a single chain and padlock, the door was secured with more than half a dozen! The announcers speculated that this was the work of the McMahon-Helmsley regime attempting to prevent Cactus Jack from fulfilling his promise to go to the top of the cage and jump onto Triple H. Instead, Cactus unleashed a series of punches on Triple H, and the WWE Champion returned blows in kind.

Cactus tried to use a foreign object on Triple H, but The Game was able to avoid contact. Triple H heaved the challenger into the steel steps and then tossed the steps at Cactus Jack. He then placed the steps on Cactus and drove the steps even further into Jack's body. Triple H hit his opponent several times, but the challenger managed to kick out of three pinning attempts. Cactus Jack responded by first landing a low blow on the Champion and then attacking The Game with a DDT and a Russian Leg Sweep. Fighting outside the ring, Cactus Jack caused the Champion to bleed by raking his face across the steel wall of the cell.

Cactus Jack threw the steel steps at Triple H, but The Game ducked out of the way. The steps hit the wall of the cage, causing it to break away from the structure. For Cactus, it was the opening he needed. He threw his body into the wall to make the breach large enough to fit through, and the battle spilled out of the cell. Jack pulled a barbed-wire two-by-four from under the ring. Triple H, looking to escape the barbaric weapon, climbed to the top of the cage. Cactus Jack followed him, but when the challenger tossed the board to the top, Triple H took it and used it to knock Cactus off the cage and through the announcers' table. To the Champion's surprise, Cactus Jack got up from the fall and climbed to the roof once again, where the two men continued to slug it out.

Recovering the barbed-wire two-by-four, Jack made it an even more dangerous weapon by setting it on fire. He blasted The Game with it, and then laid the object on top of the cage and made his intentions clear. He planned to piledrive Triple H onto the flaming board. Triple H reversed the move into a back body drop and broke the roof of the cage, sending Cactus crashing down to the mat below. The impact was so great that Cactus created a divot in the ring. Triple H climbed down, but was dismayed to see Jack still moving. He grabbed the challenger and delivered a Pedigree, pinning Cactus Jack and ending Foley's career, or so it appeared...

THE AFTERMATH

Triple H thought he would be defending his Title against Big Show at *WrestleMania 2000*, but Mr. McMahon decided that The Rock should be in the match as well, making it a Triple Threat Match. Linda McMahon took it a step further, adding Mick Foley to the fray and making the main event of *WrestleMania 2000* a Four-Way Elimination Match with a McMahon in every corner. Linda McMahon supported Mick in the match, but Foley, Big Show, and The Rock were all eliminated as Triple H retained the WWE Championship. After *WrestleMania 2000*, Mick Foley did not compete in a WWE ring for almost four years.

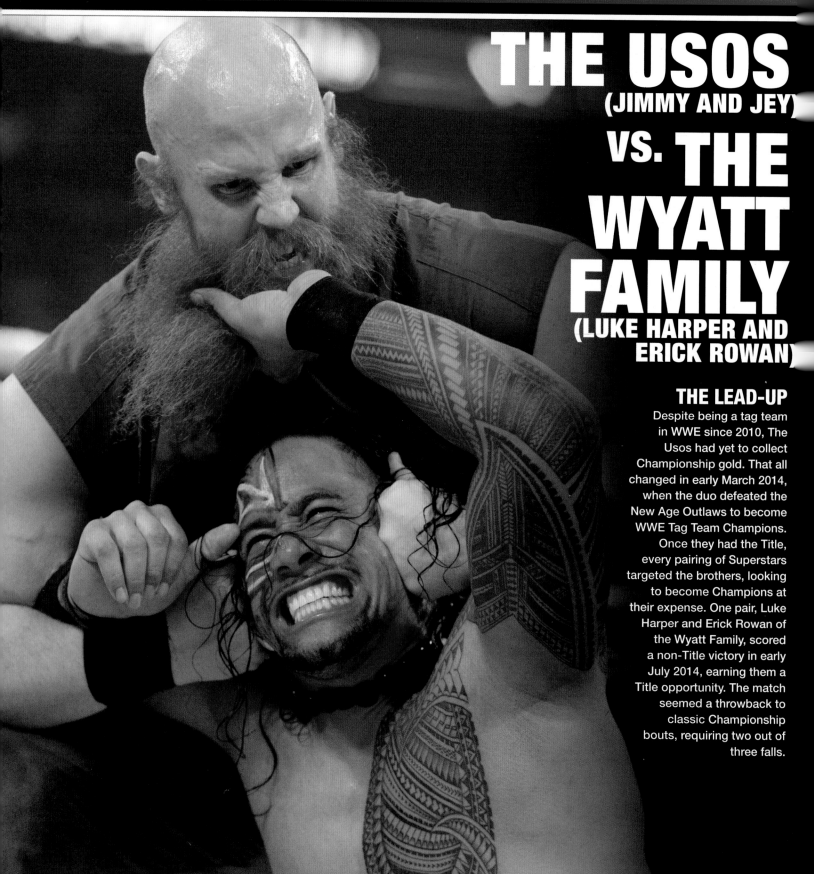

THE USOS
(JIMMY AND JEY)
VS. THE WYATT FAMILY
(LUKE HARPER AND ERICK ROWAN)

THE LEAD-UP

Despite being a tag team in WWE since 2010, The Usos had yet to collect Championship gold. That all changed in early March 2014, when the duo defeated the New Age Outlaws to become WWE Tag Team Champions. Once they had the Title, every pairing of Superstars targeted the brothers, looking to become Champions at their expense. One pair, Luke Harper and Erick Rowan of the Wyatt Family, scored a non-Title victory in early July 2014, earning them a Title opportunity. The match seemed a throwback to classic Championship bouts, requiring two out of three falls.

THE MATCH

Jey opened the match, slapping Erick Rowan so hard that Rowan's creepy sheep mask came off. The move angered Rowan, who dropped Jey with a shoulder block and a headbutt. He tagged in his partner Harper, who used his size to step on Jey. Jey made a comeback and dropkicked Harper out of the ring, while his brother kicked Rowan down off the apron as well. Back in the ring, Harper and Rowan began to dominate Jey Uso. The Wyatt Family members isolated Jey from his corner and made quick tags to keep a fresh man in the ring. Jimmy finally tagged in, but Harper ducked his big splash attempt and hit Jimmy with a boot to the face. This led to the first pin of the match, putting the Wyatt Family up 1-0.

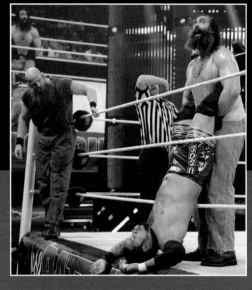

With Jey down and recovering, it fell to Jimmy to survive the Wyatt Family onslaught and to tie the match. Harper landed a big avalanche on Jimmy in the corner, getting a two-count. Rowan tagged in and hit a big splash, leading to another near fall. Rowan tried to get Jimmy to submit with

a head vice, but Jimmy would not give up. Jimmy attempted to scoop slam Rowan, but his weight was too great and it led to another near fall by Rowan. Harper reentered the ring and tried to slam Jimmy, but he floated over the top and tagged in his brother Jey. The fresh brother grabbed Harper and rolled him up for a three-count, tying the match at one fall apiece.

The deranged Wyatt Family double-teamed Jey Uso until the official regained control of the match. Harper and Rowan returned to their strategy of isolating Jey in their corner, but Jey ducked corner attacks by both men, injuring Rowan's shoulder and sending Harper to the floor below. Jey finally tagged in his brother and Jey executed suicide dives onto both Harper and Rowan, as well as a cross body off the top rope onto Harper for a two-count. An enziguri sent Harper down in a corner, and Jimmy made the WWE Universe think of his father Rikishi by driving his backside into Harper's face. Jimmy managed a two-count with a corkscrew moonsault.

Harper demonstrated amazing agility for a man his size by diving through the middle ropes onto Jimmy on the floor below.

Harper drove Jimmy into the mat with a Powerbomb, but Jimmy kicked out at two. Rowan tried to splash Jimmy from the top rope, but Jimmy rolled out of the way and tagged in his brother. Jey hit his top-rope splash on Rowan, but only managed a near fall. Rowan astounded the crowd by Superplexing both Usos at the same time, but somehow Jimmy, who had tagged himself in, kicked out at two. The Uso brothers hit a tandem kick and double splash on Harper to complete the comeback, winning the match two falls to one.

THE AFTERMATH

The Usos continued to defend the WWE Tag Team Championship through September, when they were finally dethroned by Goldust and Stardust. The Uso brothers regained the Championship before the year was over, but that reign only lasted two months. The Wyatt Family went their separate ways in the fall of 2014, and Harper and Rowan developed a rivalry over the Intercontinental Championship. Eventually the Wyatt Family regrouped, with Harper first rejoining Bray Wyatt along with new member Braun Strowman. Eric Rowan also returned to the group in October 2015, giving the Family four members for the first time ever.

RANDY ORTON vs.
RIC FLAIR

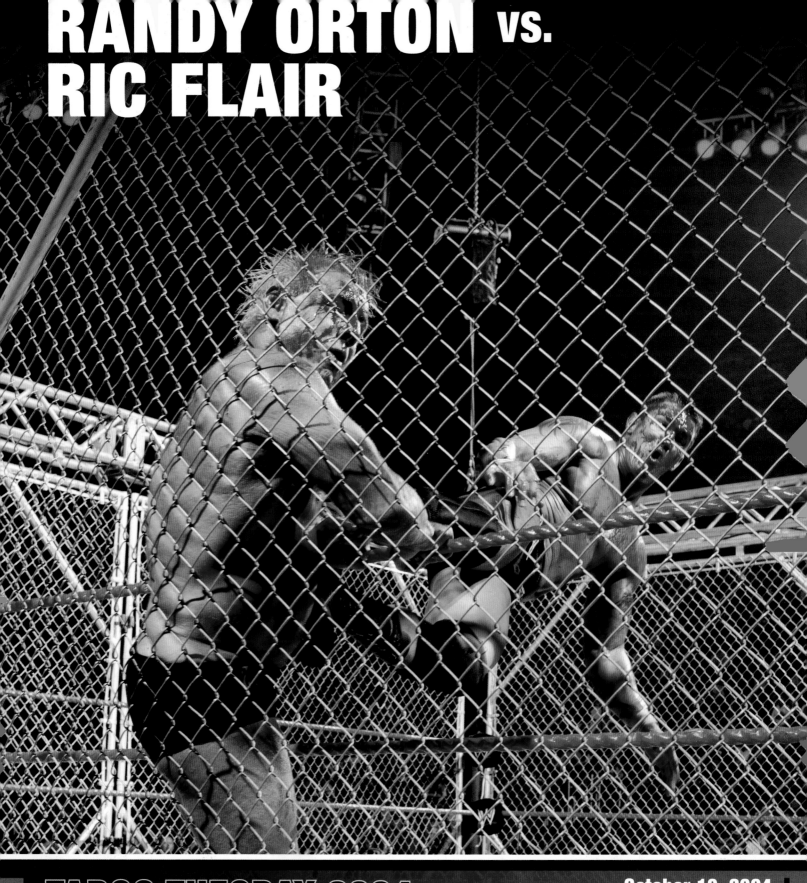

TABOO TUESDAY 2004
STEEL CAGE MATCH

October 19, 2004
Bradley Center
Milwaukee, Wisconsin

THE LEAD-UP

As a member of Evolution, Randy Orton captured the World Heavyweight Championship at *SummerSlam 2004*. Rather than support their Champion, Triple H and the rest of Evolution turned on Orton, kicking him out of the group. Ric Flair and Batista also helped Triple H defeat Orton for the Championship and prevented Orton from getting another shot at *Taboo Tuesday*. Orton decided to take out his frustration on Flair, as well as add to his "Legend Killer" résumé. The WWE Universe was given the opportunity to choose what type of match the two should have, and they overwhelmingly voted for a Steel Cage Match.

THE MATCH

Orton went right after Flair once they were both in the cage, dropping the Nature Boy twice to the mat. Flair got in some offense of his own, backing the Legend Killer into a corner and blistering his chest with a few knife-edge chops. Orton reversed their positions and landed a series of punches on Flair. Having enough, Flair headed to the opposite side of the ring and started to climb out of the cage, but Orton clambered up beside him and told him he wasn't going anywhere. Flair thumbed Orton in the eye and knocked him off the top rope.

Flair demonstrated why he's considered the Dirtiest Player in the Game when he shocked Orton with a low blow and then tossed Orton face first into the wall of the steel cage. The move cut open the Legend Killer's face and Flair made the cut worse with a series of punches as well as raking his face along the steel cage wall. Orton looked to get back into the match, trading punches with chops. The Legend Killer reversed an Irish Whip and tossed the Nature Boy into the steel cage wall, which led to Flair also bleeding from his forehead.

Again the Nature Boy looked to ascend and escape the cage, but Orton followed him to the top rope and repeatedly slammed Flair's head into the top of the cage. Flair fell to the mat, but not before his groin was driven into the top rope. Orton drove Flair into the corner of the ring and then rained down a series of punches as the delighted crowd counted along. Orton then started to kick Flair repeatedly, but the Nature Boy changed the flow of the match with a second low blow, one that caused Orton to fall to the mat. Flair chopped Orton some more, but the Legend Killer recovered, punched Flair repeatedly and then scoured Flair's face across the steel cage.

Flair put on a pair of brass knuckles that he had hidden in his trunks. He knocked the Legend Killer down with them and went to pin Orton. Somehow, Orton managed to kick out at two, so Flair instead looked to escape out of the cage door. Orton pulled him back in, but not before Flair pulled a foreign object into the ring. He swung it at Orton, but the Legend Killer ducked and instead countered with an RKO. He pinned the Nature Boy, holding Flair down for the three-count that secured the victory.

THE AFTERMATH

Orton continued to remain a thorn in the side of Triple H and Evolution. At *Survivor Series 2004*, a team captained by Orton defeated a team captained by Triple H in a four-on-four elimination match. Each member of Orton's winning team was given a week to control *Raw*. Orton tried to force Triple H to defend the Title in a Battle Royal, but Mr. McMahon changed it to a Battle Royal in which the winner got a Title opportunity. Chris Benoit and Edge went over at the same time, so they both faced Triple H in a Triple Threat Match for the Championship. That match led to Triple H vacating the Title, resulting in a new Champion being crowned in an Elimination Chamber Match—a match Triple H won, to once again become Champion.

THE BRITISH BULLDOGS
(DAVEY BOY SMITH & THE DYNAMITE KID)
VS.
NIKOLAI VOLKOFF & IRON SHEIK

THE LEAD-UP

The British Bulldogs were an extremely popular tag team combination that amazed fans with their high-flying action and incredible technical skills. For years, tag team gold eluded them until the second *WrestleMania*, when they finally defeated the Dream Team (Brutus Beefcake and Greg Valentine) for the Titles. Coming off that Championship victory, the Bulldogs faced a formidable duo on the sixth installment of *Saturday Night's Main Event*—the pairing of Iron Sheik and Nikolai Volkoff. The menacing team was led by "Classy" Freddie Blassie and they had previously won the World Tag Team Titles at the first *WrestleMania*, the first time a Title had changed hands at the event. They were now looking to repeat the feat and have *Saturday Night's Main Event*'s first Title change as well.

SATURDAY NIGHT'S MAIN EVENT

May 3, 1986

Providence Civic Center,
Providence, Rhode Island

TWO-OUT-OF-THREE FALLS MATCH FOR THE WORLD TAG TEAM CHAMPIONSHIP

THE MATCH

Nikolai Volkoff antagonized the Providence crowd by singing the Soviet national anthem and Iron Sheik praised the Soviet Union and Iran, while insulting the United States. The crowd was eager to see the Bulldogs take apart their challengers when Volkoff and Smith started the match. Volkoff charged Smith, but he dodged out of the way and both Bulldogs headbutted Volkoff, but Nikolai easily kicked out of Smith's pinfall attempt. Volkoff countered a running Smith by grabbing Davey Boy and dropping him over the ropes. Iron Sheik tagged in and hit a belly-to-back overhead suplex, and then locked in his dreaded Camel Clutch submission hold. Smith had no choice but to tap and the challengers took the first fall.

Again, the second fall started off with Smith and Volkoff. Blassie's charges kept Smith isolated in their corner, and Sheik tagged in again and gave Smith a back body drop. He picked up Davey Boy and delivered a running clothesline. Sheik tried to end the second fall with another submission maneuver, the abdominal stretch. Smith broke the hold with a hip toss, but when Smith went to drop an elbow, Sheik rolled out of the way. Volkoff tagged in and stomped Smith. Then Davey Boy turned an Irish Whip into a sunset flip but the official was arguing with Iron Sheik and did not make the count right away, giving Volkoff time to recover.

Sheik tagged in, and performed another suplex on Smith to get a two-count. Smith was finally able to counter a big boot into an atomic drop, but Iron Sheik kicked out at two. After some quick tags, Volkoff tried to pin Smith off of a body slam, but Davey Boy got his foot on the ropes and the official waved off the pin. Thinking he had won, Volkoff celebrated, only to be rolled up by Smith for a three-count that tied the match at one fall a piece. The third fall again saw Smith and Volkoff begin in the ring. After speculating why the Dynamite Kid had not been in the ring yet, the announcers learned that the Kid had torn ligaments in his knee. So Smith was working the majority of the match by himself.

Both Sheik and Volkoff tried to use submission moves to win the third fall versus Smith. Sheik locked Davey Boy in a Boston Crab, but Smith reached the ring ropes. Volkoff locked Smith in a bear hug, but Davey Boy punched his way out of that move. After a running powerslam of Sheik only got a two-count, Smith tagged in the Dynamite Kid. Volkoff and Sheik began double-teaming the Kid, with Volkoff using a crushing bear hug and Sheik suplexing him to the mat. Sheik locked Dynamite in the Camel Clutch, but before he could

submit, both Volkoff and Smith entered the ring. While the official was forcing Volkoff back to his corner, Smith used a series of forearms to get Sheik to break his hold. He then rolled Sheik up in a small package, and the official, not realizing that Smith was not the legal man, counted the pinfall to give the Bulldogs a 2-1 victory in the match.

THE AFTERMATH

The Bulldogs continued to defend the Tag Team Championship, including another memorable Two-Out-of-Three Falls Match at the next installment of *Saturday Night's Main Event* against former Champions, The Dream Team. The Bulldogs successfully retained their Championship that night and went on to face old rivals, The Hart Foundation. The Bulldogs had no idea how much the deck was stacked against them, as The Hart Foundation's manager, Jimmy Hart, paid off a crooked official, Danny Davis, to ensure that his team won the Championship.

THE DUDLEY BOYZ vs. THE HARDY BOYZ vs. EDGE & CHRISTIAN

THE LEAD-UP

In the Attitude Era, tag-team competition was largely defined by three trios—the Hardys, the Dudleys, and Edge & Christian. In total, the three teams won 23 Tag Team Championships in WWE. And when the teams faced each other, they continued to raise the bar. One innovative match created during this era is the Tables, Ladders, and Chairs Match. The three teams competed in the first-ever TLC Match at *SummerSlam* 2000, which Edge & Christian won. For *WrestleMania X-Seven*, the three duos were set for a most-anticipated sequel, one in which the Dudleys' Tag Team Titles would be suspended over the ring. The first team to retrieve both Titles would become the Tag Team Champions.

WRESTLEMANIA X-SEVEN

April 1, 2001

**Reliant Astrodome
Houston, Texas**

TLC II FOR THE WWE TAG TEAM CHAMPIONSHIP

THE MATCH

The three teams began brawling, with the Hardys and Dudleys dumping Edge & Christian out of the ring. The strategy was short-sighted, as the duo re-entered the ring with a ladder and used it as a weapon. Edge then set up a foreign object and, with the help of Christian, launched Jeff Hardy into it. Edge set up the ladder to make the first attempt to retrieve the Titles, but Jeff Hardy dropkicked him off the ladder. The Hardys then set up a second ladder and delighted the crowd with a leg drop/splash combo onto Christian.

It was no surprise the Dudleys were the first to introduce tables into the match, stunning the crowd when Bubba Ray drove Jeff Hardy onto Edge and through a table. All six men started climbing the three ladders in the ring's center for the Titles. Due to the Superstars battling and jockeying for position, it wasn't long before all six men came crashing down. Edge and Christian were the first to recover, but before they could climb a ladder, an injured Spike Dudley appeared and hit both men with Dudley Drops. Rhyno then also interfered, taking out the Dudleys and Matt Hardy. This led to the emergence of Lita, who knocked Edge off a ladder and delivered a Hurricanrana to Rhyno. Both Rhyno and Spike ended up on tables outside the ring, and Jeff Hardy delivered a Senton on Rhyno and Spike, taking them out of the match. Lita was also sidelined when the Dudleys hit her with a 3-D.

Jeff Hardy stepped across a series of ladders and grabbed at the Titles, but Bubba Ray took a ladder away, leaving Hardy hanging from the Championships. Edge leapt off another ladder and speared the dangling Hardy to the ring below. Matt Hardy and Bubby Ray Dudley climbed a large ladder and attempted to reach the Titles, but Rhyno made a surprising return and knocked the ladder over, sending both men plummeting out of the ring and through two stacked tables on the floor below. Rhyno then put Christian on his shoulders and propelled him up a ladder to the Titles. Christian grabbed the two Titles, and Edge & Christian won TLC for the second time.

THE AFTERMATH

While Edge & Christian left *WrestleMania* as Tag Team Champs, they did not hold the Title long. Less than three weeks later, The Brothers of Destruction (Kane & Undertaker) beat them for the Tag Team Championship. In May, all three teams would challenge Chris Benoit and Chris Jericho for the Titles in *TLC III*, but the Champions would retain their Titles. Thanks to the efforts of the three teams, TLC matches have become an exciting part of the WWE landscape, often featured as the Main Event of the annual TLC pay-per-view.

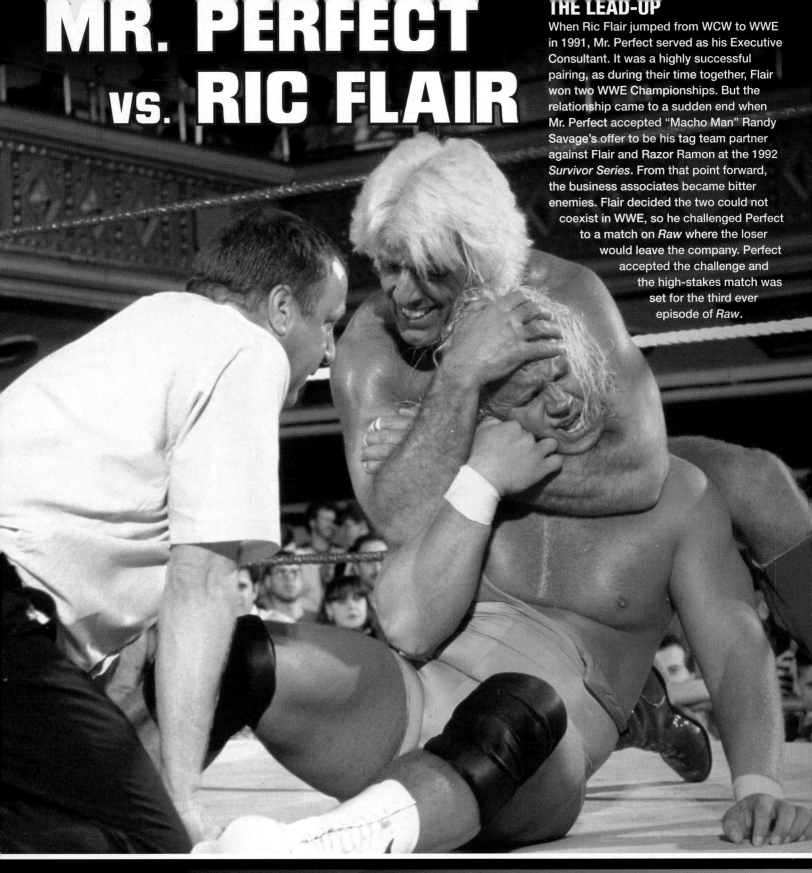

MR. PERFECT vs. RIC FLAIR

THE LEAD-UP
When Ric Flair jumped from WCW to WWE in 1991, Mr. Perfect served as his Executive Consultant. It was a highly successful pairing, as during their time together, Flair won two WWE Championships. But the relationship came to a sudden end when Mr. Perfect accepted "Macho Man" Randy Savage's offer to be his tag team partner against Flair and Razor Ramon at the 1992 *Survivor Series*. From that point forward, the business associates became bitter enemies. Flair decided the two could not coexist in WWE, so he challenged Perfect to a match on *Raw* where the loser would leave the company. Perfect accepted the challenge and the high-stakes match was set for the third ever episode of *Raw*.

MONDAY NIGHT RAW
LOSER LEAVES WWE MATCH

January 24, 1993
Manhattan Center
New York, New York

THE MATCH

After sizing each other up a bit, Flair worked Mr. Perfect into a corner and delivered a pair of his signature knife-edge chops. But Perfect quickly reversed positions with the Nature Boy and delivered a few chops of his own. The two continued to tentatively feel each other out, as each knew the stakes of the match were so high. Despite being known as two of the greatest mat wrestlers in the game, the pair resorted mostly to punches and chops. Perfect seemed to be getting the better of the exchanges, so Flair went for an eye poke to stop his opponent's momentum. Flair then tossed Perfect out of the ring. Flair attempted to hit Perfect with a foreign object, but the official grabbed it before any damage could be done.

Flair tossed Perfect into a ring post, causing Perfect to bleed from his forehead. After some more offense, Flair tried to pin Perfect—using the ropes for extra leverage—but Perfect kicked out repeatedly. The two then exchanged blows with Perfect getting the better of the exchange. Perfect got a two-count with a backslide of the Nature Boy. Flair bailed out of the ring for a breather, but Mr. Perfect suplexed him back into the ring and got another

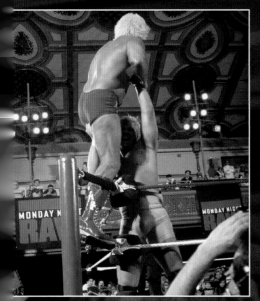

two-count. Flair raised his shoulder in time and managed to regain control of the match with a kick to Perfect's midsection. The Nature Boy then put Mr. Perfect in a sleeper hold. Flair was almost able to put Perfect away, but Perfect got his hand up before it fell for a third time. Perfect then got a number of two-counts with a side headlock, but Flair was able to counter the move into a suplex. He then put Mr. Perfect into his signature Figure Four submission move. To add to the pressure, Flair would grab the ropes whenever the official was not looking. While Perfect did not submit, the move did considerable damage to Perfect's knee. Flair looked to finish Perfect by going to the top rope, but he underestimated his opponent and Perfect slammed the Nature Boy off the top turnbuckle.

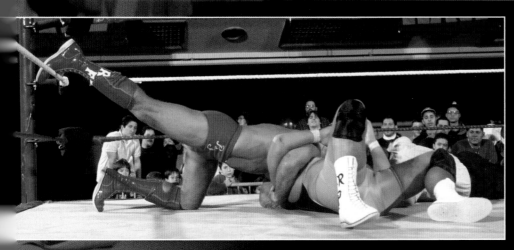

An exhausted Flair had one more trick in his bag—a pair of brass knuckles. Flair clocked Perfect, and it looked like the match would end with a miscarriage of justice. Perfect got his foot on the rope to disrupt the first pinfall attempt and kicked out of the second. Flair went for more chops, but they didn't seem to affect Perfect, who then unleashed a barrage of chops and a back body drop. Both men continued to get near falls until Perfect finally caught Flair and delivered a Perfectplex for the three-count. Perfect would stay and Flair had to go.

Mr. Perfect remained in WWE until the following year when a back injury forced him to step away from the ring. Years later, Perfect and Flair would renew their rivalry in WCW when Perfect (using his given name Curt Hennig) joined the nWo in their war with Flair's Four Horsemen. Ric Flair would not be seen in a WWE ring for almost a decade, reappearing in November 2001 as the co-owner of the WWE, having purchased Shane and Stephanie McMahon's shares in the company. This would lead to a brutal rivalry with Mr. McMahon and a Street Fight at the *2002 Royal Rumble*.

THE LEAD-UP

Shawn Michaels and Triple H had long been friends, and in the mid-to-late 90s, it often seemed like it was the two of them against the rest of the WWE locker room. But after Michaels lost the WWE Championship at *WrestleMania XIV*, a significant back injury forced him to retire. Triple H took the opportunity to shine, taking D-Generation X to new heights and becoming a multiple-time WWE Champion. Michaels made occasional appearances as Commissioner or Special Referee, but the Heartbreak Kid had not competed in the ring for more than four years. However, when his former best friend Triple H attacked him in and out of the ring, Michaels demanded a match with The Game. WWE refused to sanction the match, but the two agreed to fight at *SummerSlam 2002* anyway.

TRIPLE H VS. SHAWN MICHAELS

THE MATCH

Michaels did not wait long after the bell rang, starting things off with a series of punches aimed at Triple H's head. Michaels took the fight to The Game both inside and outside of the ring, astounding the crowd. But Triple H would not be such an easy opponent to beat. The Game made his intentions clear when he immediately began targeting Shawn's back (the reason for HBK's four-year hiatus from the ring) with back breakers, whips into the corner turnbuckles, and general assaults. He even attempted to hit Michaels with a sledgehammer, but the Heartbreak Kid thwarted the attempt.

Triple H delivered a devastating side suplex through a foreign object, but he still couldn't keep Michaels down for the three-count. Triple H continued to focus on the Heartbreak Kid's back with a sidewalk slam on the foreign object. Triple H then had Michaels set up for a Pedigree, but Michaels hit The Game with a low blow and used Sweet Chin Music to drive the foreign object into The Game's face. Now both men were bloody messes.

Michaels was now reenergized and he came up with a number of innovative ways to assault Triple H. He hit his former best friend with a trash can and lid, and the boot of one of the television announcers. Michaels further delighted the crowd when he pulled a ladder from under the ring. However, after he twice hit Triple H with the ladder, The Game was able to kick the ladder into Michaels, getting himself back into the match. Triple H attempted to finish off Michaels by hitting HBK with the ring stairs, but Michaels delivered a drop toe hold that drove Triple H's face into the steel steps. Michaels then set up a table and hit Triple H with a fire extinguisher. Triple H ended up on the table, and then Michaels delivered a flying cross-body from the top turnbuckle, driving Triple H through the table.

Knowing he could only win the match in the ring, Michaels rolled Triple H back into the ring and set up the ladder. He delivered an elbow off the ladder onto a prone Triple H and prepared for a final Sweet Chin Music. But Triple H caught HBK's leg and set Michaels up for a Pedigree. Michaels reversed the move and rolled up The Game for a three-count. Michaels' celebration was short-lived, as a bitter Triple H hit the Heartbreak Kid with a pair of sledgehammer shots to the back, forcing the winner to move on a stretcher.

THE AFTERMATH

Many assumed that Michaels' in-ring appearance would be a one-time thing, a special attraction. However, the match turned out to be the beginning of one of the most improbable second acts in wrestling history. Michaels' next match would be at *Survivor Series* 2002, when he would be one of five men to challenge Champion Triple H for the World Heavyweight Championship. Michaels completed his amazing comeback by winning the Title. Michaels and Triple H engaged in a significant rivalry for the next few years, until 2006, when they patched up their differences and re-formed D-Generation X.

TRIPLE H vs. BATISTA

THE LEAD-UP

By winning the 2005 *Royal Rumble*, Batista was guaranteed a Title opportunity and a spot in the main event at *WrestleMania 21*. He just needed to choose which Champion to challenge: *SmackDown*'s WWE Champion JBL or *Raw*'s World Heavyweight Champion (and Batista's Evolution faction-mate) Triple H. For The Game, the choice was obvious—go to *SmackDown*, beat JBL, and Evolution would control the Titles on both brands. But Batista knew that Triple H was looking to duck him, so Batista surprised his former mentor by challenging him for the World Heavyweight Championship under the bright lights of *WrestleMania 21*.

WRESTLEMANIA 21
WORLD HEAVYWEIGHT CHAMPIONSHIP MATCH

April 3, 2005

Staples Center
Los Angeles, California

THE MATCH

The two former Evolution members both tried to establish dominance by locking up and overpowering one another. Triple H had the edge in experience, but Batista had the brute strength, giving him the early advantage. Triple H attempted a Pedigree, but The Animal powered out of the move, threw the Champion into the ring ropes, and hit Triple H with a thunderous powerslam.

A third Evolution member, Ric Flair, accompanied Triple H to the ring and made life difficult for Batista. Flair frequently distracted Batista, allowing Triple H to sneak up on The Animal. And when the official was busy with Triple H in the ring, Flair would attack Batista. At one point, Triple H looked to inflict massive damage to Batista by delivering a Pedigree outside the ring on the steps. However, The Animal reversed the move and catapulted The Game into the ring post, turning Triple H's face into a bloody mess. Batista kept up the punishment by repeatedly slamming The Game's face into the steps.

Triple H rolled out of the ring, looking to catch a breather, but Batista followed. Again, Flair tried to help The Game by attacking Batista, but The Animal was fed up and clobbered The Nature Boy. Triple H tried to use the distraction to hit Batista with a foreign object, but the official grabbed it before the Champion could do any damage. With the official down, Flair tried to hit Batista with the World Heavyweight Championship, but instead got a Spinebuster for his trouble. However, Triple H grabbed the Title and used it to level The Animal. The audience groaned in unison, worried that Triple H had stolen the match, but Batista showed heart and determination to kick out of the pinfall attempt.

Batista then executed a Spinebuster on The Game and was looking to finish off the Champion. However, Triple H was not done—he delivered a low blow to the challenger. Back in control, Triple H set up for a Pedigree. Twice, the Animal blocked the attempt and instead slammed the Champion to the mat. To the delight of the crowd, Batista gave Triple H the double thumbs down and crushed The Game with a Batista Bomb, earning a three-count and winning his first World Heavyweight Championship.

THE AFTERMATH

Triple H would twice attempt to regain his Title—first in a standard rematch at *Backlash* 2005, then in a Hell in a Cell Match at *Vengeance* 2005. Batista won at *Backlash*, but Triple H had to feel confident going into *Vengeance*— four times previously he'd been in a one-on-one Hell in a Cell Match, and each time he'd won. However, Batista defended his Title once again against The Game. Ironically, Triple H got his wish, as Batista went to *SmackDown*, thanks to the 2005 WWE Draft. Unfortunately for The Game, The Animal took the World Heavyweight Championship with him.

BRET "HIT MAN" HART
VS.
THE 1-2-3 KID

THE LEAD-UP

Since winning the WWE Championship at *WrestleMania X*, Bret "Hit Man" Hart took on all comers looking to challenge him for the Title. Many of the Superstars that challenged him were larger men, but in July 1994 he faced a competitor that Hart had both a size and strength advantage over: The 1-2-3 Kid. The young challenger burst on to the scene with the stunning upset of defeating Razor Ramon. He followed that victory with wins over Ted Dibiase and IRS, and then defeated Nikolai Volkoff for an opportunity at the WWE Championship.

THE MATCH

Before the match could start, Bret's brother Owen and brother-in-law Jim Neidhart came to the ring to argue with the WWE Champion. Owen was frustrated that Bret was facing The 1-2-3 Kid when the younger Hart felt he should be getting the Title opportunity. After they left, Bret and The Kid shook hands and started the match. The two exchanged wristlocks, before Hit Man slammed The Kid to the ground. The Kid kipped up and chained a series of moves on the Champion, shifting a side headlock into a hammerlock. Hart landed a snap mare takedown on The Kid, but the challenger held on to the hammerlock through the move.

Hart took advantage of The 1-2-3 Kid, performing a scoop slam and a leg drop. Backing the challenger in the corner, Hart delivered a series of European Uppercuts as well as a knee to the face and some hard elbows to the back of The Kid's head. After a swinging neckbreaker, Hart got a two-count in the match's first pinning attempt. The Kid fought back and delivered a high crossbody, getting a near fall. The Kid tried to execute a crucifix, but Hart blocked it and pinned The Kid. Before the three-count, The Kid placed his foot on the rope. The official missed this and tried to award the victory to Hart, but Hit Man insisted the match continue.

The Champion may have regretted his act of sportsmanship, as his challenger came back strong after the match restart. The Kid executed a Backstabber and got a two-count. Hart tried to wear him down with a headlock and a DDT, but The Kid kept kicking out of pinning attempts. Hart tried to clothesline his opponent, but The 1-2-3 Kid ducked and hit the Champion with a kick. He then tossed Hit Man into the corner and delivered a missile dropkick to Hart's face. The challenger then got a series of two-counts after a succession of high-risk moves, including a Power Bomb, and a high crossbody and elbow off the top rope.

Hart tried to put The Kid into his signature Sharpshooter, but The Kid grabbed the ring rope as Hart tried to turn him over, forcing a break. Hart executed several forearms and tried to deliver a top-rope Superplex, but The Kid countered the move in-air and turned it into a high

crossbody. The Kid Irish Whipped Hart into the corner and when he leapt toward Hit Man, Hart dodged, sending The Kid into the turnbuckle. Hart nailed The Kid with a Bulldog, but when he went to the top rope, The Kid slammed the Champion to the mat. Again, The Kid tried a high-risk maneuver, but Hart caught him midair and twisted The Kid into a Sharpshooter. The Kid tapped out and Hart retained the WWE Championship.

THE AFTERMATH

Bret Hart continued to defend his Championship against all comers, with perhaps his most difficult challenge coming at *SummerSlam 1994*. That night, he was forced to face his brother in a Steel Cage Match. Hart retained the Championship and held onto the Title until *Survivor Series 1994*. The Kid eventually left WWE temporarily and joined the nWo with WCW, but he returned to WWE to join D-Generation X under the new name X-Pac. This made him the only Superstar to be an active member of both the nWo and DX during their heydays.

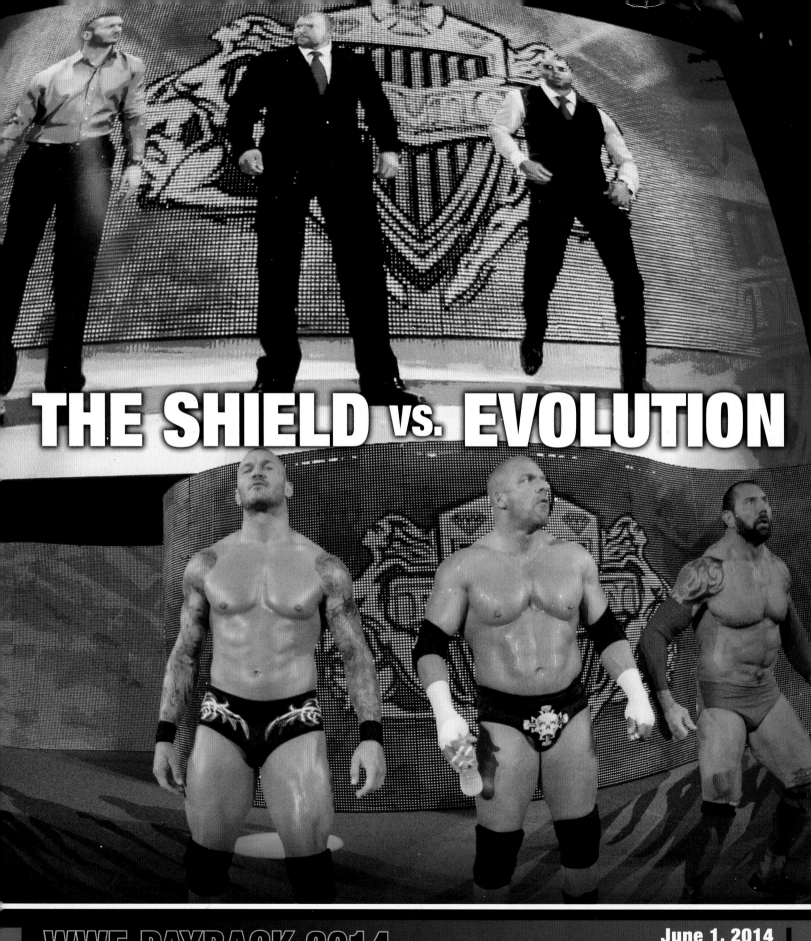

THE SHIELD vs. EVOLUTION

WWE PAYBACK 2014
NO HOLDS BARRED ELIMINATION MATCH

June 1, 2014

Allstate Arena
Rosemont, Illinois

THE LEAD-UP

For months, Triple H and The Authority could count on The Shield to do their dirty work, until the trio had enough of Triple H and his decisions. When The Game faced Daniel Bryan for the WWE World Heavyweight Championship, he tried to stack the deck in his favor by using Batista, Randy Orton, and Kane to all attack the Champion. The Shield came to the ring and attacked Triple H, evening the odds and helping Bryan win the match. Triple H, Randy Orton, and Batista reformed Evolution to fight The Shield, but the Hounds of Justice won a six-man tag match at *Extreme Rules*. The two factions decided to fight each other again at *Payback* in a no holds barred Elimination Match.

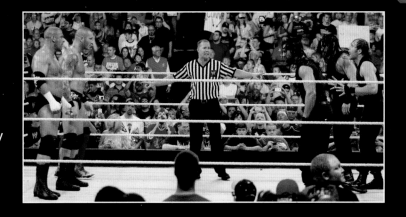

THE MATCH

Both sides stared each other down, and once the bell rang, all six men began to brawl with each other. The action spilled out of the ring and into the crowd, with The Shield gaining the early upper hand, but Evolution fighting back. It took some time, but the two teams eventually made it back to the ring with Reigns squaring off against Batista. The two teams were evenly matched, and each side isolated a competitor on the other team, using quick tags to punish their opponents. However, no one was able to gain a three-count pin, even when Evolution had Ambrose cut off from his corner and beat him in and out of the ring.

Triple H took out Rollins by slamming him with a metal sheet and Orton incapacitated Ambrose. With Ambrose and Rollins both down, the three members of Evolution focused on Roman Reigns. They raised Reigns up on Batista's shoulders and delivered a triple Powerbomb through the announcers' table. They further incapacitated Ambrose and Rollins and then turned back to deal with Reigns, beating him with kendo sticks. After he rolled out of the ring, they tried to finish him off on the entrance stage. But Ambrose fought back and Rollins dove off the top of the Titantron onto all three members of Evolution.

Batista set Rollins up for the Batista Bomb, but Rollins floated over the top of The Animal, and Batista was exposed for a Roman Reigns' spear. Rollins rolled on top of Batista and got a three-count—the first elimination of the match. Randy Orton then gave Rollins an RKO and seemed to have the Architect of The Shield down for a tying pin, but Reigns pulled him off and Dean Ambrose hit Orton in the back with a foreign object and followed that up with a Dirty Deeds to pin and eliminate Orton.

All members of The Shield were still in the match, and only Triple H remained for Evolution. The Game attempted to deliver a Pedigree to Ambrose, but Reigns hammered Evolution's leader with a Superman Punch. Batista, who should have already gone to the back, speared Reigns to prevent him from pinning Triple H. Randy Orton took advantage and handed Triple H his signature sledgehammer, and The Game pummeled Ambrose with it and was lining up Reigns. Rollins stunned Triple H by flying off the top rope and Reigns followed that up with a Spear and a pin of The Game. Not only did The Shield win the match, they achieved a clean sweep of Evolution.

THE AFTERMATH

Sick of waiting for his one-on-one Championship opportunity, Batista demanded his Title match the next night on *Raw*. When Triple H could not accommodate his request, a frustrated Animal quit and stormed off. Evolution was not the only group to dissolve that night; Seth Rollins betrayed his fellow Shield members by attacking them both and aligning with The Authority. The move paid off for Rollins. Within the next year, he ended up winning the Money in the Bank Championship opportunity and, at *WrestleMania 31*, cashed it in to win the WWE World Heavyweight Championship by pinning his former Shield teammate, Roman Reigns.

WRESTLEMANIA 13
NO DISQUALIFICATION SUBMISSION MATCH

March 23, 1997

Rosemont Horizon
Rosemont, Illinois

BRET "HIT MAN" HART VS. STONE COLD STEVE AUSTIN

THE LEAD-UP

Bret "Hit Man" Hart took a sabbatical from WWE after his overtime loss of the WWE Championship to Shawn Michaels at *WrestleMania XII*. When Hit Man returned, he found himself embroiled in a bitter rivalry with Stone Cold Steve Austin. The Texas Rattlesnake cheated Hart at the 1997 Royal Rumble Match, and he cost Hit Man his WWE Championship a month later. The two decided to have a Submission Match at *WrestleMania 13*. To keep the peace, the World's Most Dangerous Man, Ken Shamrock, was appointed the Special Guest Referee.

THE MATCH

Austin did not even wait for the bell—he attacked Hart as soon as he entered the ring. Hart and Austin rolled around on the mat exchanging blows. The fight then moved out of the ring, where Hart tossed Austin into a ring post. Austin and Hart continued to battle into the crowd. Shamrock tried to keep the crowd at bay while the two brawled deeper into the audience. Hart and Austin eventually made it back to the ring area, and Stone Cold tossed Hit Man into the steel stairs.

The match finally moved back into the ring and Hit Man floored Austin with a swinging neckbreaker. Hart then specifically targeted Austin's knee with his moves. Austin briefly stemmed Hit Man's momentum with a few moves, but Hart went for Austin's knee and continued his assault, including a brutal Figure Four that bent Austin's legs around the ring post. Hart brought the ring bell and a foreign object into the ring and inflicted further punishment to Austin's ankle. Hart climbed to the top turnbuckle, clearly planning to leap from the top rope and bring all his weight down on the same ankle. Austin freed himself and plastered Hart with a foreign object, knocking him off the top turnbuckle. Austin took control of the match, suplexing Hit Man and then dropping an elbow from the top rope.

Austin wrenched Bret's neck in a bruising submission move, but Hart would not submit. Austin then locked Hart in a Boston Crab, but Hart made the ropes and Shamrock forced a break. Austin tried to insult Hart by putting him into a Sharpshooter, but Hart thumbed Austin's eye to stop the maneuver. Hart launched a series of punches to Austin's midsection, so Austin tossed Hart out of the ring to gain some breathing room. Austin tried to Irish Whip Hart into the timekeeper's area, but Hart reversed the move, tossing Austin into the area instead. The move busted open Austin's face, and the Texas Rattlesnake began to profusely bleed.

Hart attempted to make the bleeding worse by kicking and punching Austin's face. Hart grabbed the foreign object Austin had used earlier and targeted Austin's knee with some additional shots. Hart looked to finish off the Texas Rattlesnake with a Sharpshooter, but Austin raked Hart's face to force a break of the move. It seemed inevitable that Hart would win, but Austin bought himself some time with a low blow. Austin stomped a cornered Hart repeatedly and followed it with a Superplex. Austin tried to choke Hart with an extension cord, but Hart used the ring bell to knock Austin down. Hart then locked Austin in the Sharpshooter, but Austin would not submit. Austin almost broke the move, but Hart kept the Sharpshooter locked in. The Texas Rattlesnake passed out from the pain, so Shamrock awarded the decision to Bret "Hit Man" Hart.

THE AFTERMATH

The rivalry between Hit Man and Stone Cold did not end at *WrestleMania*. The battles between the two amped up over the following months, particularly when Bret recruited family and friends Owen Hart, The British Bulldog, Jim "The Anvil" Neidhart, and Brian Pillman to form a new version of The Hart Foundation to battle Austin and his allies. Through it all, Austin's popularity with the WWE Universe continued to explode, and the Texas Rattlesnake reached the top of his profession just one year later, when he captured the WWE Championship at *WrestleMania XIV* by defeating Shawn Michaels.

TRIPLE H, MR. MCMAHON, AND SHANE MCMAHON VS. THE ROCK, UNDERTAKER, AND KANE

THE LEAD-UP

The McMahon-Helmsley faction ran roughshod over WWE in early 2000. Consisting initially of WWE Champion Triple H and his wife Stephanie McMahon-Helmsley, they were joined post-*WrestleMania* by WWE Chairman Mr. McMahon, Shane McMahon, and D-Generation X. The only member of the McMahon family not in the faction was Linda, and she tried to undo much of the damage done by the rest of the family. With three viable contenders for the WWE Championship, Linda set a Six-Man Tag Match with The Rock, Kane, and Undertaker facing Triple H, Mr. McMahon, and Shane McMahon. Linda enraged her son-in-law by announcing that if any member of Triple H's team was pinned, he would lose the WWE Title.

KING OF THE RING 2000

SIX-MAN TAG MATCH FOR THE WWE CHAMPIONSHIP

June 25, 2000

Fleet Center
Boston, Massachusetts

THE MATCH

Both teams entered the match with significant internal issues. Triple H was worried that Vince or Shane getting pinned would lead to him losing his Championship. Vince was confident because it was clear the members of the other team were not getting along. It made sense—only the man getting the pin could be WWE Champion, and all three Superstars wanted the Title. This conflict was apparent from the beginning of the match, as all three men wanted to start. Kane eventually began things for his team, going straight for Shane McMahon. A combination of punches and a military press had Shane in trouble, but Vince broke up an attempted Chokeslam and Triple H attacked Kane from behind.

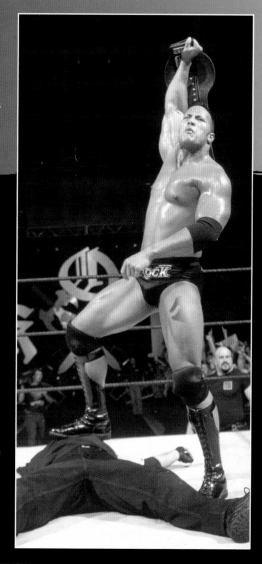

Once the match returned to a one-on-one situation, The Rock tagged himself in and delivered his own punishing blows to Shane-O-Mac. Again though, The Rock's team demonstrated a lack of cohesion when Undertaker slapped The Rock on the back to tag himself in. The Deadman hit a massive Chokeslam on the younger McMahon and would have recorded the pin, but his own teammate, The Rock, broke things up. Triple H entered the match, but did not fare much better. He was soon on the canvas, thanks to a wicked DDT from The Phenom. Undertaker's pinning attempt was then interrupted by Kane. It looked like Mr. McMahon's pre-match confidence was well placed.

The action eventually spilled out of the ring and all six men got involved, with Undertaker beating up Shane, Kane taking care of Mr. McMahon, and The Rock and Triple H pairing off. When order was restored (as much as it could be), The Rock found himself in trouble with all three members of the opposing faction working together smoothly. Kane even had to save The Rock from a Triple H pinning attempt. Again the action spilled outside the ring with The Brothers of Destruction taking out the McMahons. Alone in the ring, The Rock looked to pin Triple H, but Kane broke it up and gave The People's Champ a Chokeslam. Triple H thought he had Kane back on his side, but that notion was quickly dispelled when Kane gave the WWE Champion a Tombstone Piledriver. Undertaker pulled his brother out of the ring before the pin could be counted, and again the action spilled out of the ring.

Vince made his way back in the ring and prepared to give The Rock his version of the People's Elbow, but The Rock popped up and delivered a Rock Bottom to the Chairman of WWE. With everyone occupied outside the ring, no one broke up the pinfall attempt. The Rock won the WWE Title, and he didn't even pin the Champion to do it.

THE AFTERMATH

Triple H had an opportunity to regain the WWE Championship at *SummerSlam*, but he faced two opponents, as *King of the Ring* tournament winner Kurt Angle was also granted a Title opportunity. The Rock held off both men, but Kurt Angle would eventually defeat The Rock for Angle's first WWE Championship at *No Mercy 2000*. Two years later, Triple H would once again reign as WWE Champion, as he won the Title a fifth time at *WrestleMania X8* in March 2002.

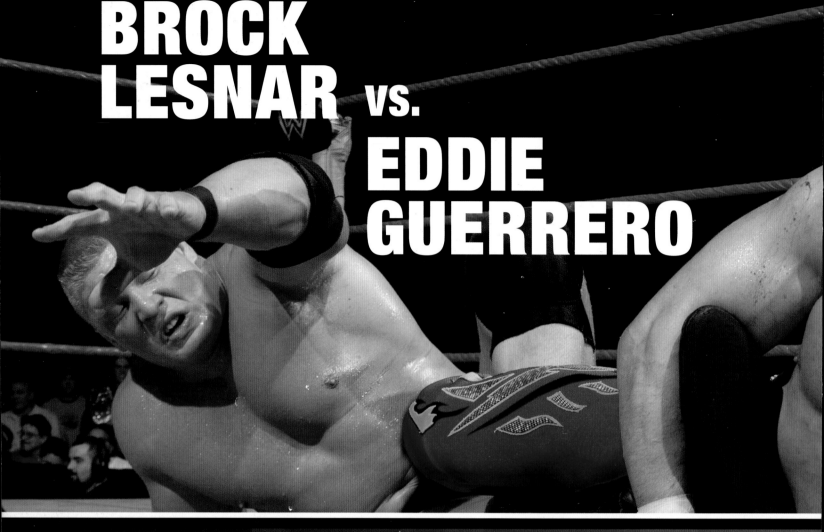

BROCK LESNAR vs. EDDIE GUERRERO

NO WAY OUT 2004
WWE CHAMPIONSHIP MATCH

February 15, 2004

Cow Palace
San Jose, California

THE LEAD-UP

After losing his job at WWE, Eddie Guerrero overcame a number of demons, battling to win his position back. After holding the Intercontinental, United States, and Tag Team Championships, Guerrero set his sights on a bigger prize—the WWE Championship. Winning a 15-Man Royal Rumble on *SmackDown*, Guerrero earned the opportunity to challenge WWE Champion Brock Lesnar at *No Way Out*. The bout would be daunting, as Lesnar had more than 60 pounds on Guerrero. But the crowd was clearly behind Latino Heat, and they knew he'd be willing to lie, cheat, and steal to achieve his goal.

Lesnar took full advantage of his power dominance early in the match. He won several lockups, throwing Guerrero to the mat, and delivered powerful punches, kicks, and knees to the challenger. Lesnar executed a devastating overhead belly-to-belly suplex, and followed with a knee to Guerrero's jaw. Lesnar tossed Latino Heat out of the ring and rejected Guerrero's attempts to reenter. Guerrero responded by leaping from the ring apron and pulling Lesnar's throat onto the top ring rope, snapping Lesnar back to the mat. Guerrero then drove the Champion's knee into the ring post twice. He went to do it a third time, but Lesnar used his strength to pull Guerrero's body into the post. Back in the ring, Lesnar continued to dominate with his power, but he made a crucial mistake. Lining Guerrero up in the corner, Lesnar took a running leap to deliver another knee to the jaw of the challenger. Latino Heat dodged and the Champion's momentum sent him crashing to the arena floor.

Now Guerrero began to execute his game plan—targeting Lesnar's knee in order to sap him of power. In addition to kicks directed at the knee, Guerrero also put the Champion in several painful submission holds that targeted the legs, including a Figure-Four Leglock and two STF holds. The Champion refused to submit and used his immense power to break each hold, but it was clear Guerrero had done some damage. The Beast winced after executing a suplex and continued to be visibly in pain when using his leg. Lesnar then attempted to slow down the match and ground the challenger by putting him in a Sleeper Hold. Guerrero finally broke the hold when he stumbled into the corner, driving Lesnar into the second turnbuckle.

Lesnar continued to wear down Guerrero, but he could not get Guerrero to give up. Guerrero finally launched some offense when he hit the Champion with his Three Amigos consecutive suplexes. Thinking he had the Champion finished, Guerrero went to the top rope for a match-ending Frog Splash. But Lesnar rolled out of the way and Latino Heat came crashing to the mat. Lesnar picked up Guerrero and delivered an F-5, but the move knocked down the official and took him out of the match.

With the official down, Lesnar looked to take advantage. He left the ring and grabbed the WWE Title. He brought it into the ring, set on knocking Guerrero out with it. But Bill Goldberg appeared and speared Lesnar, causing the Champion to drop the Title. Guerrero then picked it up, intending to hit Lesnar with it and live up to the "cheat" part of his motto. Just as Guerrero attempted to use the Title, Lesnar hit him in the gut and lifted the challenger for an F-5. However, Guerrero reversed the move into a DDT, driving Lesnar onto the Championship's faceplate. Guerrero then performed his Frog Splash and pinned Lesnar, winning the WWE Championship.

THE AFTERMATH

After his emotional win, Eddie Guerrero went on to successfully defend his Championship at *WrestleMania XX*. He held the Title until *The Great American Bash*, where he fell to JBL. Guerrero continued to compete in WWE rings until he passed away in November 2005. His early passing shocked and saddened the world. Lesnar pursued revenge at *WrestleMania XX* with a match against Goldberg, but Goldberg defeated Lesnar. It was The Beast's last match in WWE until he made his shocking return eight years later in April 2012.

SHAWN MICHAELS
VS.
KURT ANGLE

THE LEAD-UP

In 2005, Kurt Angle was looking to win his first Royal Rumble Match in order to ensure a spot in the main event of *WrestleMania 21*. But the Heartbreak Kid, Shawn Michaels, eliminated the Olympic Hero. Angle did not take his elimination well and reentered the match to return the favor and put Michaels in a painful Ankle Lock outside the ring. Even though the two men were on different WWE brands, Michaels challenged Angle to an Interpromotional Match at *WrestleMania 21*. Angle, obsessed with showing the world he was better than Michaels, accepted the challenge.

THE MATCH

With his Olympic background, Angle was considered the finest mat wrestler in WWE. However, it was Shawn Michaels that came out displaying a deep arsenal of moves and counters, including a side headlock and a short arm scissors. Angle tried to break the latter move unsuccessfully and even tried to roll Michaels into a pinning predicament. Finally, Angle used his strength to pick Michaels off the mat, but the Heartbreak Kid countered the move into a sunset flip, getting a near fall. When Michaels cinched another side headlock, Angle's frustration was palpable. The anger boiled over into a barrage of blows from both men.

Once the men were separated, Angle tried to apply his Ankle Lock submission move. However, Michaels was able to flip out of the move and then clothesline Angle (and himself) out of the ring to the mats below. Angle looked to suplex Michaels onto the announcers' table, but when the Heartbreak Kid blocked the move, Angle settled on using the Angle Slam to drive Michaels' back into the steel ring post. Angle looked to further damage his opponent's back with the use of punches and kicks. Angle then followed with a devastating overhead belly-to-belly suplex, but Michaels kicked out at the two-count.

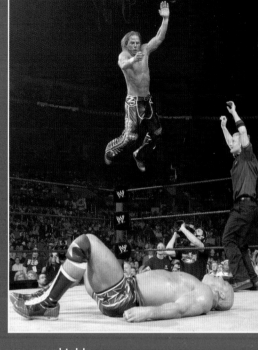

Michaels was able to stem the momentum by interrupting an Angle Slam, tossing Angle from the top turnbuckle. After missing a top-rope elbow, Michaels kept the momentum going by back-body dropping Angle out of the ring. He then demonstrated his high-risk offense by hitting a cross body from the top turnbuckle on to Angle on the floor below. He upped the ante by hitting a flying elbow onto a prone Angle, driving both men into the announcers' table.

Michaels executed a flying elbow and tried to perform Sweet Chin Music, but Angle caught the leg and turned it into an Ankle Lock. In response, Michaels was able to reach the ropes and force a break. Angle looked to finish Michaels with an Angle Slam, but Michaels countered. On his second attempt, Angle hit his namesake slam, but Michaels kicked out. Angle then missed a moonsault, and both men, exhausted and battered, struggled to continue. Michaels went to the top rope, but Angle used the moment to hit a top-rope Angle Slam. Then Michaels showed why he is Mr. WrestleMania and kicked out of the pinfall, following with a perfectly executed Sweet Chin Music.

Angle put Michaels into the Ankle Lock one more time. Repeatedly, the Heartbreak Kid tried to flip out of the move or drag himself to the ropes to force a break. But Angle would not let go and kept pulling the Showstopper away from the ropes. Angle upped the pressure by grapevining Michaels down to the mat, and Michaels finally had no choice but to tap out.

THE AFTERMATH

While both men returned to their respective brands, they would eventually appear on the same show when Angle was drafted to *Raw* in June 2005. Michaels took the opportunity to challenge the Olympic Hero to a rematch at *Vengeance* 2005. Michaels would even the score on their rivalry by defeating Angle in the rematch. Eventually both men would challenge John Cena for the WWE Championship in a Triple Threat Match at *Taboo Tuesday* 2005, but Cena was able to retain the Title.

THE LEAD-UP

For two years, Bayley pursued her singular goal of becoming the NXT Women's Champion. On multiple occasions, she earned Title opportunities, but fell short. The Champion, Sasha Banks, won the Title in February at *NXT TakeOver: Rival* by pinning Charlotte in a Fatal Four-Way Match for the NXT Women's Championship, a match that also featured Becky Lynch and Bayley. Returning from a hand injury in July, Bayley defeated Charlotte and Becky in one-on-one matches to become the #1 contender to Banks' Title. The two longtime rivals would meet in Brooklyn in a historic Co-Main Event to *NXT TakeOver: Brooklyn*.

SASHA BANKS vs. BAYLEY

THE MATCH

Banks began the match by berating Bayley, but the Ultimate Underdog would not take it, launching herself at the Champion. The two competitors rolled around the ring, brawling, with Bayley getting the better of things. Bayley followed up with a clothesline on Banks for the first pinfall attempt of the match. Bayley then hung Banks upside down in the corner and hit her with a springboard elbow. Banks rolled out of the ring to collect herself, but Bayley demonstrated her innovative offense by executing a drop kick from the floor and through the ring on the Champion.

Banks changed the momentum of the match by kicking Bayley on the knee and knocking her to the floor. After Bayley returned to the ring, Banks tried to hit Bayley with a double-knee in the corner, but Bayley countered. However, Banks soon had the challenger draped across the top rope and successfully double-kneed Bayley, earning a two-count from the move. With Bayley down in a corner, Banks again belittled the challenger. But this was a mistake, as Bayley kicked Banks in the midsection and then drove her into the turnbuckle.

Banks reversed a move and tossed Bayley out of the ring. Banks then took the bandages off Bayley's hand and attacked the injury. Banks even drove foreign objects into Bayley's hand. With Bayley outside the ring trying to recover, Banks dove over the official and the top rope onto Bayley below. Banks stopped her own momentum with a high-risk move that ended with her falling from the top rope to the floor below. Bayley recovered and hit Banks with a corner shoulderbreaker and a suplex. She went for the Bayley-to-Belly, but Banks countered and eventually locked Bayley into her Banks Statement submission move.

Bayley stunned the crowd by reversing the move into a submission hold of her own. The Champion barely escaped by draping her leg over the bottom rope. Bayley finally hit her Bayley-to-Belly Suplex, but Banks kicked out at the two-count.

Bayley set Banks on the top turnbuckle for a top rope hurricanrana, but Banks was able to shove her to the mat below. Banks then hit the challenger with a double-knee drop off the second rope, but Bayley again kicked out. Banks looked to finish off the challenger by taking her to the top rope. But Bayley was able to counter Banks and hit a reverse top-rope hurricanrana. She then hit a second Bayley-to-Belly and pinned Banks to become the NXT Women's Champion.

THE AFTERMATH

In an emotional scene, NXT alumni Charlotte and Becky Lynch entered the ring to celebrate with Bayley. Even Banks congratulated her longtime rival and the four women shared an emotional hug. But Banks was guaranteed a rematch, and for the first time ever, two women competed in a 30-minute Iron Man Match, the Main Event of *NXT TakeOver: Respect*. Bayley was able to retain her Championship by beating Banks, three falls to two.

HULK HOGAN VS. ANDRE THE GIANT

THE LEAD-UP

Hulkamania continued to run wild on WWE. Ever since early 1984, Hulk Hogan had been the WWE Champion and defended the Title against all comers. But in early 1987, his most difficult challenger would emerge. Andre the Giant, who had been undefeated for more than a decade, was tired of Hulk getting more recognition than him, so the Giant aligned himself with manager Bobby "The Brain" Heenan. On a Piper's Pit interview show, Andre demanded a WWE Championship Match, emphasizing his point by ripping off the Hulkster's shirt and crucifix necklace. Although saddened by the betrayal of his former friend, Hogan accepted the Title challenge.

WRESTLEMANIA III

WWE CHAMPIONSHIP MATCH

March 29, 1987

Pontiac Silverdome
Pontiac, Michigan

THE MATCH

The clash between Hulk Hogan and Andre the Giant was so anticipated that a record 93,173 fans filled the Pontiac Silverdome to witness the clash. After being so beloved for years, the WWE Universe expressed their anger at Andre and Heenan, pelting their cart with trash on its way to the ring. The Hulkster didn't wait for the cart to take him to the ring—he marched to the ring with his eyes locked on the massive Giant the entire time.

The two men traded early shots, but then Hogan went for the early slam. The choice was unwise, as he collapsed under the weight of the massive Giant, and Andre almost earned the pinfall victory then and there. Hogan may have gotten his shoulder up before the third count, but Andre stayed on the offensive. He slammed the Champion twice to the ring and then started launching him into the turnbuckles, following up each with shoulder blocks into Hogan's chest. Just as the announcers remarked that Andre was making it seem easy, Hulk was able to escape the corner and hit Andre with a series of powerful punches. But Andre was still not done, as he delivered a kick to Hogan that completely derailed the Champ's momentum.

Hogan was finally able to knock the Giant off his feet. Then, as Andre tried to recover, Hogan did what no one thought was possible—he picked up the Giant and body slammed him. The packed Silverdome and the millions watching around the world were stunned. The Hulkster then hit Andre with his signature Leg Drop and pinned the massive Giant to retain his WWE Championship. As a distraught Heenan and furious Andre the Giant left the ring, Hulk Hogan gave the 93,173 fans one final treat as he celebrated and posed in the ring for the jubilant crowd.

The match went back and forth with Hogan attempting to bring the Giant down, and Andre using his massive power to club the Champion at every opportunity. Andre almost won the Title a second time when he put Hogan in a punishing Bear Hug. Andre wrenched his beefy arms around Hogan, constricting the flow of air into Hogan's lungs and slowly draining the champion of all energy. Twice, the official lifted Hogan's arm and it limply fell back. One more and Andre would have won the Title. But Hogan fed off the energy of his Hulkamaniacs and was able to break the hold and begin his comeback.

THE AFTERMATH

Over the next year and a half, Andre remained a thorn in Hulk Hogan's side. WWE would create its second-ever pay-per-view tradition in November of 1987, when Andre and Hulk each captained five-man teams in the main event of the inaugural *Survivor Series*. Andre was the sole survivor of the match, sending the message to the WWE Champion Hogan that the Giant was still a threat to take the Championship. Almost eleven months after their *WrestleMania III* match, the two would meet again for the WWE Championship in a match that would have perhaps one of the most controversial endings in the history of sports-entertainment.

THE LEAD-UP

After being named the inaugural World Heavyweight Champion in September, Triple H made a number of enemies, all of whom wanted to take The Game's Championship. To accommodate the number of challengers, and to top *SmackDown*'s Hell in a Cell from the previous month, *Raw* General Manager Eric Bischoff introduced a new type of match—the Elimination Chamber. Six men are locked in an unforgiving steel structure, with four sealed in pods and two starting off the match. Every five minutes, one of the pods opens and a new competitor enters the match. The match continues until only one competitor remains. For Triple H to retain his Title, he would have to outlast Chris Jericho, Booker T, Kane, Shawn Michaels, and Rob Van Dam.

TRIPLE H
vs. SHAWN MICHAELS
vs. CHRIS JERICHO
vs. KANE
vs. BOOKER T
vs. ROB VAN DAM

THE MATCH

Things did not start well for the Champion, as Triple H was one of the two Superstars chosen to begin, along with Rob Van Dam. Van Dam enacted some of his innovative offense early. To make his moves even more devastating, RVD executed them on the solid steel floor surrounding the ring. Chris Jericho was the next Superstar to enter the match and he immediately attacked Rob Van Dam. The two traded blows, and then RVD attempted to leap at Jericho. Y2J ducked, but RVD showed incredible athleticism, holding on to the cage wall and then leaping back onto Jericho. Triple H and Jericho then worked together, double teaming RVD. Van Dam fought back valiantly, but the two men were too much to overcome.

The odds evened a bit more when the fourth man, Booker T, entered the match. Booker hit both Triple H and Jericho with a series of punches and kicks. With those two recuperating outside the ring, Booker and RVD squared off. With RVD getting the better of the exchange, Van Dam then turned his attention to Triple H. He knocked the Champion down, and looked to perform his Five-Star Frog Splash. Instead of leaping from the top turnbuckle, RVD executed the move from the top of a pod. The move took something out of RVD as well, leaving him open for a top-rope Missile Dropkick from Booker T. Booker pinned RVD, making him the first Superstar eliminated from the match.

Kane now entered the contest. The Big Red Monster pounded everyone in the ring, until turning his focus on the Champion. Jericho used the opportunity to hit Booker T with a Lionsault and pin him, the second elimination of the match. As the clock began to count down for the last time, the crowd eagerly anticipated the final entrant, Shawn Michaels. While Michaels started off strong, Kane reemerged by delivering three Chokeslams. The other three competitors worked together to eliminate Kane after he suffered Sweet Chin Music, a Pedigree, and a Lionsault. The three remaining Superstars were all now bleeding,

and Triple H and Jericho tried to work together to eliminate the Heartbreak Kid. Jericho thought he had eliminated Michaels with a Lionsault, but Michaels kicked out at two. Jericho also almost eliminated Triple H with The Walls of Jericho, but Michaels took advantage and delivered Sweet Chin Music, pinning and eliminating Jericho.

The last two Superstars in the match were former friends, now turned bitter rivals, Michaels and Triple H. Michaels tried to give Triple H a Pedigree on the steel floor, but The Game countered it into a slingshot, sending HBK crashing through one of the pods. Triple H attempted to Pedigree Michaels, but HBK reversed it and catapulted the Champion into the steel wall of the chamber. Michaels then delivered an elbow off a pod ceiling and went to hit a Superkick. But Triple H countered it into a Pedigree, and nearly won the pinfall. Triple H then tried to hit a second Pedigree, but HBK countered the move, hit Triple H with Sweet Chin Music, and pinned The Game to become the new World Heavyweight Champion.

THE AFTERMATH

For Triple H and Shawn Michaels, their rivalry was just catching fire. The two would face each other one month later in a Three Stages of Hell Match at *Armageddon* 2002. Triple H won the Street Fight and Michaels captured the Steel Cage Match. The third stage and deciding match was a Ladder Match, where Triple H won the Title back from his bitter rival. The two would battle for the next four years, until they put their differences aside and reformed D-Generation X in the summer of 2006.

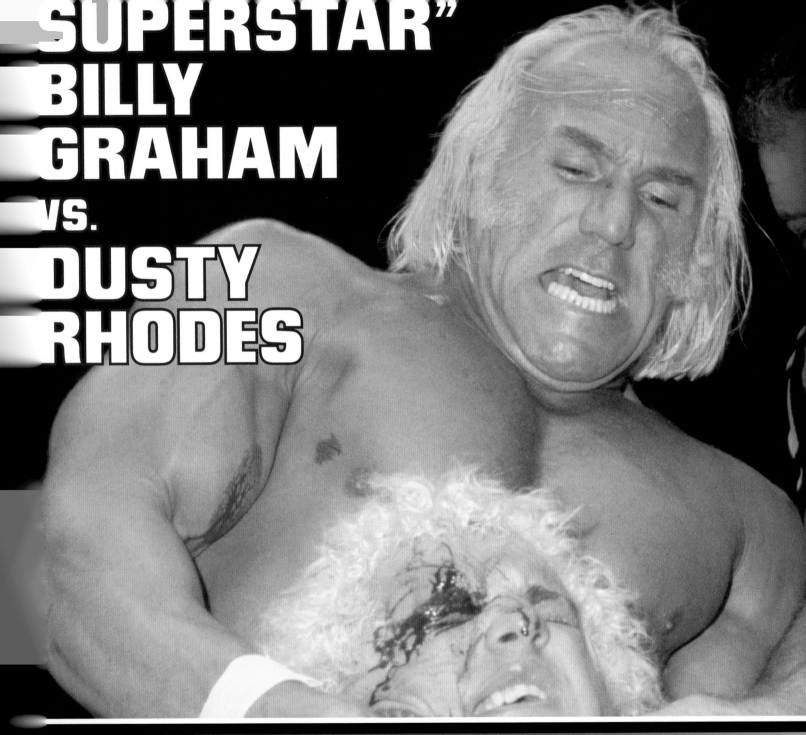

"SUPERSTAR" BILLY GRAHAM
vs.
DUSTY RHODES

TEXAS DEATH MATCH
FOR THE WWE CHAMPIONSHIP

October 24, 1977

Madison Square Garden
New York, New York

THE MATCH

The WWE Champion, accompanied by his manager the Grand Wizard, came to the ring after Rhodes. The Wizard was reverently removing Graham's shirt when Rhodes decided he didn't want to wait any more and attacked the Champion. Rhodes made the mistake of not pressing his advantage, instead arguing with The Grand Wizard. This allowed Superstar to sneak up on Dusty and attack him with a double axe-handle. Graham followed with a couple of boots to the downed challenger, but the American Dream delighted the crowd by popping back up and hitting several of his trademark bionic elbows. Graham begged for mercy, but the Dream gave him a couple of right crosses instead.

Graham tried to collect himself outside the ring, but Rhodes gave chase and forced him back inside. Rhodes dropped the Champion to the canvas with another bionic elbow, and Graham left the ring again. The Champion looked like he was going to head back to the dressing room, but he decided to re-enter the ring. Graham locked up with his challenger and delivered a stinging right, one that sent Rhodes out of the ring. Superstar followed him out and was ready to bulldog the Dream onto the floor, but Rhodes countered and sent the Champion flying back into the ring.

Rhodes landed a series of blows on the Champion, but made a tactical error by assuming the Champ was down for the count. Getting too close to the Superstar allowed Graham to hit the Dream in the midsection and toss Dusty out of the ring. There Graham took advantage of the no holds barred stipulation of a Texas Death Match, ramming the Dream into the ring post and slamming him on the metal guardrail. The Champion found a rope under the ring and started choking the challenger with it. This was particularly damaging because Rhodes was bleeding from a cut above his eye. Rhodes finally broke away from Graham with a series of elbows to the top of Superstar's skull. The Dream managed a measure of revenge by now choking the Champion, who was also bleeding, with the same rope. Rhodes dropped elbows on the prone Champion and hit him with a splash, but Graham got his legs under the bottom rope before the official could count to three.

Graham raked the eyes of his challenger and hit Rhodes with a series of punches. Getting back to his feet first, Graham stomped at the Dream, but Rhodes also made it to his feet and dropped Graham to the canvas with a big elbow. Rhodes tried to pin the Champion, but the official saw that Dusty had his feet on the ropes and waived off the count before he got to three. Rhodes, thinking he had pinned the Champion, began to jump around the ring in excitement, but then argued with the official when he explained what had happened. Instead of debating the official, Dusty should have been focused on the Champion, who snuck up on the Dream and dropped him to the mat. Graham draped one arm over the challenger and managed the three-count to win the match and retain the Title.

THE AFTERMATH

While Rhodes came close to defeating Graham for the Title, The American Dream never claimed the WWE Championship. Graham held the Title for four more months, as he lost the Championship to Bob Backlund in February 1978, never to regain it again. The rivalry between Graham and Rhodes transcended the Title as the two competed in a brutal Texas Bullrope Match in 1978. Although the Championship wasn't on the line, Rhodes defeated Graham in that match.

BATISTA
VS.
UNDERTAKER

THE LEAD-UP

By winning the 2007 *Royal Rumble*, the first Royal Rumble Match win in his storied career, Undertaker could choose which Champion to face at *WrestleMania 23*: ECW Champion Lashley, WWE Champion John Cena, or World Heavyweight Champion Batista. Undertaker chose Batista and punctuated that selection with a devastating Chokeslam. Despite the unprovoked attack, Batista was initially honored The Deadman chose him, but those feelings dissipated in the buildup to the match as The Animal lost respect for Undertaker and his tactics. Batista gained a measure of revenge when he gave Undertaker a Spinebuster at *No Way Out* where the duo were tag-team partners, but it only served to increase the tension heading into the match.

THE MATCH

Immediately after the opening bell, Batista speared Undertaker. He then backed The Deadman into the corner and unleashed a barrage of punches. Undertaker was briefly dazed, but then tossed Batista into the corner and exploded with a series of punches of his own. Not to be outdone, The Animal tossed Undertaker back in the corner and hit a series of shoulder blocks into Undertaker's midsection. Batista clotheslined Undertaker out of the ring, but The Deadman landed on his feet and dragged the Champion out with him. Batista demonstrated his resolve and aggression by throwing Undertaker into the steel stairs and then, back in the ring, Batista executed a top-rope shoulder tackle on The Deadman.

Batista scoopslammed Undertaker and attempted a kick to the challenger's skull, but Undertaker countered with numerous punches to Batista's midsection, followed with an uppercut. The two men traded blows, with the Ford Field crowd cheering Undertaker's punches and booing Batista's offense. Undertaker got on a roll with a Snake Eyes, a big boot to the Champion's face, and a Leg Drop. He went for the pin, but Batista kicked out on the two-count. The Deadman delighted the crowd by going Old School, but the Champion then fought his way out of Undertaker's Chokeslam attempt. Undertaker dropped a leg on Batista while he was prone on the ring's apron. Undertaker then gave the crowd a genuine *WrestleMania* moment by leaping over the top rope and onto Batista outside the ring.

Batista made it clear that he was not done yet by reversing a whip and tossing The Deadman into the time keeper's area. He then delivered a running powerslam that put Undertaker through one of the announcers' tables. Undertaker seemed out of it, so Batista rolled the challenger back into the ring and went for the pinfall, but The Deadman kicked out. Batista tried to position Undertaker for the Batista Bomb, but the challenger countered by driving the Champion into the turnbuckles. Undertaker looked to whip Batista into the opposite corner, but Batista countered the move into a belly-to-belly suplex and another near fall.

Batista backed Undertaker into a corner and started punching him while standing on the second rope. This wasn't wise, as it allowed The Deadman to pick up Batista and deliver a Last Ride. This time Batista kicked out at the two-count. Batista then hit a Spinebuster, but Undertaker sat up before he could proceed to the Batista Bomb. Instead, Undertaker Chokeslammed Batista, but again Batista kicked out of the pinfall. Batista blocked a Tombstone attempt, and hit the challenger with a spear and Batista Bomb. The Animal was sure he'd won the match, but again Undertaker kicked out. Batista tried a second Batista Bomb, but Undertaker countered it with a back body drop and a Tombstone Piledriver to pin Batista and win the World Heavyweight Championship.

THE AFTERMATH

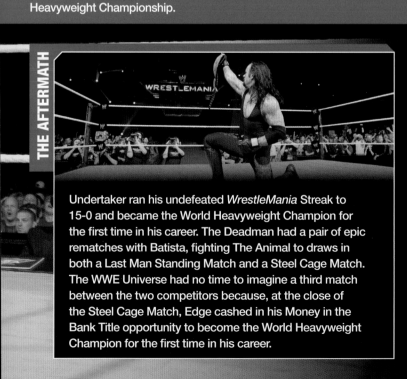

Undertaker ran his undefeated *WrestleMania* Streak to 15-0 and became the World Heavyweight Champion for the first time in his career. The Deadman had a pair of epic rematches with Batista, fighting The Animal to draws in both a Last Man Standing Match and a Steel Cage Match. The WWE Universe had no time to imagine a third match between the two competitors because, at the close of the Steel Cage Match, Edge cashed in his Money in the Bank Title opportunity to become the World Heavyweight Champion for the first time in his career.

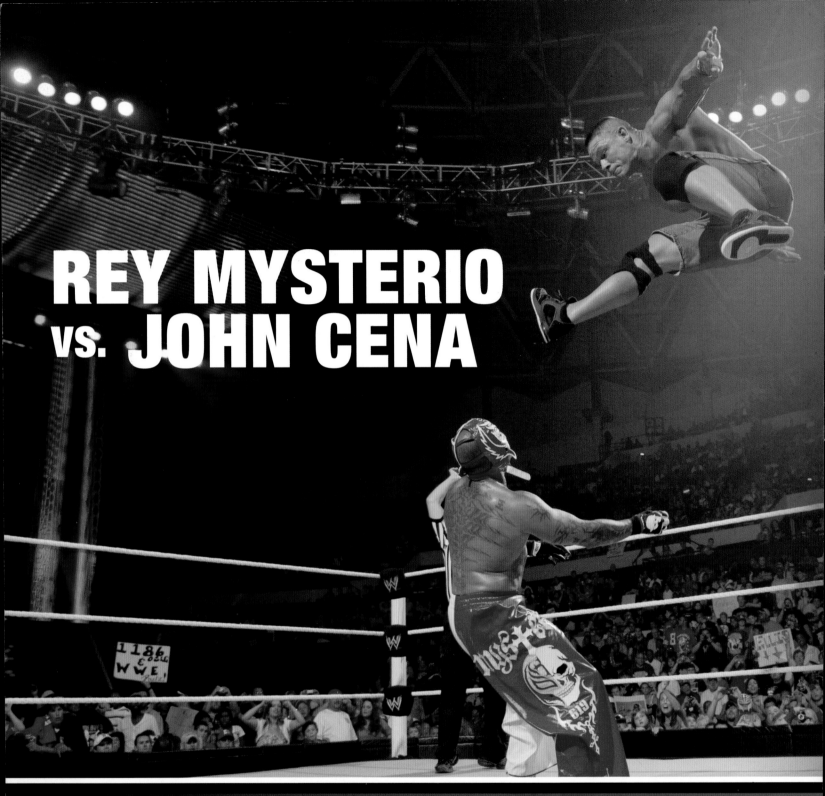

REY MYSTERIO
VS. JOHN CENA

THE LEAD-UP

When CM Punk won the WWE Championship and left WWE at *Money in the Bank 2011*, the WWE Chairman had two priorities. First was to crown a new WWE Champion, and Mr. McMahon set up an 8-man tournament to do just that. Second, he had to fulfill his promise of firing John Cena for losing the Title to Punk. The tournament was a success, as Rey Mysterio won the WWE Title for the first time in his career. However, Mr. McMahon's threat to end Cena's tenure with the company convinced the WWE Board of Directors to remove their Chairman from power and put Triple H in charge instead. Not only did The Game undo Cena's firing, he gave Cena a Title opportunity against Mysterio the same night Rey won the Championship.

THE MATCH

The assumption was that Cena would have the early advantage, as he hadn't yet competed, while Mysterio faced The Miz earlier in the night in the finals of the WWE Championship tournament. Mysterio tested that theory early with some quick kicks to the back of Cena's legs. The challenger's other advantage was his power, and he demonstrated that with a crushing clothesline, and an early near fall. Mysterio showed that he could win the match early as well when he got a two-count from a victory roll. Rey tried to sap Cena's power with an extended side headlock, but the challenger dropped Mysterio to the mat with a side suplex. Cena attempted to hit Mysterio with a splash in the corner, but Rey moved away and the challenger crashed into the turnbuckle. Cena rolled out of the ring to collect himself, but Mysterio jumped onto the second rope and dove onto Cena outside.

Outside the ring, Cena tried to whip Mysterio into the ring steps, but the Champion instead ran up the steel steps and tried to hit Cena with a Hip Hop Drop. Cena ducked the move and clobbered Rey with a devastating clothesline. Cena rolled Mysterio back in the ring, but could only get a two-count. Cena tried to wear down Mysterio with a waist lock, but Rey countered it into a DDT and a near fall. Rey attempted a 619, but Cena caught him and reversed the move into a Powerslam and another two-count. Cena landed a shoulder block and looked to hit a second, but Rey countered with a drop kick to Cena's chest. Twice Cena attempted an Attitude Adjustment, but Rey blocked it both times, the second by countering the move into a hurricanrana. Rey managed a near fall with the move.

Cena almost had Mysterio in the STF, but Rey flipped Cena over and put Cena in the STF. Cena managed to lift Mysterio and again attempt an Attitude Adjustment, but Cena's knee buckled and he fell to the ropes. Mysterio ran from the opposite side of the ring and connected with an STF. Rey dove off the top rope at the prone challenger, and Cena raised his knees to block the move. Mysterio then worked Cena into the corner to attempt another hurricanrana, but Cena grabbed the Champion and tossed him to the mat. Cena hit his top-rope leg drop, but Mysterio kicked out at two.

Cena hoisted Mysterio onto his back for an Attitude Adjustment, but Rey countered it by dropkicking Cena in his back so that the challenger went face first into the ropes, a perfect position for Mysterio to deliver his 619. As Rey ran into the far ropes to execute the move, Cena popped up and grabbed Rey for the Attitude Adjustment. The official counted the pin, and John Cena was once again WWE Champion, ending Mysterio's reign at less than two hours.

THE AFTERMATH

John Cena barely had time to celebrate with his new Championship when Living Colour's "Cult of Personality" began playing. Cena did not recognize the classic rock anthem as anyone's entrance theme. He did, however, recognize the man that emerged from the back—CM Punk had returned, and he was wearing his WWE Championship. The two faced off in the ring, each holding a Title. Triple H set a match at *SummerSlam* where the two faced each other to determine the true WWE Champion. CM Punk repeated his Money in the Bank feat and beat John Cena in controversial fashion. But he did not leave as Champion that night; Alberto Del Rio cashed in his Money in the Bank opportunity and won the Title.

RANDY ORTON vs.
BATISTA vs. DANIEL BRYA[N]

WRESTLEMANIA 30
WWE WORLD HEAVYWEIGHT CHAMPIONSHIP MATCH

April 6, 2014

Mercedes-Benz SuperDome
New Orleans, Louisiana

THE LEAD-UP

It was supposed to be a straightforward one-on-one match—
Randy Orton would defend his WWE World Heavyweight
Championship at *WrestleMania 30* against the winner of the
2014 *Royal Rumble*, Batista. But a large contingent of the WWE
Universe known as the "Yes!" Movement had other ideas. After
months of rivaling with The Authority, Bryan's fans finally let their
voices be heard. Bryan was awarded a match with Triple H to
open *WrestleMania 30* with the winner added to the main event
Title match. Bryan won and, despite his injured shoulder and arm,
became part of the WWE World Heavyweight Championship Match.

THE MATCH

Bryan jumped on the offense first, hitting Orton with a running kick to the face. Bryan then countered an attempted Batista Bomb and flipped Batista out of the ring. Continuing his offense, Bryan hit Orton with a series of kicks before The Viper attacked Bryan's injured arm to stem his momentum. Orton tossed Bryan out of the ring, and then Batista and Orton focused on each other with devastating power moves. The Animal looked to hit Orton with a Batista Bomb on the steel steps, but Orton reversed it into a Back Body Drop. With both of his challengers down, The Viper took the time to pose for the Superdome crowd.

Rolling Batista back into the ring, Orton looked to pin The Animal, but he was not able to get the three-count. With Batista and Orton focused on each other, Bryan surprised both men and downed them with a Double Missile Drop Kick, following with a series of kicks to each of them. But Orton caught Bryan's leg and suplexed him. Bryan managed to recover and perform a series of Running Knees on both Orton and Batista. While Bryan had Orton in the "Yes!" Lock, Stephanie McMahon and Triple H approached the ring. Triple H removed the match's official and inserted his hand-picked crooked referee. Batista hit Bryan with a Batista Bomb, but Bryan did not succumb to the three-count. Bryan then kicked the new official in the head, sending him out of the ring. With Triple H, the official, and Stephanie below, Bryan leaped from the ring, taking out all three of them. A furious Triple H went under the ring to retrieve a sledgehammer, but Bryan ended up using it on The Game.

Orton and Batista then decided to work together. After hammering Bryan with a series of punches and blows, the two former Evolution faction mates delivered the brutal combination of a Batista Bomb into an RKO onto an announcers' table. Medical officials came to help Bryan—it looked like his challenge for the Title was over. Batista then started to dismantle Orton. Batista attempted to roll Orton back in the ring to pin him, but the Champion was able to hit Batista with a DDT from the ring apron to the floor below. Meanwhile, Bryan was being carted out of the ring on a medical board, but he somehow made his way back into the match. Orton was set to deliver an RKO on Bryan, but Bryan reversed it into a "Yes!" Lock. Batista made the save to prevent the Champion from tapping out.

Orton tried to finish the match by punting Batista, but The Viper collided with a Bryan Running Knee. Batista then delivered a Batista Bomb to Orton. But before Batista could cover Orton, Bryan hit Batista with a Running Knee and then maneuvered him into the "Yes!" Lock. Batista tapped out, and Bryan was the WWE World Heavyweight Champion.

THE AFTERMATH

Bryan's post-match celebration to close *WrestleMania 30* was one of the most heartfelt and emotional moments in WrestleMania history. However, the joy did not last—after defending the Title for a month, Bryan's injuries forced him to vacate the Championship to have neck surgery. Bryan would be out of action until January 2015. Orton and Batista worked with Triple H in order to reform Evolution and take on The Shield. After two unsuccessful matches against the trio, Batista quit WWE and Rollins betrayed his two Shield faction mates to align himself with Triple H and The Authority.

BRET "HIT MAN" HART vs. SHAWN MICHAELS

WRESTLEMANIA XII
60-MINUTE IRON MAN MATCH FOR THE WWE CHAMPIONSHIP

March 31, 1996

Arrowhead Pond
Anaheim, California

THE LEAD-UP

Bret "Hit Man" Hart and "The Heartbreak Kid" Shawn Michaels had some epic battles over the years, but none compared to the war of attrition that they had at *WrestleMania XII*. Hart was in his third reign as WWE Champion, having defeated Michaels' former bodyguard Diesel for the Title at *Survivor Series 1995*. Michaels had never won the WWE Championship, but he did win the 1996 Royal Rumble to earn a Title opportunity for the second straight year. This was no ordinary match, but a 60-Minute Iron Man Match. The man that recorded the most decisions in the 60 minutes would be crowned Champion. It was to be the ultimate test of stamina, will, and determination.

THE MATCH

Two of Shawn Michaels' nicknames are the Showstopper and Mr. WrestleMania, and he demonstrated why he earned both with a spectacular ring entrance. Not content to walk to the ring, the Heartbreak Kid ziplined from the top of the arena down to the ring. The Champion Hart took a more traditional route. After the official provided instructions, the two locked up. Understanding that it would be a long and challenging match, both Hart and Michaels started with submission moves designed to wear down their opponents. Hart cinched in a side headlock and Michaels used an arm bar. The match became a little less scientific when Hart and Michaels exchanged blows in a ring corner.

Fifteen minutes into the match, Hart slammed Michaels to the mat and tried to lock in the Sharpshooter. Before the Hit Man could succeed, Michaels grabbed the ring ropes, forcing a break. The two went outside the ring to brawl, and the first casualty of the match was not Hart or Michaels, but the timekeeper, who was accidentally superkicked by HBK when Hart ducked out of the way. Hart came close to getting the first fall of the match when he slingshot the challenger into the turnbuckles, but Michaels kicked out. At the halfway mark, Michaels powerslammed Hart, but he also could only get a two-count. The back and forth continued, as each man failed to gain too much of an offensive advantage.

Michaels was nearly counted out when Hart sent him over the turnbuckles to the floor below. Hart targeted HBK's back by ramming it into the steel post, as well as delivering kicks, punches, flying elbows, and a backbreaker. For the next fifteen minutes, Hart dominated in and out of the ring, but he could not get a pinfall or submission. Michaels finally managed some offense with some punches at the 53 minute mark, but Hart took control again with a superplex. Hart tried to perform the Sharpshooter, but Michaels blocked the move. With two minutes remaining, Michaels climbed to the top rope to hit a moonsault on the Hit Man. Again, Hart kicked out of the pinfall attempt. Michaels leapt off the second rope for a victory roll, but Hart was able to kick out. Hart caught Shawn's legs when HBK went for a missile dropkick from the top rope and locked in the Sharpshooter with 32 seconds remaining. Michaels was clearly in pain, but he refused to submit and the clock expired.

With the two tied at no falls, Hart assumed he'd retained the Title thanks to the draw, but the president of WWE, Gorilla Monsoon, announced sudden death overtime to determine a winner. Hart argued with Monsoon, giving Michaels time to recover. The bell rang again and Hart targeted Michaels' lower back with punches, knees, and kicks. Hart followed it up with a back body drop and a backbreaker. Out of nowhere, Michaels landed Sweet Chin Music on Hart. The two men remained prone for several seconds. When the two struggled to their feet, Michaels hit a second Sweet Chin Music, pinning Hart for the 1-0 overtime decision and becoming the WWE Champion.

THE AFTERMATH

Shawn Michaels had finally achieved his "Boyhood Dream," but there were no shortage of Superstars lining up to make that dream a nightmare. Throughout the summer, Michaels defended the Title against former friends and rivals like Diesel, the British Bulldog, Mankind, and more. His luck finally ran out at *Survivor Series 1996*, when Sid seized the Title from him. Bret took a hiatus from WWE for several months before returning at *Survivor Series* to face a new nemesis, Stone Cold Steve Austin. Michaels and Hart had one more major PPV fight, and it would go down in history as WWE's most controversial match.

CHRIS BENOIT
VS. CHRIS JERICHO

THE LEAD-UP

For close to a year, Chris Benoit and Chris Jericho had an intense rivalry. Both had pinned each other in a Three-Man Two-Fall Match at *WrestleMania 2000* for the European and Intercontinental Championships, with Jericho winning the European Title in the first fall and Benoit claiming the Intercontinental Title in the second. The two met at three additional pay-per-views with Jericho beating Benoit by disqualification, and Benoit winning both a Submission Match and a 2-out-of-3 Falls Match. Jericho wanted to face Benoit one more time after Benoit and Perry Saturn attacked Y2J. This time, Jericho wanted the encounter to be a Ladder Match for Benoit's Intercontinental Championship.

ROYAL RUMBLE 2001
LADDER MATCH FOR THE INTERCONTINENTAL CHAMPIONSHIP

January 21, 2001

New Orleans Arena
New Orleans, Louisiana

THE MATCH

The Superstars began exchanging blows before the bell even rang. Early on, Benoit tried to put Jericho in his Crippler Crossface, but Y2J countered and attempted The Walls of Jericho. Benoit then kicked Jericho and tossed him into a ring post. The high intensity action spilled outside the ring when Jericho tried to springboard off the ropes and Benoit ducked out of the way. Benoit grabbed a ladder and, after dodging a baseball slide from Jericho, set it up in the ring.

Benoit's climb was not successful, as Jericho slammed him to the mat. Jericho then got his hands on the ladder, ramming Benoit with it. Y2J set up the ladder in the corner, but Benoit reversed an Irish Whip and drove Jericho into the ladder and out of the ring. Benoit then attempted to leap from the ring, but Jericho blasted him with a foreign object. A stunned Benoit moved at the last second to avoid Jericho launching himself and the ladder onto him. The two continued to battle in and out of the ring, often using the ladder to retaliate against each other: Benoit dropkicked the ladder into Jericho, and Jericho used the ladder as a lever, driving it into Benoit.

Jericho finally set the ladder up and tried to reach the Title, but Benoit knocked him off and then suplexed Y2J out of the ring. Benoit started climbing the ladder and was close to the top, but Jericho recovered and put the Champion into a modified version of The Walls of Jericho over the ladder's top rung. Jericho then dumped Benoit off the ladder and tried to reach the Title. Benoit had enough ring presence to knock the ladder over, causing Jericho to bounce off the ropes below. Benoit then applied the Crippler Crossface and forced Jericho to tap out, but he could not win the match that way. Benoit attempted a diving headbutt off the top of the ladder, but Jericho dodged.

Jericho set the ladder up again, pinning Benoit to the mat under it, and started to climb. In response, Benoit tipped the ladder over, sending Jericho crashing to the mat. When Benoit went to retrieve the Title, Jericho headed him off at the pass and knocked him off the ladder, all the way to the ringside floor. With Benoit out of the ring, Y2J took advantage and grabbed the Intercontinental Championship once again.

THE AFTERMATH

Jericho and Benoit managed to put aside their differences in May 2001 and form a tag team. The pair defeated the World Tag Team Champions Triple H and Stone Cold Steve Austin to win the Championship. They successfully defended the Title for more than a month. Soon after, Jericho saw his career skyrocket—in November 2001, he unified the WWE and WCW Championships, becoming the first Undisputed Champion in history. Jericho defended that Title until *WrestleMania X8*, where he lost it to Triple H.

JOHN CENA
VS.
KEVIN OWENS

THE LEAD-UP

After winning the United States Championship at *WrestleMania 31*, John Cena wanted to show the world he was a fighting Champion, so he created the United States Open Challenge, where each week anyone could step up and face him for the Title. Cena defended the Championship against an eclectic mix of Superstars, including Dean Ambrose, Cesaro, and Kane, as well as rookies from NXT like Sami Zayn and Neville. The boldest challenger, however, was NXT Champion Kevin Owens, who actually said he had no interest in the United States Championship, since he already possessed the NXT Title. Owens said he would fight Cena, but on his own terms—a Champion vs. Champion match at *Elimination Chamber 2015*.

ELIMINATION CHAMBER
CHAMPION VS. CHAMPION MATCH

May 31, 2015

American Bank Center
Corpus Christi, Texas

THE MATCH

Meeting John Cena in a Champion vs. Champion Match for his WWE debut bout was a bright spotlight for Kevin Owens, but he displayed no signs of intimidation. He put Cena in a headlock to open the match, but Cena showed the newcomer his power with a shoulder tackle that knocked Owens to the ground. Owens responded with forearms, punches, and kicks to knock Cena to the mat. Cena countered with a Running Bulldog, but when he tried to follow with a back body drop, Owens kicked Cena in the face. Owens then looked to wear down the United States Champion with a headlock, but Cena almost turned it into an Attitude Adjustment. In response, Owens delivered a DDT to Cena.

After dropping Cena with a boot to the face, Owens antagonized the crowd. The premature celebration was almost a huge mistake, as Cena rolled up the NXT Champion and managed a two-count. Owens responded with a clothesline and a near fall against Cena. Cena hit a shoulder tackle, but when he went for a second, Owens caught him, spun him, and turned the move into a fallaway slam. Again, Cena managed to kick out, as he did when Owens hit a cannonball in the corner. Again, the two exchanged blows, and Owens tried to execute his Pop-Up Powerbomb. Cena responded by floating over Owens, hitting two shoulder tackles, a side slam, and a Five-Knuckle Shuffle. Cena attempted an Attitude Adjustment, but Owens reversed it into a Pop-Up Powerbomb. Cena kicked out at the two-count.

Owens went to the top rope, but Cena hit the ropes, dropping Owens onto the top turnbuckle. Owens tossed Cena off the top rope and attempted a moonsault, but Cena moved and grabbed Owens for an Attitude Adjustment. Owens showed some resilience of his own by kicking out of the pinfall attempt. Owens hit Cena with a Superkick and then tried to mock Cena with a Five-Knuckle Shuffle. Cena countered the move into an STF. Cena tried to pull Owens away from the ropes, but Owens used the opportunity to kick Cena. Owens then delivered Cena's own Attitude Adjustment to the United States Champ, but Cena kicked out of the pinfall attempt. Cena then executed a second-rope Tornado DDT, but Owens would not be pinned.

Cena thought he'd won the match with a top-rope leg drop, but Owens resisted the three-count. Owens then reversed an attempted Attitude Adjustment into a twisting side Powerbomb. Cena performed a Springboard Stunner on Owens, but Owens again kicked out of the pinfall attempt. Cena then tried to superplex Owens, but Owens countered and executed a top-rope Swanton Bomb. Cena tried to hit Owens with a big running clothesline, but Owens turned Cena's momentum against him and executed another Pop-Up Powerbomb. Owens was able to keep Cena down for the three-count, gaining a massive upset victory for his debut WWE match.

THE AFTERMATH

The rivalry between John Cena and Kevin Owens was merely beginning. The two would meet again a month later at *Money in the Bank* 2015 with Cena winning the rematch in another instant classic. The two had one more match at *Battleground* 2015 to break their 1-1 tie. Once again, the back-and-forth action did not disappoint and Cena came out on top. In early July 2015, Owens lost his NXT Championship to Finn Balor, but he wasn't without gold for long, winning the Intercontinental Championship in September. Cena briefly lost the United States Championship to WWE World Heavyweight Champion Seth Rollins, but he regained it the same night Owens won the Intercontinental Championship. A returning Alberto Del Rio defeated Cena for the United States Championship at *Hell in a Cell* 2015.

RANDY ORTON
VS.
CACTUS JACK

THE LEAD-UP

In early 2004, an intense rivalry developed between Mick Foley and Randy Orton. Foley eliminated Orton from the Royal Rumble Match, and an enraged Legend Killer returned to the ring to remove Foley from the contest. A Handicap Tag Team Match with Orton, Batista, and Ric Flair against Foley and The Rock did not end the rivalry, as Orton repeatedly attacked Foley and challenged his manhood. The Viper even knocked The Hardcore Legend down a flight of stairs. Foley finally turned the tables by demanding a match for Orton's Intercontinental Championship, but only under Foley's rules— no holds barred and falls count anywhere.

BACKLASH 2004
NO HOLDS BARRED, FALLS COUNT ANYWHERE MATCH
FOR THE INTERCONTINENTAL CHAMPIONSHIP

April 18, 2004
Rexall Place
Edmonton, Alberta, Canada

THE MATCH

Orton approached the ring carrying a trash can filled with weapons, including a two-by-four wrapped in barbed wire. Mick Foley only brought "Barbie," his barb-wire-wrapped baseball bat. Foley immediately attacked Orton with the bat, repeatedly hitting the trash can as Orton used it for protection. Outside the ring, the Champion managed to grab the bat from Foley. The two men fought over the bat until Orton used his dented trash can to deliver three blows to The Hardcore Legend.

Foley then reversed the momentum and took control in and out of the ring. After performing a baseball slide and a swinging neckbreaker on Orton, Foley attempted to drop an elbow from the middle rope while Orton recovered on the floor below. But Orton escaped up the entrance ramp and Foley followed him, where the two traded blows and slams onto the unforgiving steel ramp. Back in the ring, Orton tried to drive Barbie into Foley's face, but a low blow by the challenger allowed him to grab the weapon and cut Orton's face with it. Foley then inflicted more pain with Barbie, even driving it with a leg drop into Orton's groin. Foley attempted to light the bat on fire, but *Raw* General Manager Eric Bischoff stopped him. Instead, Foley introduced a board covered in a bed of barbed wire into the match.

Orton was able to save himself from the barbed-wire bed by throwing powder into Foley's face and slamming him onto the bed. Randy then spread thousands of thumbtacks onto the mat and attempted to RKO The Hardcore Legend into the tacks. Foley countered the RKO and dropped Orton onto the tacks, driving them into the Champion's back and legs. Again Orton tried to leave the ring, but Foley chased him and then threw the Champion off the entrance stage. Officials tried to keep Foley away while they checked on the status of the Champion, but Foley tossed them aside and leapt off the stage, driving an elbow into Orton. Somehow, Orton kicked out of the pinfall attempt.

THE AFTERMATH

Back in the ring, Orton hit Foley repeatedly with Barbie. When Orton wound up to strike Foley one last time, The Hardcore Legend countered with the Mandible Claw. Orton faded, but was able to free himself with an uppercut and a low blow. Foley reapplied the Mandible Claw, and Orton ended the hold a second time by using his RKO signature move. Orton attempted a pinfall but could not get the three-count. Orton then executed a second RKO—this time driving Foley onto the barbed-wire bat. Orton pinned Foley and retained his Intercontinental Championship.

Orton continued to defend the Intercontinental Championship until July, when Edge defeated The Legend Killer for the Title. But Orton would go on to bigger things that summer, as he became the #1 contender to the World Heavyweight Championship. At *SummerSlam 2004*, Orton became the youngest World Heavyweight Champion in WWE history. Foley's hardcore antics in the match had the crowd chanting "ECW," which would serve as an omen of the future. Just one year later, The Hardcore Legend would provide color commentary for ECW's return to television, the *One Night Stand* pay-per-view event.

SHAWN MICHAELS
vs. CHRIS JERICHO

THE LEAD-UP

Growing up, Chris Jericho always wanted to be a professional wrestler. As he trained to achieve his goals, he patterned himself after Shawn Michaels. But Jericho joined WWE a few years after the Heartbreak Kid was forced to leave WWE due to a debilitating back injury, so it looked like the two would never meet in the ring. However, Michaels made an incredible return to the ring four and a half years after his last match, so Jericho challenged his former idol to a bout at *WrestleMania*. But Jericho was no longer looking at Michaels with stars in his eyes—the arrogant Y2J wanted to prove he was better than HBK. And what better place to do it than *WrestleMania*?

WRESTLEMANIA XIX
SINGLES MATCH

March 30, 2003

Safeco Field
Seattle, Washington

THE MATCH

The match began with an almost even exchange of moves and holds, including headlocks, wristlocks, single leg takedowns and more. Michaels then gained the upper hand and tossed Jericho out of the ring. Michaels attempted to dive over the top rope onto Jericho, but Y2J ducked out of the way. Rather than crashing to the floor, Michaels had enough presence to land on the ring apron. He then grabbed the second rope and propelled himself back into the ring, gaining momentum to nail Jericho with a running baseball slide. Michaels then tossed Y2J back into the ring and hit Jericho with a cross body off the top rope. But Jericho used Michaels' momentum to roll through and get a two-count.

Michaels attempted to weaken Jericho's legs with a pair of Figure-Four Leglocks. Jericho fought through them both and then tried to toss Michaels out of the ring. HBK held onto the ring ropes and countered into a hurricanrana, throwing Jericho to the floor below. Michaels then performed a Suicide Dive onto Jericho. The Heartbreak Kid made a tactical error when he tried to deliver a dropkick. Jericho reversed the kick into The Walls of Jericho. Y2J broke the hold to get back into the ring and end the official's 10-count. Jericho then went back outside the ring and slammed Michaels into a ring post twice, targeting Michaels' surgically repaired back. After Michaels recovered, he tried to reenter the ring, but Jericho hit him with a springboard missile dropkick. Jericho's offense continued to target Michaels' back and gained Jericho several near falls.

Jericho mocked HBK by mimicking some of Michaels' most famous moves, including the flying forearm, the kip up, and Michaels' signature pose. Michaels responded by showing how the original does it, executing his own flying forearm. Jericho stemmed HBK's momentum and hit a Bulldog/Lionsault combination. Michaels resisted the pinfall attempt and raised his shoulder at two. Jericho then locked Michaels in The Walls of Jericho, but a desperate HBK made it to the ropes, forcing a break. Jericho then nailed Michaels with HBK's own Sweet Chin Music. Again, Michaels managed to kick out at two.

Jericho locked Michaels into another Walls of Jericho. To Y2J's frustration, the Heartbreak Kid again reached the ropes, forcing another break. After arguing with the official, Jericho ran directly into a Sweet Chin Music. It was Michaels' turn to be frustrated, as Jericho kicked out of the pin at two. Jericho then Irish Whipped Michaels into a corner and attempted a suplex. Michaels flipped over Y2J's head, landed on his feet, and rolled up Jericho for the three-count to end this incredibly competitive match.

THE AFTERMATH

After such a hard-fought match, Michaels extended his hand as a sign of respect. Jericho went further, giving the Heartbreak Kid a hug. But Jericho could not stay classy—he ended the hug with a kick to the groin. This was an indication that things were not over between the two men. Over the next few years, they would have some classic confrontations, including an Unsanctioned Match at *Unforgiven 2008* and a Ladder Match for the World Heavyweight Championship at *No Mercy 2008*.

BRUNO
SAMMARTINO vs.
LARRY ZBYSZKO

SHOWDOWN AT SHEA 1980
STEEL CAGE MATCH

August 9, 1980

Shea Stadium
Flushing, New York

THE LEAD-UP

In addition to being the longest-running WWE Champion in history, Bruno Sammartino was a teacher, helping the next generation of Superstars refine their craft. Perhaps his greatest pupil was Larry Zbyszko, who would go on to be World Tag Team Champions with his partner Tony Garea. But Zbyszko was frustrated at only being looked at as Sammartino's student, so he asked the former WWE Champion for a match to prove himself. Sammartino reluctantly agreed, but when it was clear that Bruno had the advantage, an irate Zbyszko attacked his mentor with a foreign object, leaving Bruno a bloody mess. Sammartino vowed revenge, and the two were slated to meet in a steel cage at Shea Stadium.

THE MATCH

Zbyszko tried to catch Bruno unaware by attacking him as he entered the cage, but Sammartino kicked his former student away. Bruno picked up Zbyszko and tossed him into the cage wall twice and then stomped on Zbyszko repeatedly. Sammartino continued the punishment with repeated kicks to the midsection, as well as throwing Zbyszko into the last two cage walls. Larry had enough, and he tried to escape the cage through the front door, but Sammartino grabbed him and raked his face along the ropes and then the metal of the cage. Zbyszko begged for mercy, but only got a running boot to the face.

Just when it seemed like the mentor would dominate the entire match, Zbyszko hit a low blow on Sammartino to halt his momentum. Zbyszko nailed a downed Bruno with a series of kicks to the chest and midsection. Thinking Sammartino was down, Zbyszko tried to win the match by leaving the cage, but Sammartino pulled him back into the ring before he was out. Zbyszko tossed his former teacher into the cage wall and then stomped and kicked him several times. Again, Zbyszko tried to escape the cage, this time by climbing out, but Sammartino pulled Zbyszko off the top turnbuckle and down to the canvas.

Zbyszko doled out more punishment to Bruno, but Sammartino changed the match's course with a knee to Zbyszko's backside. Unlike his former protégé, Sammartino seemed to have little interest in escaping the cage, instead looking for retribution for Zbyszko's earlier attack. Bruno choked Zbyszko and then lifted him by his trap muscles and slammed Larry to the mat. Bruno had Zbyszko down and continued to attack him, but Zbyszko halted Sammartino's attack by thumbing him in the eye. Again, Zbyszko tried to flee the cage. Sammartino grabbed him and bodyslammed him, but Sammartino's right arm was clearly injured as he kept favoring it.

Sammartino clearly had had enough of his former pupil, so he upped his level of aggression. He repeatedly slammed Zbyszko's skull into the ring posts and the cage, to the delight of the crowd. His arm now covered in blood, Bruno indicated to the outside official to open the cage door. Sammartino returned to his downed opponent and gave him an additional stomp for good measure. Bruno walked to the cage door and turned to give Zbyszko one last disgusted look. Larry struggled to his feet as his former mentor stepped out of the cage to win the match. A bloody Zbyszko staggered out of the cage and received another pair of punches from Sammartino before Zbyszko reluctantly raised Sammartino's hand to signify his victory.

THE AFTERMATH

After gaining revenge against his former student, Sammartino stepped away from the ring for a few years. He focused more on a broadcast career, but he seconded his son at the first *WrestleMania* and appeared in a Battle Royal at *WrestleMania II*. After a long separation from WWE, Sammartino returned in 2013 to be inducted into the WWE Hall of Fame. Shortly after his match with Sammartino, Zbyszko left to make his name in the NWA, AWA, and WCW. He eventually returned to WWE as well to be inducted to the Hall of Fame in 2015. That night, he was inducted by his old mentor, patching up their relationship.

January 21, 2001

New Orleans Arena
New Orleans, Louisiana

ROYAL RUMBLE MATCH

THE LEAD-UP

The WWE Universe was eagerly anticipating the 2001 Royal Rumble Match for a number of reasons. In addition to the non-stop action and the chance for the winner to fight in the main event at *WrestleMania*, fans were eagerly anticipating Stone Cold Steve Austin's return to the Royal Rumble. The previous year Austin had missed the Rumble after being run over by a car driven by Rikishi at *Survivor Series 1999*. Both Austin and the previous year's winner, The Rock, were confident they would win. However, the hint that the Brothers of Destruction, Undertaker, and Kane were going to work together also kept the WWE Universe guessing as the event approached.

THE MATCH

The first two entrants in the match were Jeff Hardy and Bull Buchanan. The two battled back and forth, with Buchanan seeming to have the upper hand until Matt Hardy entered as number three. The brothers teamed up to eliminate Buchanan before they started to fight each other. Once the countdown for the fourth competitor started, the brothers waited for the new contestant, Faarooq. Once he entered they worked together again to eliminate him before once more turning their sights on each other. As Drew Carey became the fifth entrant, the Hardy Boyz eliminated each other, leaving the comedian by himself. That did not last, as Carey found himself face-to-face with the Big Red Demon, Kane. After a handshake and a bribe did not work, Carey decided to eliminate himself.

At this point, the Rumble match took a turn for the hardcore, with Raven introducing several trashcans filled with weapons to the ring. New entrants Al Snow, Perry Saturn, and Steve Blackman all used the various signs, cans, and sticks, but Kane eventually eliminated all four men, as well as Grand Master Sexay and the Honky Tonk Man, leaving him alone in the ring until the next entrant, The Rock, appeared. The two men battled each other back and forth, only stopping to quickly eliminate the next two entrants, The Goodfather and Tazz. As more competitors entered the ring, many tried to make their name by eliminating the previous year's winner, The Rock. The crowd was surprised as Big Show entered at #23. He eliminated two competitors and Chokeslammed five others. He tried to Chokeslam The Rock, but The Great One instead eliminated Big Show. In retaliation, the angry giant pulled The Rock out of the ring and Chokeslammed him through the announcers' table.

The remaining competitors decided to work together to eliminate Kane. But the next entrant, Undertaker, pulled the men off his brother and the two joined forces to eliminate all other competitors in the ring. Unlike the Hardys earlier, these two brothers did not attack each other when alone, choosing to wait for each new competitor. Stone Cold was supposed to enter next, but he was ambushed from behind by Triple H, who beat the Texas Rattlesnake into a bloody pulp. Rock finally returned to the ring, as did new entrants Billy Gunn and Haku. Austin made it into the ring at last when the final competitor, Rikishi, entered. Rikishi eliminated Undertaker, Stone Cold took out Haku, and The Rock knocked Rikishi out, leaving four men.

The final four were three favorites: Kane, Stone Cold, and The Rock, as well as Billy Gunn. Austin took out Gunn, and then the three remaining men tried to eliminate each other. Austin and The Rock were tied up in the ropes when Kane attempted to dump both men out of the ring. He eliminated Rock, but Stone Cold hung on. The Rock's elimination was Kane's 11th of the match—a new record. He almost had Austin out as well, but Stone Cold landed a Stunner, three brutal shots, and a clothesline to eliminate Kane and win the Royal Rumble.

THE AFTERMATH

With Austin's position in the main event at *WrestleMania* set, he and Triple H finally settled their longstanding rivalry at *No Way Out* where the two Superstars met in a Three Stages of Hell Match. While Triple H won the match 2-1, Austin turned his attention to *WrestleMania*. *No Way Out* also produced his opponent, as The Rock beat Kurt Angle for the WWE Championship. For the second time in three years, Stone Cold and The Rock would meet in the main event of *WrestleMania*.

EDGE vs. RIC FLAIR

RAW

TABLES, LADDERS, AND CHAIRS MATCH FOR THE WWE CHAMPIONSHIP

January 16, 2006

RBC Center
Raleigh, North Carolina

THE LEAD-UP

At *New Year's Revolution 2006*, John Cena defended the WWE Championship against five other competitors and managed to retain the Title. Even so, his night was not over, as Edge cashed in his Money in the Bank Contract to defeat a bloodied and exhausted Cena and claim his first WWE Championship. The next night on *Raw*, Ric Flair interrupted Edge and Lita's lude celebration, only to be brutalized by the Rated-R Superstar. The following week on *Raw*, Edge was compelled to make his first formal Title defense in a Tables, Ladders, and Chairs Match against the Intercontinental Champion, Ric Flair.

THE MATCH

The announcers acknowledged that the Nature Boy faced long odds, particularly since TLC Matches were completely new to Flair, while his opponent specialized in them. Still, it was hard to discount the 16-time World Champion. He got the crowd chanting "Woooooo!" with each of the blistering knife-edge chops he used to redden the Champion's chest. Edge used a right hand to drop Flair to the mat, and the Rated-R Superstar followed that up with some kicks and an elbow. With Flair down, Edge exited the ring and retrieved a ladder. Edge used the ladder to knock down Flair, and then sandwiched Flair with the ladder, driving it into the challenger's body.

Flair rolled out of the ring and Edge followed him, only to receive more chops from the Nature Boy. The two brawled into the crowd until Edge gave Flair a back body drop over the guardrail. Edge draped Flair on a table and prepared for a Conchairto, but the Nature Boy gave the Champion a low blow and tossed him onto a guardrail. Before Flair could go after Edge, Lita jumped on the challenger's back and distracted him long enough for Edge to grab a foreign object and blast Flair with it. Edge put Flair back on the table on the ring floor and Lita held the Nature Boy in place. Edge took a second ladder, set it up in the ring, and dove off the top of the ladder, splashing Flair through the table.

Back in the ring, a bloodied Flair changed the momentum of the match with a low blow to Edge. The Nature Boy now put Edge between the sides of the ladder and drove the ladder into the body of the Rated-R Superstar. He also knocked down the Champion, as well as hit the ladder into his ribs again. Before Flair could climb the ladder after the Title, Edge started stirring, so Flair put the ladder in the corner, perhaps looking to deliver a big move off

the top onto his opponent. Unfortunately for the challenger, it was Edge with the big move, as he superplexed Flair from the top of the ladder. Edge went for a missile dropkick from the ladder, but came up short, leaving both men lying on the mat.

Edge climbed the ladder and had his fingers on the Title, when Flair recovered enough to push the ladder over. The action sent Edge flying out of the ring and through a table on the ring floor. Flair climbed the ladder to the Title and had almost reached the top when Lita interfered, pulling the Nature Boy down and punching him repeatedly. Flair considered hitting back, but instead he put her in the Figure-Four Leglock until she begged for mercy.

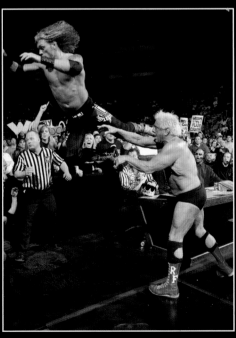

Once again, Flair ascended the ladder, but Lita's distraction gave Edge the time he needed to recover. Edge climbed the opposite side of the ladder, and he punched the challenger until Flair fell to the mat below. This allowed the Rated-R Superstar to finish the climb and grab the Title, retaining the WWE Championship.

THE AFTERMATH

Not content to just win the match, Edge descended the ladder and delivered a spear to Flair. He then prepared to deliver further damage but Edge's *Royal Rumble* challenger, John Cena, ran to the ring to stop the Rated-R Superstar, chasing off Edge and Lita. At the Rumble, John Cena regained the WWE Championship from Edge, but it was just the start of a year-long rivalry between the two, one that culminated in their own Tables, Ladders, and Chairs Match at *Unforgiven 2006*, where Cena emerged victorious.

JOHN CENA VS. CM PUNK

THE LEAD-UP

The 2013 *Royal Rumble* saw two crucial developments in the road to *WrestleMania 29*. The Rock became WWE Champion for the eighth time by ending CM Punk's 434-day reign as WWE Champion. John Cena won the Royal Rumble Match and decided to challenge the WWE Champion at *WrestleMania*. Punk tried to regain the Title at *Elimination Chamber*, but was unsuccessful as The Rock retained it in controversial fashion. The next night, when Cena spoke of his match, Punk interrupted, claiming that he had been screwed and he deserved the Title match, particularly because John had never beaten him in a match. Cena, wanting to silence his critics, proposed a match between the two of them in the main event that night.

WWE RAW
MATCH TO DETERMINE WHO WOULD FACE THE ROCK AT WRESTLEMANIA 29

February 25, 2013

American Airlines Center
Dallas, Texas

THE MATCH

The announcers noticed that Cena looked nervous to start the match, probably due to two factors: first, he had never beaten Punk in a big match, and second, he had everything to lose in the match, while Punk risked nothing. Cena brought Punk down with a side headlock, but Punk broke the hold with a leg scissors. Punk then put Cena in a similar headlock, but Cena could not execute the head scissors as his opponent did just moments before. Punk's strategy seemed to be negating Cena's power by grounding him, so he put The Champ in another leg scissors, this time around John's head. But Cena's strength was apparent when he stood up and dropped the Straight Edge Superstar to the mat, breaking the hold.

Punk tried to keep Cena to the mat, but Cena got back to a vertical base and landed a flying shoulder block. He went for a second one, but Punk dropped down and Cena went crashing out of the ring to the floor below. The Straight Edge Superstar then followed that up with a suicide dive onto Cena outside the ring. Cena recovered to line Punk up for an Attitude Adjustment, but Punk countered it into a DDT. Cena returned to his feet and hit two more shoulder blocks, but when Cena went for the scoop slam, Punk reversed the move into his Anaconda Vice submission maneuver. Cena turned Punk over and the official started counting Punk's shoulders on the mat, so the Straight Edge Superstar released the move to prevent being pinned.

Punk took to the air, hitting a high cross body on Cena, but it only garnered a two count. Punk repeated the move, but Cena caught him midair, and put the Straight Edge Superstar in the STF submission move. Punk battled to counter the move back into the Anaconda Vice, but The Champ reversed the move again back into the STF. Like Cena before him, Punk rolled Cena on to his shoulders, so Cena had to break the move in order to prevent being pinned. The two traded punches and Cena slammed the Straight Edge Superstar to the mat and tried to land a Five-Knuckle Shuffle, but Punk blocked the move with a kick to the head. Cena then succeeded with a Five-Knuckle Shuffle and followed it with an Attitude Adjustment, but Punk countered the move into a Go To Sleep attempt that Cena reversed into a Power Bomb and a two count.

Punk performed another Go To Sleep and went for the pin, but Cena kicked out at two. The Straight Edge Superstar went for a second GTS, which Cena countered into an STF, but Punk reached the ropes to force a break. Punk caught The Champ with a Piledriver, but Cena kicked out. A frustrated Punk went to the top rope to finish off Cena, but The Champ rolled out of the way, surprised Punk with a hurricanrana, and finally executed an Attitude Adjustment to pin Punk and retain his WWE Championship opportunity at *WrestleMania*.

John Cena went on to *WrestleMania 29*, and he avenged the previous year's *WrestleMania* loss to The Rock by beating The Great One for the WWE Championship. Cena held the Title until *SummerSlam 2013* when Daniel Bryan shocked the world by defeating The Champ for the WWE Championship. CM Punk, still looking for a signature match on the grand stage of *WrestleMania*, challenged Undertaker's 20-0 mark. Although he came dangerously close to pinning The Deadman on several occasions, Punk eventually became victim #21 in Undertaker's incredible *WrestleMania* streak.

For Bret "Hit Man" Hart, 1993 was a year with significant highs and lows. After starting the year as the WWE Champion, Hit Man lost the Title at *WrestleMania IX* in controversial fashion to Yokozuna. When the Japanese giant then lost the Title to Hulk Hogan moments later, Hart had to wait for another Title opportunity while Yokozuna got his Title rematch at *King of the Ring*. So Hart entered the *King of the Ring* tournament, an eight-man bracket, where he defeated Razor Ramon in the quarterfinals and Mr. Perfect in the semifinals. In the final match, Hart's opponent was Bam Bam Bigelow. After Bigelow defeated "Hacksaw" Jim Duggan in the quarterfinals, he got a bye into the finals, thanks to a Tatanka/Lex Luger draw. So after two grueling matches, Hit Man faced a well-rested opponent in the finals.

BRET "HIT MAN" HART
vs.
BAM BAM BIGELOW

KING OF THE RING 1993
KING OF THE RING FINAL MATCH

June 13, 1993

Nutter Center
Dayton, Ohio

THE MATCH

Bigelow took the early advantage, using his strength and power on Hart. Bam Bam press-slammed Hart out of the ring, and then delivered a number of devastating head-butts. Bigelow focused many of his attacks on Hart's back, including a number of Irish Whips into the unforgiving turnbuckles. By weakening the back, Bigelow set Hart up for his devastating Bear Hug. But Hart would not quit, and he kicked out of a number of pinning attempts.

Bigelow again dumped Hart out of the ring and looked to deliver more punishment. But Hart was able to reverse a move and toss Bigelow into the guard rails. Hart was finally able to mount some offense against Bam Bam, but Hit Man made a mistake as he launched himself at Bigelow. Bigelow caught Hart and slammed him into the ring post.

Bigelow slammed Hart onto the bare aisle way's floor. The move was devastating, as the floor was not covered with any mats. Bigelow made his way back into the ring and argued with the official. While the two men were focused on each other, Bigelow's valet, Luna Vachon, came down the aisle with a foreign object. Just as Hart was attempting to recover, she smacked the object across his back, knocking him down again. Bigelow then dragged Hart back into the ring. He slammed Hart, gave him a diving head-butt off the top rope, and pinned him for the three-count. It looked as if Bigelow would be the King of the Ring.

Before the ring announcer could relay the official's decision, a second official arrived and explained what Vachon had done. After a brief conference, the decision was made to continue the match. Bigelow was enraged, but continued to dominate Hart with power moves. Hart was able to escape a backbreaker and give Bigelow a side suplex, but Bigelow still remained in command. However, he went for one move too many, and Hart rolled away from Bigelow's posterior drop, causing Bam Bam to crash to the ring. With the extra time to recover, Hart launched his offense, including a sleeper hold, a drop kick, a second-rope bulldog, and a victory roll that led to an improbable three-count. Hit Man had overcome the odds to become the King of the Ring.

Immediately following the match, Hit Man was brought to a stage for a coronation ceremony. Standing in front of a throne, Hart was presented with a robe, a crown, and a scepter. Before Hart could make an acceptance speech, he was confronted by Jerry "The King" Lawler, who angrily proclaimed he was the only true king of WWE. Hart mocked Lawler for not even entering the tournament, but then made the mistake of turning his back on Lawler. Lawler took this opportunity to attack Hit Man. Lawler told Hart he would have to kiss the feet of the true king, and backed up his point by kicking Hart in the face. The two would engage in an on-again off-again rivalry for the next few years.

THE ROCK vs. STONE COLD STEVE AUSTIN

THE LEAD-UP

At *Survivor Series 1998*, The Rock turned his back on the WWE Universe and aligned himself with Mr. McMahon's Corporation, winning the WWE Championship and giving Mr. McMahon a Champion he wanted, as opposed to the Texas Rattlesnake, Stone Cold Steve Austin. Mr. McMahon even entered and won the *Royal Rumble* to prevent Austin from earning the Title opportunity. However, Austin beat Mr. McMahon for the chance to face The Rock at *WrestleMania XV*. There would also be a Special Guest Referee decided by a match between Mankind and Mr. McMahon's hand-picked choice, Big Show. Mankind won the match, but Big Show incapacitated him so that it seemed impossible that he'd be able to work the match later that night.

WRESTLEMANIA XV

NO DISQUALIFICATION MATCH FOR THE WWE CHAMPIONSHIP

March 28, 1999

First Union Center
Philadelphia, Pennsylvania

THE MATCH

With Mankind out of commission after his match with Big Show, the main event needed a new guest referee, and Mr. McMahon came out to take the job. But the commissioner, Shawn Michaels, came out and banned both McMahon and his Corporation from ringside, evening the odds for Stone Cold Steve Austin. The Corporate Champion tried to psych out Austin by talking trash, but the Texas Rattlesnake responded with a series of punches. The two continued to fight inside and outside the ring. They even brawled into the crowd. Once Austin started to get the upper hand, Rock tried to escape back to the ring.

The Rock took advantage of the no disqualification stipulation by trying to choke Austin with a ring cable as well as hitting a back body drop onto a lighting support structure. Austin countered with a slam and cable choke of his own. The Texas Rattlesnake also tossed the Brahma Bull into the *WrestleMania XV* sign, and tried to suplex The Rock onto the metal ramp, but The Great One blocked the move and instead slammed Austin. Austin recovered and dropped a series of elbows onto The Rock on the announcers' table, with the second elbow breaking the table.

Austin rolled The Rock back into the ring, but he surprised the challenger with a Rock Bottom. Austin kicked out at two. The Rock intended to finish Austin by grabbing a foreign object, but Austin wrested it from The Great One. He tried to use it against the Champion, but The Rock pulled the official in front of him and Austin nailed the official instead. The Rock then battered Austin repeatedly and called for a second official to count the pin. To the amazement of The Great One, Austin kicked out. The Rock then gained another two-count with a Samoan drop. The Rock, frustrated with the two-count, took out the second official with a Rock Bottom, but the Champion then ate a Stone Cold Stunner from Austin. Initially, there was no official to count Austin's pin attempt until a third one came into the ring, but the delay gave The Rock enough time to recover and kick out.

Austin prepared another assault, but Mr. McMahon returned to the ring and punched the third official. Mr. McMahon and The Rock double-teamed Austin until Mick Foley came to the ring and knocked Mr. McMahon down. The Rock started to hit Foley, but the distraction allowed Austin to roll up the Champion for a two-count. Rock regained the advantage and dropped Austin with a Rock Bottom. He tried to follow it up with the Corporate Elbow, but Austin rolled out of the way. The Texas Rattlesnake dodged a second Rock Bottom and instead delivered a Stone Cold Stunner to pin the Brahma Bull, winning the match and the WWE Championship.

THE AFTERMATH

Stone Cold celebrated in the ring, drinking beer and saluting the crowd. He even shared a beer with one of the officials. Outside of the ring, Mr. McMahon seethed and even yelled at Austin when the Texas Rattlesnake started to head to the back. Austin punched McMahon and gave him a Stone Cold Stunner for his trouble. The Rock was owed a rematch, and he exercised the right the following month at *Backlash: In Your House*. However, Austin retained the Title against The Great One and defended the WWE Championship until May, when he lost the Title to the Undertaker.

TRISH STRATUS
VS.
MICKIE JAMES

THE LEAD-UP

Mickie James came to WWE not only looking to become a successful Diva, but also to be near her idol, WWE Women's Champion Trish Stratus. She teamed with Trish in several matches, and even got a chance to face Trish for the Women's Championship at *New Year's Revolution 2006*, but she was unsuccessful in her pursuit of the Title. It soon became clear that Mickie was obsessed with Trish, telling Trish she loved her and giving the Women's Champion an unwanted kiss. When Trish finally had enough and tried to get Mickie to back off, Mickie attacked Stratus and informed her she would destroy her and take her Title at *WrestleMania 22*.

WRESTLEMANIA 22
WWE WOMEN'S CHAMPIONSHIP MATCH

April 2, 2006

Allstate Arena
Rosemont, Illinois

THE MATCH

Stratus entered the match having held the Women's Title for more than 15 months, but she was focused on getting revenge on her challenger for all the insults and indignities that James had heaped upon her over the past few months. The two locked up to start the match, and James gave the back of Trish's head a few slaps until Trish responded with an elbow to Mickie's skull as well as a few rights. Trish took Mickie to the mat with a Lou Thesz Press and continued to rain punches on her challenger. Mickie briefly got away, but then Trish backed her into the corner with a kick and a few knife-edge chops.

Mickie tried to kick Trish, but the Champion grabbed her leg before it connected and forced James into a painful split. The challenger tried to get a breather, but Trish kicked her off the apron and onto the floor. Trish followed her out and tried to kick Mickie, but Mickie ducked and Trish's kick connected with the ring post. This shifted the momentum to James, who kicked Stratus and then slammed Trish's already injured leg into the ring post. Back in the ring, the two exchanged punches until Mickie took Trish to the mat with a low drop kick. James then continued to focus her offense on Trish's injured leg.

Mickie tried to get the Champion to submit by putting Stratus in a half Boston Crab. She pulled Trish's hair back to gain some **additional leverage,** but that illegal act spurred the official to make her break the hold. Mickie continued to target the leg, and Trish was only able to **stem the** challenger's momentum by locking both legs on Mickie's head and executing a head scissors. Despite favoring her injured leg, **Trish fought back,** hitting James with several rights as well as a pair of clotheslines. The rebellious Chicago crowd made their allegiances clear when **they lustily** booed fan-favorite Trish for dropping rule-breaker James to the mat with a spinebuster. James kicked out and then countered **Trish's attempted** top-rope hand spring elbow by driving the Champion into the mat.

James again attempted to pin the Champion, but Trish kicked out at two. Trish pursued an inside cradle pin, but James kicked out **at two.** James went to the top rope again, but Trish caught her and turned it into a running Powerbomb and a two-count. Trish had James **set up for** Stratusfaction, but James countered the move and delivered the Mick Kick. James pinned Stratus to become the new WWE **Women's Champion.**

James and Stratus continued their rivalry for the next several months. Although she made several attempts, Stratus did not recapture the Title from James. Lita defeated Mickie for the Women's Championship, ending James' Championship reign at just over four months. Ironically, Trish beat Lita for the Title in Stratus's last match as an active member of WWE. James became WWE Women's Champion for the second time when she beat Lita two months later in Lita's last match as an active member of WWE. In total, Trish Stratus held the Women's Championship seven times, while Mickie held it five times, as well as the Divas Championship once.

TEAM SAVAGE vs. TEAM HONKY TONK

THE LEAD-UP

With the success of the first three *WrestleMania* events, WWE decided to add another big pay-per-view event to its calendar. In 1987, Thanksgiving night saw the first ever *Survivor Series*, where teams of five Superstars fight to survive. That night's main event featured teams captained by Hulk Hogan and Andre the Giant, as their *WrestleMania III* match had not cooled their rivalry over the WWE Championship. The first match of the night included a team captained by the Honky Tonk Man, the reigning Intercontinental Champion. His cocky attitude made a number of enemies, including former Champions Randy "Macho Man" Savage and Ricky "The Dragon" Steamboat, as well as Title challenger Jake "The Snake" Roberts. Both teams filled out their squads and launched a new WWE tradition that continues to this day.

THE MATCH

Savage appointed Beefcake to start the match for their squad and he was initially opposed by Hercules. Angered by Beefcake's early strutting, the powerful Hercules hit the Barber with a clubbing blow to his back and took Beefcake to the mat with a snapmare takedown. The Barber locked Hercules into his Sleeper move early, but Hercules made his corner and tagged in Davis. The Dangerous One was on the bad end of some punishment from multiple members of Savage's team as their squad used quick tags to keep Davis isolated. He finally managed to tag in Race and Duggan entered for Savage's team. The two men ended up outside the ring brawling and ignoring the count. Both men were eliminated via countout, dropping each squad to four men.

Bass and Savage continued in the ring, with Savage's squad getting an early advantage, followed by Bass taking the offensive momentum. However, Savage tagged in Beefcake without Bass seeing it, and Bass ran into a high knee from the Barber, leading to a pin and Honky Tonk Man's squad being down a man, 4-3. They negated that advantage by keeping Beefcake in their corner and tagging in and out between Honky Tonk Man and Hercules. The Barber started to make a comeback, but the Intercontinental Champion pummeled him with his Shake, Rattle and Roll move and pinned Beefcake, evening things up again to three men a side.

Honky Tonk's team continued to function well as a unit, isolating first Savage and then Roberts in their corner with quick tags and the occasional double-team maneuvers. Danny Davis tagged in and went to work on the Snake, backing him into a corner with a series of punches and kicks. The blows seemed to have no effect on Roberts, and he actually encouraged Davis to keep hitting him. Finally the Snake pulled Davis in and dropped him with a short-arm clothesline and then planted the former official with his signature DDT. After the pinfall, Savage's side was up again, three men to two.

Hercules re-entered the ring and dropped Roberts with a wicked leaping clothesline. He then dropped two elbows on the Snake and went for the pin, only managing a two-count. Hercules tagged in Honky Tonk Man and he kept working over Roberts while his teammates and the crowd yelled encouragement for the Snake.

Roberts finally broke Hercules' chinlock with a jaw-jacker and tagged in Steamboat. Steamboat dropped Hercules to the mat and tagged in Savage, who eliminated Hercules with a top-rope elbow and a pin. This left Honky Tonk Man on his own against three men. As all three of his rivals took out their aggression on the Intercontinental Champion, he rolled out of the ring and decided to fight another day, allowing himself to be counted out and making Savage, Steamboat, and Roberts the survivors of the match.

THE AFTERMATH

Although the format has changed over the years, *Survivor Series* remains a popular feature that the WWE Universe looks forward to every year. After several years on either Thanksgiving or the night before, *Survivor Series* became a Sunday event in 1995. Some notable WWE debuts occurred in *Survivor Series*, including Undertaker in 1990, Kurt Angle in 1999, and The Shield in 2012. Undertaker, Big Show, and The Rock all won their first WWE Championships at *Survivor Series* events. In addition, the first Elimination Chamber happened at *Survivor Series 2002*. The "Teams of Five Fight to Survive" event is a rich part of WWE history.

JOHN CENA vs. ROB VAN DAM

THE LEAD-UP

By winning a Money in the Bank Match, a Superstar is allowed to cash in his contract for a Championship opportunity at the time of his choosing. For most Superstars, this means picking a most opportune spot, particularly after the Champion has just finished a grueling match. Most winners also use the element of surprise, so the Champion cannot prepare. But after winning the Money in the Bank Match at *WrestleMania 22*, Rob Van Dam announced his plans in advance—he wanted to challenge WWE Champion John Cena at *ECW One Night Stand*. He planned to use his "home-field advantage" to beat Cena for the Title and rechristen it as the ECW World Championship.

THE MATCH

As WWE Champion, John Cena had to compete in a number of hostile environments, but few venues could contend with the intensity of the Hammerstein Ballroom. The place was packed with ECW diehards, complete with signs like "If Cena Wins, We Riot." The match's start was delayed for a few minutes when Cena attempted his tradition of throwing his t-shirt into the crowd—the crowd kept throwing the shirt back.

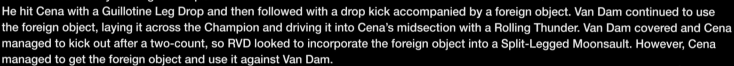

Cena took early control of the match with his power, but the crowd was not impressed. Cena demonstrated some innovation, leaping out of the ring from the top turnbuckle to nail RVD with a forearm. Van Dam showed his innovative offense as well, hitting Cena with a Corkscrew Leg Drop while Cena was draped over the guard rail. The action spilled into the ECW crowd and then back to the ring.

Van Dam was clearly feeding off the partisan crowd. He hit Cena with a Guillotine Leg Drop and then followed with a drop kick accompanied by a foreign object. Van Dam continued to use the foreign object, laying it across the Champion and driving it into Cena's midsection with a Rolling Thunder. Van Dam covered and Cena managed to kick out after a two-count, so RVD looked to incorporate the foreign object into a Split-Legged Moonsault. However, Cena managed to get the foreign object and use it against Van Dam.

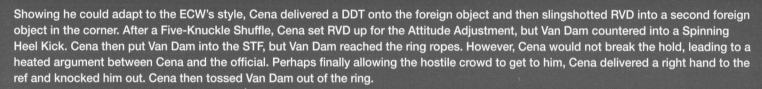

Showing he could adapt to the ECW's style, Cena delivered a DDT onto the foreign object and then slingshotted RVD into a second foreign object in the corner. After a Five-Knuckle Shuffle, Cena set RVD up for the Attitude Adjustment, but Van Dam countered into a Spinning Heel Kick. Cena then put Van Dam into the STF, but Van Dam reached the ring ropes. However, Cena would not break the hold, leading to a heated argument between Cena and the official. Perhaps finally allowing the hostile crowd to get to him, Cena delivered a right hand to the ref and knocked him out. Cena then tossed Van Dam out of the ring.

A man in a motorcycle helmet snuck into the ring and speared John Cena through the table RVD had set up earlier. The helmeted man then knocked out the second official and removed his helmet—it was Edge. RVD returned to the ring, went to the top turnbuckle, and executed a Five-Star Frog Splash on Cena. With no referee available, Paul Heyman appeared and made the three-count. RVD was WWE Champion and the Hammerstein Ballroom was overjoyed. The ECW competitors filled the ring to celebrate their new Champion.

THE AFTERMATH

Instead of renaming the WWE Championship the ECW Championship, RVD was awarded a new Title by Paul Heyman. Van Dam decided to keep both Titles, making him the WWE Champion and the ECW Champion. Edge, who helped RVD win the Title, was the first challenger for the WWE Championship at *Vengeance*, but RVD managed to retain the Title. However, RVD would lose both of his Titles in July, as Edge beat him for the WWE Championship and Big Show defeated him for the ECW Championship. The relaunched ECW managed to stick around for almost four years before it folded once again.

THE LEAD-UP

After purchasing WCW, Shane McMahon looked to poach some key WWE Superstars, as well as interfere with the actions of others. Kurt Angle was participating in a reenactment of his Olympic medal ceremony when "Shane-O Mac" interrupted the proceedings. Angle took exception and put the junior McMahon in the Ankle Lock. The two continued to have problems over the next few weeks, leading Angle to challenge McMahon to a Street Fight at *King of the Ring*, despite the fact that Angle would have one or two other matches the same night.

KURT ANGLE vs.
SHANE MCMAHON

THE MATCH

Shane McMahon had already inserted himself into Angle's first two matches of the night. He helped Angle win his Semifinal Match, in order to force Angle to wrestle an extra match before they met. However, McMahon then interfered in the Finals, ensuring that Angle would not win the King of the Ring. Perhaps anger from this led Angle to charge McMahon early in the match. Twice Angle would put himself in the crouching amateur wrestling position, inviting McMahon to take the initiative. The first time Shane did, Angle easily countered and rained punches on McMahon. The second time, Shane took the opportunity to kick Angle in the midsection.

The two continued to trade the advantage back and forth. Angle executed a variety of suplexes, while Shane used a kendo stick on the former Olympic Champion. Shane took further advantage of the Street Fight rules by bringing a board, trash cans, and a street sign into the ring. McMahon repeatedly hit Angle with the sign and then used Angle's own Ankle Lock on him. The Olympic Hero was able to counter the move, but McMahon tried another submission move, the Sharpshooter. Angle was able to break the move by hitting Shane with a kendo stick. McMahon fought back and tried to drive a trash can into a prone Angle by performing a top-rope Shooting Star Press, but Angle rolled out of the way.

As the two battled to the Superstars' entrance, Angle grabbed McMahon in a belly-to-belly overhead suplex that bounced Shane off one of the set pieces. Angle repeated the act, and this time the glass shattered as McMahon went through it. Angle followed McMahon inside the set and suplexed McMahon two more times off a second glass panel. He finally tossed McMahon through the second glass panel, leaving Shane a bloody mess on the entrance stage. An exhausted Angle, realizing he couldn't carry McMahon back to the ring for the pinfall attempt, loaded Shane onto a cart and wheeled him to the ring.

Angle looked for the pinfall, but an exhausted McMahon still managed to kick out before the three-count. Angle, incredulous that Shane would kick out, went to hit McMahon with a garbage can lid. McMahon responded and delivered a low blow, a series of shots with the garbage can lid. McMahon then followed with The Olympic Hero's own Angle Slam, but Angle kicked out of the pinfall. Angle then draped McMahon on the top turnbuckle. Placing a board across the ropes as a platform, Angle stood on the board and delivered a top-rope Angle Slam to pin McMahon and win the match.

THE AFTERMATH

Despite his loss, Shane continued to push his WCW product and received an additional boost when ECW, now owned by his sister Stephanie McMahon, combined forces for a full-fledged invasion of WWE. Angle first fought for the side of WWE, even winning the WWE Title from WWE turncoat Stone Cold Steve Austin. In October, Angle joined the side of The Alliance, stunning the WWE Universe and Superstars. However, the defection was just a ruse, as Angle proved he was on the side of WWE during the Winner Take All Match between The Alliance and WWE at that year's *Survivor Series*.

JOHN CENA

VS.

SHAWN MICHAELS

April 23, 2007

Earl's Court
London, England

THE LEAD-UP

John Cena and Shawn Michaels had a classic confrontation at *WrestleMania 23*, a match that saw Cena retain the WWE Championship by forcing the Heartbreak Kid to submit to the STF. At the time, the two were co-holders of the World Tag Team Championship, but Michaels screwed over his partner the night after *WrestleMania*, allowing the Hardys to win the Tag Titles. The tension and animosity between the two ran high, particularly with the announcement that Michaels would get another shot at Cena's Title at *Backlash* in a Fatal 4-Way. Before that happened though, the two faced off on *Raw* in a non-Title match.

THE MATCH

Michaels grabbed the early advantage in the match by using his superior technical skills. Before the match, Michaels had asserted to Cena that he, HBK, was the better man and he seemed determined to prove it in the match, taking Cena down to the mat twice with fireman carry takedowns. Cena countered Michaels with a drop toehold and came close to locking Michaels in the STF, the move he'd used to win the match at *WrestleMania*. Michaels tried to return to his technical moves, but Cena clearly got under HBK's skin by going for the STF two more times. The two started trash-talking each other in the ring, and Michaels twice shoved Cena, but the WWE Champion responded by decking Michaels with a right.

Cena aimed to negate Michaels' quickness advantage by taking HBK to the mat with a series of side headlocks. Michaels fought out of the headlock, and tried to hip block the Champion, but Cena countered the move into a short-armed clothesline and a near fall. Michaels seemed to daze Cena by hitting an elbow and a knife-edge chop, followed by ramming Cena's head into a turnbuckle. Cena had to know that Michaels can perform Sweet Chin Music at any time, so when Michaels whipped Cena into the ropes, Cena held on to prevent the kick from connecting. Cena then grabbed Michaels for an Attitude Adjustment, but Michaels latched onto the ropes and ended up on the apron before falling to the mats below.

Back in the ring, Cena got a few near falls and then went for a suplex, but Michaels countered the move with a swinging neckbreaker. The two exchanged blows, Cena with punches and Michaels with chops, and then Michaels dropped the Champion with a flying forearm. Michaels drove a top-rope elbow into Cena's chest, and started tuning up the band for Sweet Chin Music. Instead HBK tried a backslide that got a two-count and then ducked a Cena shoulder block that sent the Champion crashing out of the ring. Back in the ring, Cena performed a series of shoulder blocks, landed his Five-Knuckle Shuffle, and raised Michaels up for the Attitude Adjustment. HBK fought out of the move and tried to hit Sweet Chin Music, but Cena ducked it and then executed the Attitude Adjustment. Somehow, Michaels kicked out of the pin before three.

Cena continued to focus on Michaels' lower back, while Shawn went after Cena's left arm. Cena hit a top-rope leg drop and got another near fall. Cena tried to deliver an Attitude Adjustment from the top rope, but Michaels reversed it into a Powerbomb. Cena almost locked Michaels in the STF a third time, but HBK again fought his way out of it. After the two brawled outside the ring, Cena finally managed to put Michaels in the STF. With herculean effort, Michaels reached the ropes to force a break. Cena went for another Attitude Adjustment, but Michaels countered it into Sweet Chin Music. Michaels covered Cena, but The Champ grabbed the rope before the three-count. Cena tried to execute yet another Attitude Adjustment, but Michaels landed on his feet, hit Cena with a second Sweet Chin Music, and covered Cena for the three-count.

THE AFTERMATH

Michaels may have hoped his one-on-one victory over Cena would give him momentum leading into the Fatal 4-Way Match at *Backlash*, but John Cena retained the WWE Championship by pinning Randy Orton. In fact, Cena held on to the WWE Championship until a torn pectoral muscle in October 2007 forced him to relinquish the Championship. Michaels was injured by The Viper, Randy Orton, during their match at *Judgment Day 2007* and was out of action until October of that year when he returned to confront the man who injured him, newly crowned WWE Champion Orton.

KURT ANGLE vs. TRIPLE H vs. RIKISHI vs. UNDERTAKER vs. STONE COLD vs. THE ROCK

THE LEAD-UP

Kurt Angle had completed one of the most spectacular debut years in history by capturing the WWE Championship in October 2000. Among the five men with compelling cases for a Championship shot, there was incredible animosity. In order to clarify the Title situation and settle the numerous grudges, WWE Commissioner Mick Foley decided to put all six men into Hell in a Cell at *Armageddon*. It was the first time ever six men would compete in the demonic structure. Mr. McMahon was furious—he knew the lasting damage the cell could do, so he tried to talk the competitors out of the match. For his trouble, he got a Stone Cold Stunner, a Rock Bottom, and a Last Ride.

ARMAGEDDON 2000

SIX-MAN HELL IN A CELL MATCH FOR THE WWE CHAMPIONSHIP

December 10, 2000

Jefferson Civic Center
Birmingham, Alabama

One by one, the competitors were introduced and made their way into the cell. Kurt Angle did not initially enter the cage, trying to avoid his fellow competitors. But the last man introduced, Stone Cold Steve Austin, went straight for Angle and dragged him into the cell. Once the cage was locked, the competitors largely paired off in shifting groups. Stone Cold Steve Austin focused on The Game, raking Triple H's face across the walls of the cell. It made sense, as the Texas Rattlesnake had been out of action for almost a year because of a hit-and-run—Rikishi may have been the driver, but Triple H was the mastermind of the plan. Austin wanted his pound of flesh from Triple H.

The in-ring action intensified, leading to a sequence that highlighted the problems inherent in getting a pinfall in a six-man, everyone-for-himself match. Triple H hit Rikishi with a Pedigree, but The Rock broke up the pin. He then hit Triple H with a DDT, but Kurt Angle prevented the three-count and dropped The Rock with an Angle Slam. However, Stone Cold pulled Angle off and gave the former Olympic champion a Stunner. It was then Undertaker's turn to interrupt the decision and the Texas Rattlesnake received a Chokeslam for his trouble until Triple H stopped that pinfall.

Mr. McMahon and Stooges then showed up with a contractor and his pickup truck. They tied a chain to the cell door and ripped it off its hinges. Mr. McMahon wanted the entire cell pulled down, but Commissioner Foley arrived and had McMahon arrested for interfering with the match. However, the missing door allowed the competitors to spill out of the cell. If Vince was trying to prevent his Superstars from getting hurt by getting them out of the cell, his idea backfired—the six men started slamming each other on the cars at the entrance ramp. Soon all six competitors were bruised and bloody.

Triple H decided to climb to the cell's top to avoid the wrath of the Texas Rattlesnake, but Austin followed him. The two battled dangerously close to the edge of the cell, and then the other four competitors joined them on the top. Once again, Undertaker made a Superstar famous by throwing him off the top of the cell—this time it was Rikishi, who landed in the bed of the truck Mr. McMahon had brought ringside. But the match could only be won in the ring, so the competitors made it back inside. Stone Cold thought he had the match won when he hit The Rock with a Stunner. But Triple H pulled Stone Cold off The Rock and looked to finish Austin off. While they were battling, Angle stole the pin on The Rock and retained the WWE Championship.

THE AFTERMATH

After defending his Championship in the brutal cell, Kurt Angle would go on to defend the Title at the *Royal Rumble* and *No Way Out*. Angle's luck would run out at the latter event, and The Rock would regain the Championship. Mr. McMahon was finally able to get his revenge on Commissioner Foley—once the Chairman regained control of the WWE, he fired Foley from the position and replaced him with William Regal.

Hell in a Cell continues to be a signature event on the WWE calendar, but there has never again been a six-man contest like the one at *Armageddon 2000*. Based on the carnage unleashed at that event, it is probably for the best.

OWEN HART vs.
BRITISH BULLDOG

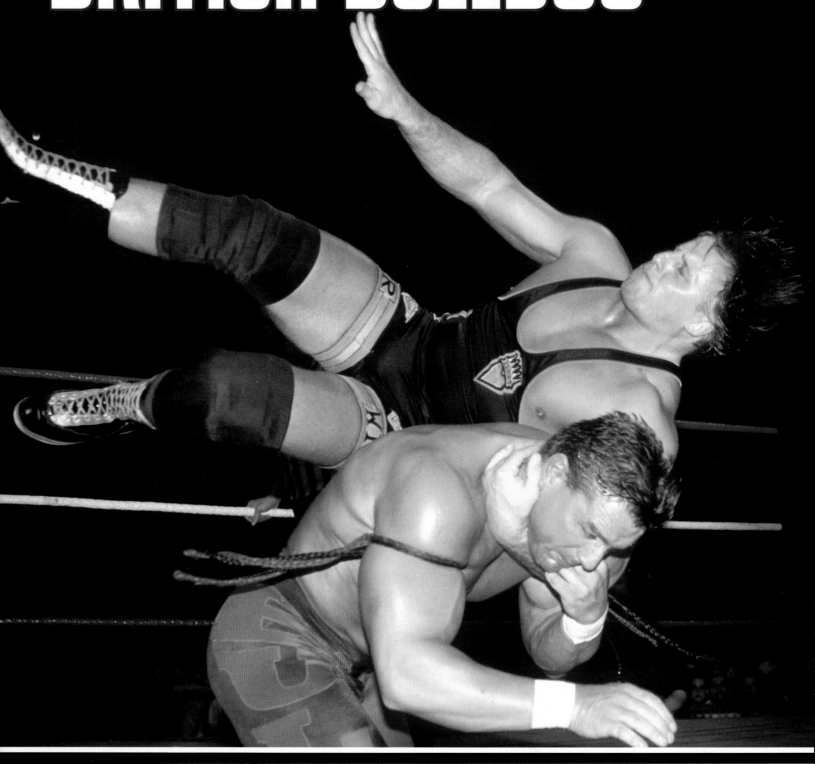

WWE RAW
FINAL MATCH TO CROWN THE FIRST EUROPEAN CHAMPION

March 3, 1997

Deutschlandhalle
Berlin, Germany

THE LEAD-UP

WWE decided to add a new Championship in early 1997, its first in 20 years. To crown the European Champion, an eight-man tournament was set up. On one half of the bracket, the British Bulldog advanced to the finals by beating Mankind and Vader. On the other half of the bracket, Owen Hart defeated Flash Funk and his brother Bret "Hit Man" Hart. As Owen and Bulldog prepared to meet in the tournament final, it set up a unique match as the two men were not only brothers-in-law, but co-holders of the World Tag Team Championship.

THE MATCH

The announcers speculated that this match would fracture the partnership of the Tag Team Champions, and that both men would use devious tactics to win. There was no sign of that at the beginning of the match, as the two competitors exchanged scientific holds and countering wristlocks, as well as Smith impressively countering a monkey flip by landing on his feet. Owen gave Smith a hip toss and then attempted to execute a victory roll, but Bulldog countered it into a Powerbomb before catapulting Owen out of the ring. Bulldog demonstrated sportsmanship by refusing to attack Owen, instead holding the ropes open so Hart could re-enter.

Bulldog tried to suplex Owen, but Hart landed on his feet and rolled up Smith for a two-count. Smith locked Hart in a crucifix, but Owen kicked out of the pinning attempt at two. Owen countered an Irish Whip attempt and he dumped Bulldog out of the ring. Owen returned the sportsmanship that Bulldog displayed earlier, staying in the ring while Smith recovered and then holding open the ring ropes for Bulldog to re-enter. Smith then hit a snapmare takedown and gained a two-count. Owen feigned a knee injury and used the advantage to launch some offense at his tag-team partner. Owen tried to lock Smith in the Sharpshooter, but Bulldog used his leg strength to kick Owen away. Bulldog executed an Irish Whip on Hart, but Hart ducked Bulldog and nailed Smith with a spinning heel kick.

Owen tried to finish off Bulldog with a top-rope superplex, but Smith adjusted his body in midair to turn the move into a high cross body, earning a two-count. Smith followed that up with three clotheslines and a suplex to earn another near fall. Owen countered a Smith Suplex into a German Suplex and a two-count. Owen countered an attempted powerslam into another near fall on Bulldog. Hart dropped his tag-team partner with a perfectly executed enziguri, followed by a Sharpshooter, but Bulldog used his considerable strength to reach the ropes and force a break of the move.

Bulldog whipped Owen into the ropes and looked to hit a side suplex on Hart. Owen countered the move into an attempted Piledriver but Bulldog had a counter of his own when he got Hart up on his shoulder and delivered a picture-perfect running Powerslam. To Bulldog's astonishment, Hart kicked out at two. While Smith argued with the official, Owen leapt on Bulldog's back and hit a Victory Roll. Bulldog rotated their positions and put Owen in a pinning predicament. The official counted to three, and Bulldog won the match, becoming the first European Champion in WWE History.

THE AFTERMATH

Four weeks later the two men met for a rematch, which did not display the same sportsmanship of the tournament final. Owen attacked his brother-in-law before the match even started. The two competitors were prepared to use dangerous foreign objects on each other when Bret Hart came to the ring and begged them to reconcile and help the Hit Man with his war on America. The three men hugged, and the new Hart Foundation began to form. Bulldog held the European Championship for seven months before losing the Title in September to Shawn Michaels during a controversial match in Birmingham, England.

TRIPLE H VS. RANDY ORTON

THE LEAD-UP

The week before *No Mercy*, WWE Champion John Cena tore his pectoral muscle, an injury that sidelined him for months and forced him to forfeit the WWE Championship. Mr. McMahon announced that he would address the issue at *No Mercy*, promising a new WWE Champion. He didn't wait long, opening the show with a ceremony awarding the WWE Championship to Randy Orton. However, Triple H goaded the Chairman into granting him a Title match, and The Game took the Title from Orton. Mr. McMahon made Triple H defend the Title twice that night—first against Umaga and then in a Last Man Standing Match with Orton.

NO MERCY 2007

October 7, 2007

**Allstate Arena
Rosemont, Illinois**

LAST MAN STANDING MATCH FOR THE WWE CHAMPIONSHIP

THE MATCH

There would be no disqualifications, count-outs, submissions, or pinfalls in the match—the point of the contest was to beat your opponent so bad that they would not be able to answer a 10-count. Triple H had injured his ribs in his earlier match with Umaga, so Orton focused much of his early attention in that area. With no disqualifications or count-outs to worry about, the action quickly spilled out of the ring with Orton suplexing Triple H onto the security wall. After a six-count, Triple H got up. Orton looked to increase the punishment, and he tossed The Game into the steel ring steps. Again, Triple H got up on the count of six.

Back in the ring, Triple H demonstrated his incredible resiliency, hitting Orton with a Facebuster. To regain control, Orton executed a vicious Inverted Backbreaker. Taking advantage of the match's anything-goes nature, Orton wrapped a television cable around The Game's neck, trying to choke his opponent out. Triple H was not done yet, and he managed to get up at the count of nine. A furious Orton took Triple H outside the ring and hit him with a television monitor. He then attempted to RKO Triple H through a table, but The Game pushed Orton through the table and almost won the match. Orton managed to get up on the nine-count. The Champion then gave Orton a Spinebuster on the outside floor. Again, Orton barely beat the count, getting up at nine. Triple H then hit Orton with the stairs, and Orton needed another nine-count to respond.

Back in the ring, Triple H attempted to use a foreign object on Orton, but the challenger hit the Champion in his injured ribs and delivered a DDT onto the same apparatus. Orton then set up the equalizer and put The Game's face into it with an RKO. Now it was Triple H that needed a nine-count to recover. Orton tried to put Triple H out with his Legend Killing punt, but The Game caught Orton's leg and dumped him out of the ring.

Triple H attempted to finish the match by delivering a Pedigree to Orton on the announcers' table. But Orton demonstrated why he's WWE's Apex Predator, as he quickly executed an RKO, driving Triple H into the table. The referee began a new count on both men. Orton got up at three and returned to the ring. Triple H could not make it up by the 10-count, so Orton retained the Championship.

THE AFTERMATH

Orton's first opponent after *No Mercy* was Triple H's D-Generation X running mate Shawn Michaels. Five months earlier, Orton had punted the Heartbreak Kid and put him out of commission for several months. Michaels returned the night after *No Mercy* and delivered Sweet Chin Music to the new Champion. The WWE Universe chose Michaels as Orton's opponent at *Cyber Sunday 2007*, but Orton managed to retain the Championship when Orton lost by disqualification. Because of his win, Michaels received another Title shot at *Survivor Series* 2007, but Orton was able to pin Michaels and retain the Title. Triple H continued his rivalry with Umaga, as the two fought in a Street Fight at *Cyber Sunday 2007*.

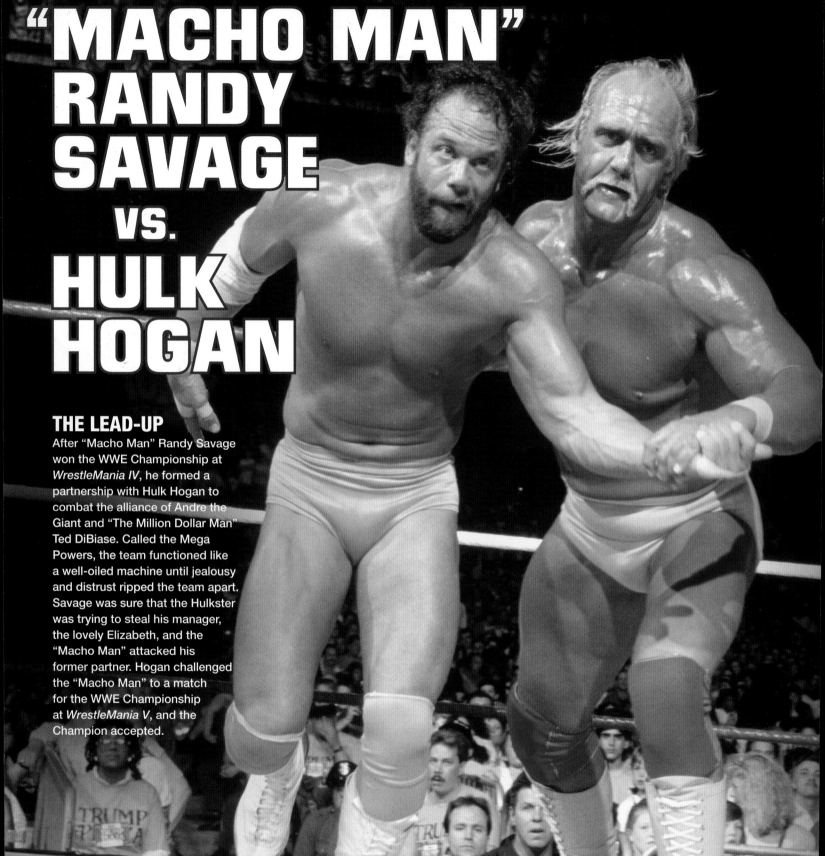

"MACHO MAN" RANDY SAVAGE VS. HULK HOGAN

THE LEAD-UP

After "Macho Man" Randy Savage won the WWE Championship at *WrestleMania IV*, he formed a partnership with Hulk Hogan to combat the alliance of Andre the Giant and "The Million Dollar Man" Ted DiBiase. Called the Mega Powers, the team functioned like a well-oiled machine until jealousy and distrust ripped the team apart. Savage was sure that the Hulkster was trying to steal his manager, the lovely Elizabeth, and the "Macho Man" attacked his former partner. Hogan challenged the "Macho Man" to a match for the WWE Championship at *WrestleMania V*, and the Champion accepted.

WRESTLEMANIA V
WWE CHAMPIONSHIP MATCH

April 2, 1989

**Trump Plaza
Atlantic City, New Jersey**

THE MATCH

The two Superstars circled each other in the ring, trying to gain a psychological advantage. When the pair locked up in a show of strength, Hogan easily tossed Savage to the mat. The Champion put the Hulkster in a headlock, but Hogan knocked the "Macho Man" down again with a shoulder block. Savage went for another side headlock, wrenching it in so that Hogan dropped to one knee. Hogan whipped Savage into the ropes, but the "Macho Man" held on and bailed out of the ring. The challenger chased Savage outside, but the Champion showed the depths to which he would sink when he grabbed Elizabeth and put her between himself and Hogan.

Hogan showed technical wrestling prowess when he chained a series of moves together, including two headlocks, a drop toe hold, and a front facelock. Savage countered the move with a suplex, but Hogan moved out of the way when Savage followed it up by dropping an elbow. Hogan then dropped the Champion to the mat with a series of punches. Savage fought back with a thumb to the Hulkster's eye and a double axe-handle off the top turnbuckle. Savage managed to get a near fall, and the "Macho Man" stayed on the offensive with an arm bar. Savage was in control until Hogan grabbed his tights and sent the Champion careening through the ropes and to the floor below.

Hogan, knowing he had to pin Savage in the ring to win the Title, followed the "Macho Man" outside the ring and rolled him back in. The challenger rammed Savage's head into two of the top turnbuckles and then dropped the Champion with a big clothesline. Hogan whipped Savage into the ropes, but the "Macho Man" kicked Hogan and made the challenger bleed with a clothesline of his own. Hogan kicked out of the pinfall attempt at two. Savage tried to then put the challenger down with a sleeper hold. Hogan forced Savage to break the hold with a series of elbows, landing a shoulder block on the "Macho Man," and then reversing the Champ's attempted kick into an atomic drop. Savage had enough presence of mind to roll away from the Hulkster's elbow drop, and the Champion earned a two-count on an attempted roll-up.

Savage, now in control, attacked the Hulkster's bleeding eye. Hogan tossed Savage out of the ring, and then attempted to ram the "Macho Man" into the steel post. Elizabeth blocked Hogan's attack, and Savage took advantage of her interference by shoving the challenger into the post. The "Macho Man" started menacing Elizabeth, so the official sent her to the back. Still in control of the match, the Champion dropped a double axe-handle from the top rope onto Hogan on the floor below. Back in the ring, Savage targeted Hogan's throat with an elbow as well as an illegal choke with his athletic tape. The crowd started urging Hogan on, and the challenger responded to their cheers. Nothing Savage did affected the Hulkster. Hogan planted the big boot in Savage's face, and dropped the leg for the three-count, beginning his second reign as WWE Champion.

THE AFTERMATH

The rivalry between Hogan and Savage continued throughout 1989. Hogan starred in a movie that year titled *No Holds Barred*. His cinematic rival, Zeus, followed the Hulkster to WWE where Zeus partnered with Savage to take out the Champion. But with the assistance of his close friend Brutus "The Barber" Beefcake, Hogan rebuffed both of his challengers. Hogan and Savage had another rematch in February 1990, but not only did Hogan win again, the "Macho Man" ran afoul of Heavyweight boxing Champion Buster Douglas, and was knocked out. Elizabeth was no longer in Savage's corner, as shortly after his *WrestleMania V* loss, the "Macho Man" enlisted the services of Sensational Sherri as his new manager.

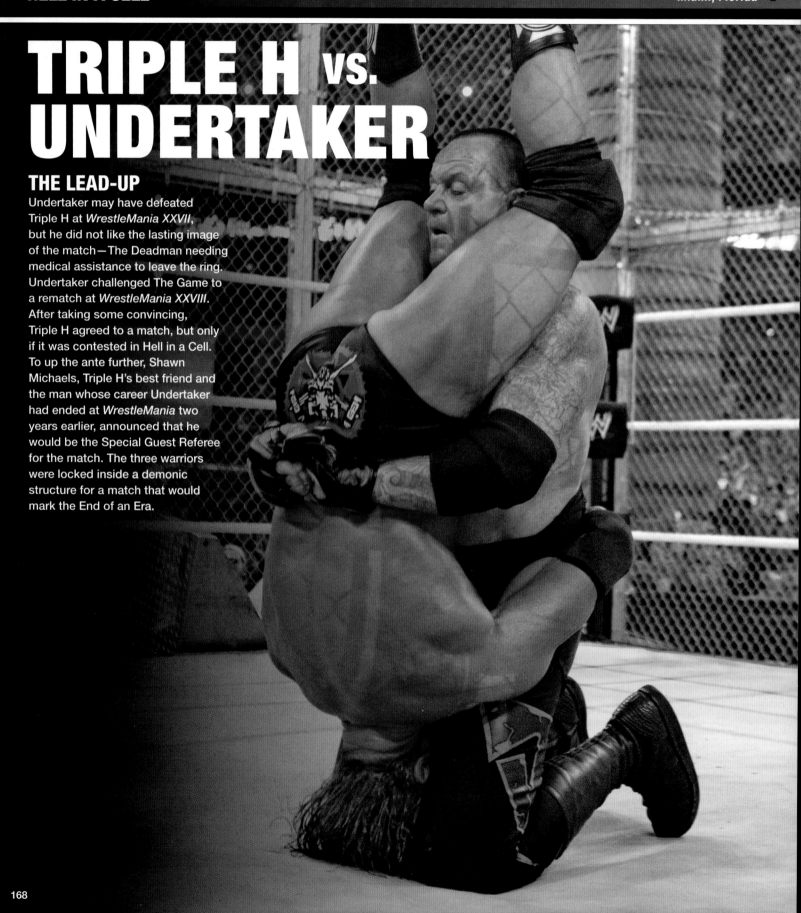

TRIPLE H vs. UNDERTAKER

THE LEAD-UP

Undertaker may have defeated Triple H at *WrestleMania XXVII*, but he did not like the lasting image of the match—The Deadman needing medical assistance to leave the ring. Undertaker challenged The Game to a rematch at *WrestleMania XXVIII*. After taking some convincing, Triple H agreed to a match, but only if it was contested in Hell in a Cell. To up the ante further, Shawn Michaels, Triple H's best friend and the man whose career Undertaker had ended at *WrestleMania* two years earlier, announced that he would be the Special Guest Referee for the match. The three warriors were locked inside a demonic structure for a match that would mark the End of an Era.

THE MATCH

Fighting outside the ring, Undertaker whipped The Game into the ring steps. Taking Triple H back in the ring, Undertaker found himself on the receiving end of Triple H's offense, including a facebuster. The move did not seem to affect The Deadman, and he dropped The Game with a clothesline, two shoulder blocks, and his Old School maneuver. The two men rolled out of the ring, and Undertaker bounced the steel steps off Triple H's skull.

Undertaker continued his methodical dismantling of Triple H, but The Game had life in him and he dropped The Deadman with a DDT. He took advantage of the steel steps Undertaker brought into the ring by bouncing The Deadman's skull off of them. But when he tried to Pedigree Undertaker on the steps, The Deadman reversed the move into a back body drop. Undertaker went to kick The Game with a big boot, but Triple H hit him with a Spinebuster onto the steel steps. He went to follow up the move, but Undertaker locked The Game in Hell's Gate, the submission move he used to win the previous year's match. Triple H demonstrated his incredible strength by lifting The Deadman, who still had the hold locked in, and slamming him to the mat to break it. The move gained Triple H a near fall.

Triple H tried to keep Undertaker down with a series of shots to The Deadman's spine. The Game was unrelenting, but Undertaker would not give up, even after Triple H hit him with a sledgehammer. Undertaker kicked out just before Michaels counted three. Michaels contemplated stopping the match, so The Deadman locked the official in Hell's Gate. To break the submission, Triple H hit the Undertaker with the sledgehammer again, but Undertaker locked The Game in Hell's Gate as well. Undertaker Chokeslammed The Game, but Triple H kicked out at two. Angry at the two-count, Undertaker Chokeslammed the replacement official as well. The Deadman went for a Tombstone, but HBK delivered Sweet Chin Music and Triple H followed up with a Pedigree. Even after taking all that punishment, Undertaker still kicked out before the three-count.

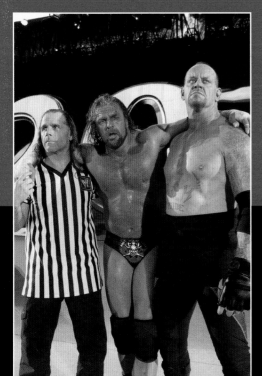

Triple H went back to the sledgehammer, and when Michaels tried to stop him from using it, Triple H tossed HBK out of the ring. This gave Undertaker time to sit up and take control of the match. He hit Triple H with Snake Eyes, a Big Boot to the face, and a leg drop. He then Tombstoned The Game, and was in disbelief when Triple H kicked out at two. Neither man would quit, as they punched each other while struggling to their feet. Triple H delivered another Pedigree, but it was only a near fall once again. Undertaker used a foreign object to pepper Triple H with a series of blows, but again Triple H kicked out. Triple H tried to use the sledgehammer one last time, but Undertaker took it away and used it on The Game. One more Tombstone later, Undertaker had increased his *WrestleMania* streak to 20-0.

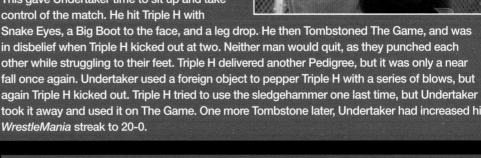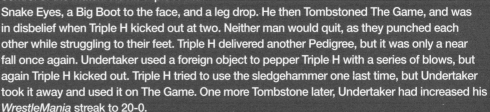

THE AFTERMATH

As the cell lifted, the toll the match took on both men was clear. Michaels helped Undertaker to his feet, and the two men embraced. HBK then turned to his fallen friend, Triple H. After celebrating his win with a fireworks display, The Deadman also walked over to Triple H, and he and Michaels helped The Game to his feet and up the entrance ramp. When they reached the stage, the three man paused to appreciate the crowd's ovation and then embraced before heading backstage. Undertaker continued his *WrestleMania* winning streak until *WrestleMania 30* when Brock Lesnar put an end to it.

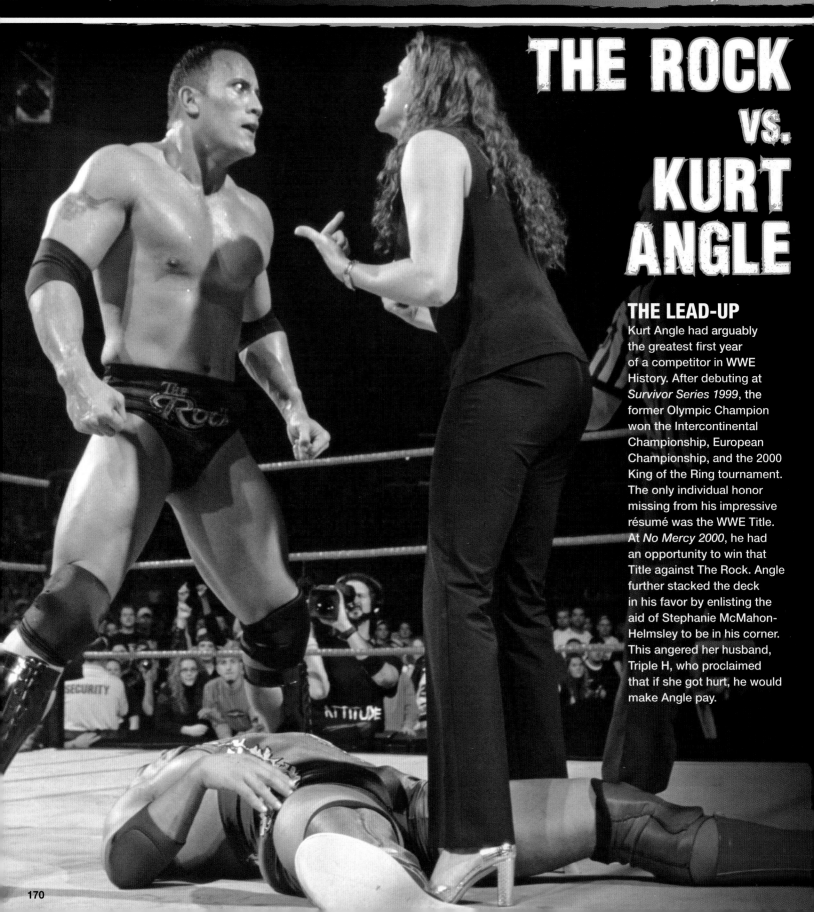

THE ROCK VS. KURT ANGLE

THE LEAD-UP

Kurt Angle had arguably the greatest first year of a competitor in WWE History. After debuting at *Survivor Series 1999*, the former Olympic Champion won the Intercontinental Championship, European Championship, and the 2000 King of the Ring tournament. The only individual honor missing from his impressive résumé was the WWE Title. At *No Mercy 2000*, he had an opportunity to win that Title against The Rock. Angle further stacked the deck in his favor by enlisting the aid of Stephanie McMahon-Helmsley to be in his corner. This angered her husband, Triple H, who proclaimed that if she got hurt, he would make Angle pay.

THE MATCH

As the ring announcer disclosed the stipulations of the match, the television announcers were surprised to learn that the bout was now a No Disqualification Match. The change to the match would pay immediate dividends to Angle's side, as Stephanie interfered in the match, distracting The Rock and allowing Angle to gain an early advantage. The Olympic Hero struck the Champion repeatedly in the ring and outside of it. Back in the ring, The Rock gained the offensive advantage with a clothesline and a Samoan Drop. Angle rolled out of the ring and headed up the ramp, looking for a breather.

The Rock followed the challenger out of the ring, and started pounding Angle up and around the entrance stage. The Champion slammed Angle in the tech area and into a guardrail and then threw him into the public staging. Angle fought back, tossing the People's Champion into a pile of equipment, but The Rock furthered Angle's indignity by punching the challenger through a cardboard standee of the Champion. Angle made his way back to the ring and distracted the official, allowing Stephanie to choke The Rock with the ring ropes. Getting frustrated, The Rock hit Angle's ankle with two shots and put a limping Olympic Hero in the Sharpshooter. Angle tapped out, but Stephanie occupied the official and he missed the submission. A frustrated Rock confronted Stephanie and chased her around the ring, but that gave Angle time to recover and he nailed the Champion with an overhead belly-to-belly suplex.

Stephanie tried to further help her business associate by dropping the WWE Title in the ring and then again distracting the official. Although Angle first missed hitting The Rock with the Title, he connected on his second attempt and managed a two-count. Angle tried to go to the top turnbuckle, but the Champion Superplexed Angle. The challenger kicked out at two. Angle suplexed Rock and attempted a moonsault, but the People's Champion rolled out of the way. The Rock gave Angle a Spinebuster, and was set to deliver the People's Elbow, but Stephanie interfered once again and got a Rock Bottom for her trouble. This led to Triple H entering the match, where he knocked down Angle, gave Rock a Pedigree, and took his wife to the back. Angle tried to pin The Rock, but the Champion kicked out at two.

Rikishi joined the fray, coming out and attacking Kurt Angle. Rikishi attempted to splash Angle in the corner, but Angle pulled The Rock in front of him, and the Champion absorbed the brunt of the blow. A frustrated Rikishi, looking to help Rock again, tried to kick Angle, but he ducked and the kick connected with the People's Champion again. Angle then gave Angle Slams to both Rikishi and The Rock, allowing him to pin The Rock and win the WWE Championship.

THE AFTERMATH

Kurt Angle's reign as WWE Champion lasted four months, and highlights included defeating Undertaker at *Survivor Series*, Triple H at the *Royal Rumble*, and five other men in a Hell in a Cell Match at *Armageddon*. He finally lost the Title at *No Way Out* when he had a rematch with The Rock. Before regaining the Title, the People's Champion had some business to settle with Rikishi, and he defeated the oversized Superstar at *Survivor Series*.

CHARLOTTE VS. BAYLEY VS. BECKY LYNCH VS. SASHA BANKS

THE LEAD-UP

After the inaugural NXT Women's Champion, Paige, was stripped of her Title due to her winning the WWE Diva's Championship, NXT set up an 8-woman tournament to crown a new Champion. Charlotte made it through the brackets to become the second NXT Champion in history, but she had no shortage of rivals. Sasha Banks, Becky Lynch, and Bayley all expressed a desire to win the Title and all three legitimized their claims through exciting in-ring victories. To settle matters, NXT General Manager William Regal decided that Charlotte would defend her Title in a Fatal 4-Way Match against her three strongest rivals.

NXT TAKEOVER: RIVAL
FATAL 4-WAY MATCH FOR THE NXT WOMEN'S CHAMPIONSHIP

February 11, 2015

Full Sail University
Winter Park, Florida

THE MATCH

From the opening bell, Charlotte was the target of all three of her challengers, with the trio of Divas punching and kicking the Champion. Charlotte knocked Banks and Lynch out of the ring, but while she was focused on them, Bayley rolled her up for a one-count. Banks then pulled the Champion out of the ring and she and Lynch tossed Charlotte into the LED board on the ring skirt, taking her out. It was clear that Becky and Sasha had formed an alliance, at least temporarily, and the duo reentered the ring and double-teamed Bayley. Bayley fought back, but then the pair rocked Bayley back and forth before tossing her into the turnbuckles.

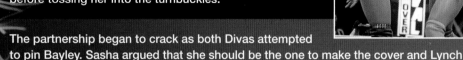

The partnership began to crack as both Divas attempted to pin Bayley. Sasha argued that she should be the one to make the cover and Lynch seemed to agree. But when Sasha turned her back on Lynch, Becky tossed her over with a pump-handle suplex. Becky landed a trio of leg drops on Bayley, managing to get a near fall. Lynch targeted Bayley's knee with a submission move, but Sasha returned to the ring to break it up. Banks worked Lynch over with a series of shoulder blocks, but when she went for the double knee drop, Lynch dodged it and nailed Banks with a missile dropkick. Lynch's pinfall attempt was halted by Charlotte, who then dropped Sasha with a neckbreaker, but Becky broke up that pin.

Banks had Charlotte draped across the second rope for a double knee, but Becky tried to break it up. Instead, Banks put her across the bottom rope and hit the double knee on both women. However, each kicked out of Sasha's pinfall attempt. Bayley snuck up on Sasha and suplexed her out of the ring. Bayley then focused on Charlotte, hitting her with several back elbows, a Bayleycanranna, and a Bayley-to-Belly Suplex on the Champion. She almost had a three-count, but Becky pulled her off the Champ and out of the ring. Bayley and Becky clashed outside of the ring. Sasha hit both of them with a suicide dive through the second and top ropes and then Charlotte leapt out of the ring onto all three challengers.

Charlotte grabbed Becky and rolled her back into the ring to focus on one challenger. But Becky surprised the Champion with a knee to the midsection and a wicked suplex. Charlotte managed to kick out of the pinfall attempt at two. Lynch put the Champion on the top turnbuckle, but before she could execute a move, she was interrupted by first Sasha, then Bayley. Bayley tossed Becky out of the ring and hit a second-rope Bayley-to-Belly Suplex, but Banks broke up the pinfall attempt and tried to pin Charlotte herself unsuccessfully. Banks twisted Charlotte's back with a crossface submission move and then flipped the Champ over to gain the three-count pinfall, becoming the new NXT Women's Champion.

THE AFTERMATH

Banks defeated Charlotte in a rematch for the Title the following month and faced other Divas, including Alexa Bliss and Becky Lynch. She also granted Charlotte another title opportunity, but retained the Championship once again. Meanwhile, Bayley become the #1 contender and defended that position until *NXT TakeOver: Brooklyn*, NXT's biggest event to date. More than 13,000 fans packed the Barclay's Center the night before *SummerSlam* to see Bayley defeat Sasha. Bayley and Sasha then became the first women to compete in an Iron Man Match, a bout won by Bayley, three falls to two. Sasha's reign as the third NXT Women's Champion lasted just over six months, and she then joined the WWE roster.

JEFF HARDY
vs. CM PUNK

THE LEAD-UP

Jeff Hardy had finally reached the top of his profession, only to see CM Punk snatch it away in a moment. Hardy defeated longtime nemesis Edge in a Ladder Match for the World Heavyweight Championship at *Extreme Rules 2009*, but Punk cashed in his Money in the Bank Championship Contract directly after the match and defeated Hardy. The two battled over the summer, with Hardy reclaiming the Title at *Night of Champions*. To truly settle the bitter rivalry, a Tables, Ladders, and Chairs Match for the Championship was set for *SummerSlam*.

SUMMERSLAM 2009
TABLES, LADDERS, AND CHAIRS MATCH FOR THE WORLD HEAVYWEIGHT CHAMPIONSHIP

August 23, 2009

Staples Center
Los Angeles, California

THE MATCH

Hardy seemed to have an advantage heading into the match, as he had participated in numerous TLC Matches throughout his career, while this would be Punk's first. Perhaps to negate the Champion's advantage, the Straight Edge Superstar began the match aggressively, knocking Hardy out of the ring and then hitting him with a foreign object. Thinking he had incapacitated Hardy, Punk brought a ladder into the ring and began to climb. Hardy recovered, however, and knocked Punk off the ladder. The challenger blocked Hardy's attempted Twist of Fate, and Hardy countered an early Go To Sleep by Punk. This made it clear that both men had work to do before climbing the ladder and retrieving the Title would be possible.

Punk continued his extreme streak, launching a Suicide Dive from the ring to Hardy on the floor below. The challenger then tried to permanently maim Hardy by slamming him into the ring post with a foreign object over Hardy's face, but Hardy fought back and avoided disaster. Still outside the ring, Hardy set Punk up on a table and leapt from the top rope, but the challenger rolled away, sending Hardy crashing through the table by himself.

Punk continued his extreme offense, Superplexing the Champion onto a ladder in the ring. The move did not leave Punk unscathed either. Hardy demonstrated his incredible resolve by blocking an additional suplex and countering the move into a Twist of Fate. He tried to follow with a Swanton Bomb, but Punk lifted his knees to injure Hardy. Punk hit a running knee, but then Hardy dropped Punk out of the ring and through a table. Hardy tried to climb the ladder once again, but Punk leapt from the top turnbuckle to hit Hardy with a double axe-handle. Both men then rolled out of the ring once more.

Hardy almost ended the match for both men when he executed one of the most incredible moves in WWE history. After again preventing Punk from tossing him into the ring post with a dangerous object wrapped around his neck, Hardy hit the Straight Edge Superstar with a television monitor. With Punk prone on the announcers' table, Hardy set up a large ladder and performed a Swanton Bomb off the ladder onto Punk and through the table. Both men seemed unconscious and medical personnel rushed to the scene, ready to take both men out on stretchers. However, Punk crawled into the ring and tried to climb the ladder, so Hardy denied medical attention and also began to climb the ladder. Both men got their hands on the Title, but Punk kicked Hardy in the ribs and knocked him off the ladder. Punk grabbed the Title and become the new World Heavyweight Champion.

After winning the Championship, CM Punk gloated over the prone body of Jeff Hardy. But the Straight Edge Superstar's night was not over. The lights dimmed, and the familiar notes of Undertaker's music filled the arena. When the lights returned, Punk frantically looked to the entrance ramp for The Deadman. He should have looked down, as Undertaker had taken the place of Hardy and reached up and Chokeslammed the new Champion. After the TLC Match, CM Punk and Jeff Hardy had one last bout. The following *SmackDown*, Jeff Hardy got his rematch in a Steel Cage Match for the Title in which the loser would have to leave WWE. Punk retained the Title and, in his mind, rid the WWE of Jeff Hardy's bad influence.

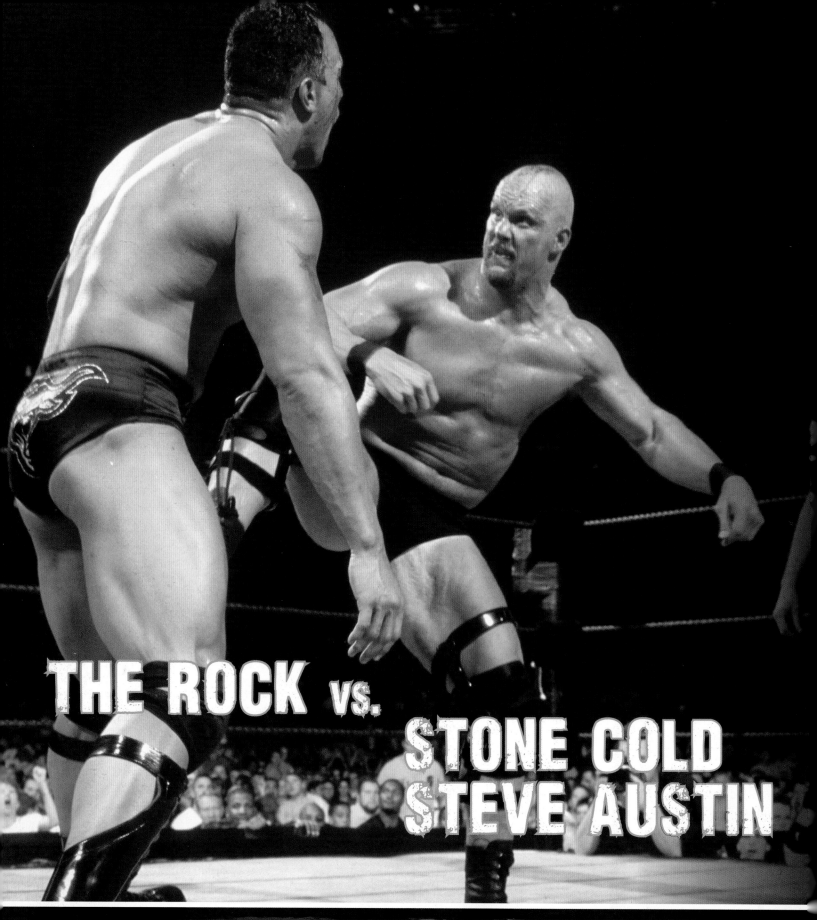

THE ROCK vs. STONE COLD STEVE AUSTIN

WRESTLEMANIA X-SEVEN
NO DISQUALIFICATION MATCH FOR THE WWE CHAMPIONSHIP

April 1, 2001
Reliant Astrodome
Houston, Texas

THE LEAD-UP

The Rock and Stone Cold Steve Austin helped define an entire era in WWE. The WWE Universe loved seeing both Superstars in action, but when they faced each other, the atmosphere was absolutely electric. The two fought for the WWE Championship for the first time at *WrestleMania XV*, and two years later, thanks to Austin's *Royal Rumble* win and The Rock taking the Championship from Kurt Angle, they were ready for a Main Event rematch. For both men, they had to win in order to define their legacy—Stone Cold needed to regain the Championship, while The Rock had to avenge his loss two years earlier.

THE MATCH

Austin wasted no time, attacking The Rock while he was posing for his fans. Attempting to take early advantage of the no disqualification rule, Austin tried to hit The Rock with the WWE Championship. The Rock ducked the move and got some punches in of his own. Both men tried to hit their signature moves early, but Austin blocked a Rock Bottom, and The Rock stopped a Stone Cold Stunner. The competitors soon started brawling outside the ring, both on the announcers' table and in the crowd.

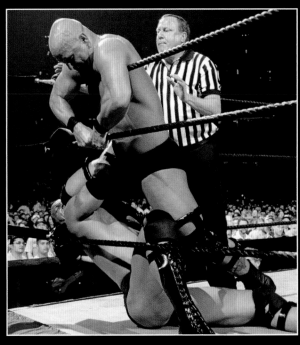

Outside the ring, Austin hit The Rock with the ring bell, causing the Champion to bleed from his forehead. Austin targeted the cut with repeated strikes looking to exploit the wound, even utilizing the ring steps and the announcers' table. Austin was in complete control until The Rock stunned the challenger with a wicked clothesline from the corner. The Rock then grabbed the ring bell and returned the favor to Austin, causing the challenger to bleed as much as the Champion. Both Superstars tried to get their opponents to submit with Sharpshooters, but each was able to reach the ring ropes and force a break.

The Rock hit a Stone Cold Stunner on Austin but didn't immediately cover, so the Texas Rattlesnake kicked out at the two-count. Then, to everyone's surprise, Mr. McMahon appeared and made his way to the ring. The announcers speculated why he was there—but his reasons would become apparent soon enough. The Rock performed a Spinebuster and People's Elbow on Austin, but before he could get the pinfall, Mr. McMahon pulled him off the Bionic Redneck. Austin then ordered Mr. McMahon to bring a foreign object into the ring and hit The Rock with it. But The Rock would not stay down. He fought back and caught Austin with a Stone Cold Stunner. Mr. McMahon distracted the official so he could not make the three-count.

At this point, Austin began taking full advantage of the no disqualification stipulation. He delivered a low blow to The Rock, followed by a Rock Bottom and another shot with a foreign object. Each time, The Rock was able to kick out before the three-count. The Rock's tenacity enraged the Texas Rattlesnake, so he wailed on The Rock repeatedly as Mr. McMahon looked on with approval, finally keeping the Champion down for a three-count. A stunned crowd sat in disbelief as the new Champion and Mr. McMahon celebrated over the prone Great One—the WWE world flipped upside down at the sight of Austin and the Chairman (his longtime archrival) on the same page.

THE AFTERMATH

The Rock would get his rematch the following night on *Raw* in a Steel Cage Match, but Stone Cold retained the Title when he revealed a second alliance besides Mr. McMahon. Austin teamed with former rival Triple H to form Two-Man Power Trip. Not only did The Rock lose the match, but Mr. McMahon then suspended The People's Champion, keeping him on the shelf for months before he finally returned to help WWE in its war with the WCW/ECW Alliance. Stone Cold and The Rock would meet at one more *WrestleMania*. At *WrestleMania XIX*, The Rock finally defeated his nemesis at the Showcase of the Immortals. It was Austin's last match to date.

MR. PERFECT vs. BRET "HIT MAN" HART

SUMMERSLAM 1991
INTERCONTINENTAL CHAMPIONSHIP MATCH

August 26, 1991
Madison Square Garden
New York, New York

THE LEAD UP

Mr. Perfect, the self-described "Greatest Intercontinental Champion in History" was in the midst of his second reign with the Title, having held it since November 1990. Entering 1991's *SummerSlam* event, Perfection was going to have to face Excellence, as Mr. Perfect's opponent was Bret "Hit Man" Hart, "The Excellence of Execution." For years the WWE Universe knew Hart as a tag-team specialist. Hart and Jim "The Anvil" Neidhart made up the Hart Foundation and the two had twice held the World Tag Team Championship. But the Hit Man decided to pursue singles competition and this was his first opportunity at a Championship.

THE MATCH

Perfect looked to take an early advantage, whipping Hart into the ropes. However, the Hit Man knocked Perfect down with a well-timed shoulder block and then hip tossed Mr. Perfect out of the ring. The Champion collected himself and then reentered the ring, only to almost be pinned by a Hart crucifix. Hart gained two additional near falls with a high-cross body and a sunset flip. Hart scoop slammed the Champion, but Perfect kicked the Hit Man away before he could follow up the move. Perfect had enough, and he and his manager The Coach decided to leave and accept a countout loss, but Hart dragged the Champion back into the ring.

The two men locked up in the corner of the ring, and while the official tried to separate the two, Perfect used the distraction to punch the Hit Man in the jaw. The Champion kicked the downed Hit Man twice in the ribs, with the second kick causing the Hit Man to roll out of the ring. Perfect followed Hart out of the ring and blistered the challenger's chest with a reverse knife-edge chop. Twice Hart tried to re-enter the ring, but both times Perfect knocked Hart off the apron, with the second attack sending Hart crashing into a guardrail. Hart finally returned to the ring and landed a series of punches on the Champion, but Perfect viciously tossed the challenger into the turnbuckles, a move that dropped the Hit Man to the mat.

Perfect looked to finish Hart off with a snap neckbreaker and a pinfall attempt that garnered a two-count. He knocked Hart out of the ring again with a dropkick. Back in the ring, Perfect tried to take Hart out with a Sleeper Hold, but the Hit Man elbowed the Champion repeatedly until he broke the hold. Hart attempted a second crucifix pinning combination, but Perfect was ready for this one, and he fell back and slammed Hart to the mat. Perfect chopped Hart some more and then tossed the Hit Man chest-first into the turnbuckles. The challenger was barely able to kick out of the pinning attempt. Perfect tried to end the match with his signature move, the Perfectplex, but Hart kicked out at two.

A clearly frustrated Perfect looked to dish more punishment to his challenger, but the Hit Man landed a few blows to the midsection and stunned the Champion with an Inverted Atomic Drop. Hart tossed Perfect from one corner to another, and then executed a textbook suplex for another two-count. Hart then attempted a small package, but the Champion kicked out at two, just like he did after Hart's neckbreaker move. Hart chained a backbreaker and a knee off the top rope, but again Perfect kicked out. Perfect looked to drop a leg into Hart's midsection, but the Hit Man grabbed the Champion's leg and rolled over into a Sharpshooter. Perfect submitted, and the Hit Man was the new Intercontinental Champion.

THE AFTERMATH

Mr. Perfect did not compete in the ring again for more than a year, although the WWE Universe continued to see him as he served as the Executive Consultant for "Nature Boy" Ric Flair, once he entered WWE. Perfect made his in-ring return at *Survivor Series 1992*, facing his former client Flair in a Tag Team Match. For Hart, the Championship was just a small taste of what was to come. Hart held the Intercontinental Championship twice, and he reached the summit of sports-entertainment when he won the WWE Championship, a Title he held on five occasions.

BROCK LESNAR vs. JOHN CENA vs. SETH ROLLINS

THE LEAD-UP

In 2014, Brock Lesnar captured the WWE World Heavyweight Championship from John Cena at *SummerSlam*. Lesnar's dominant performance included more than a dozen German Suplexes and a pair of F-5 moves. Cena showed his resiliency by winning the right to challenge Lesnar for the Title at the 2015 *Royal Rumble*. However, the match would not stay a one-on-one. After John Cena's team deposed The Authority from their position of power at the 2014 *Survivor Series*, Rollins manipulated Cena into putting them back in power. As a reward, Triple H put Rollins into the championship match at the *Royal Rumble*, making it a Triple Threat Match. Rollins had a further ace in the hole, as he was the reigning Money in the Bank winner, meaning he could cash in his Title opportunity at any time, even at the Rumble.

2015 ROYAL RUMBLE

TRIPLE THREAT MATCH FOR THE WWE WORLD HEAVYWEIGHT CHAMPIONSHIP

January 25, 2015

Wells Fargo Center
Philadelphia, Pennsylvania

THE MATCH

When the match started, Rollins hightailed it out of the ring, leading Lesnar to deliver one of his patented German Suplexes to John Cena. Lesnar hit Cena with a second one and Rollins tried to use the distraction to attack the Champion. The plan did not work and J&J Security needed to save Rollins. They paid for their interference, as Lesnar gave both men a suplex at the same time. Lesnar then proceeded to work on both of his challengers.

After a variety of suplexes, Lesnar put Cena in the Kimura Lock, a move that had broken the arms of numerous Superstars in the past, including the arm of Triple H. Cena once again demonstrated his incredible strength by standing up with Lesnar still holding onto the move. This gave Rollins an opportunity to launch some offense as he leapt off the top turnbuckle and hit both men in the head, knocking them down. Rollins then attacked the Champion with some kicks and punches, and briefly Cena and Rollins worked together to take out Lesnar. The two left Lesnar down outside the ring and battled each other. Cena thought he had the match won, but Lesnar returned to the ring and grabbed Cena, delivering another German Suplex.

Cena hit the Champion with three consecutive Attitude Adjustments, and then went for the certain pinfall victory. But Rollins interrupted the count and dumped Cena outside the ring. Rollins then delivered a Curb Stomp on Lesnar and tried to pin the Champ. This time Cena interrupted the count and all three men were down. Lesnar left the ring in order to gather himself, but Cena followed and threw the Champion into the stairs. With Lesnar sprawled on the Spanish announcers' table, Rollins flew off the top turnbuckle and crashed onto Lesnar, collapsing the table. As medical personnel attended to Lesnar at ringside, it seemed like he was out of the match.

Rollins and Cena continued to fight in what had effectively become a one-on-one contest. The match went back and forth, although Cena almost had the win when he locked Rollins in the STF. J&J security saved Rollins from submitting, but the two received an Attitude Adjustment from Cena, as did Rollins. The Money in the Bank winner barely kicked out of the pin attempt after the move. Rollins gave Cena a Curb Stomp and hit him with a corkscrew move off the top rope. He then went for the pin, but Lesnar returned to the ring and suplexed both men. Rollins then hit Lesnar twice with his Money in the Bank suitcase, and set the Champion up to Curb Stomp his head on the briefcase. But Lesnar caught Rollins and delivered an F-5 for the pinfall victory.

By retaining his Championship, Lesnar was set to defend the Title in the main event at *WrestleMania*. His opponent was determined later in the Royal Rumble Match, when Roman Reigns won and earned a Title shot at *WrestleMania*. Lesnar and Reigns hammered each other for more than 15 minutes before Rollins emerged with his Money in the Bank briefcase, turning the match into a Triple Threat Match. Rollins delivered Curb Stomps to both Lesnar and Reigns, and then pinned Reigns, shocking Levi's Stadium and the WWE Universe. Seth Rollins had become the Champion without even pinning Brock Lesnar.

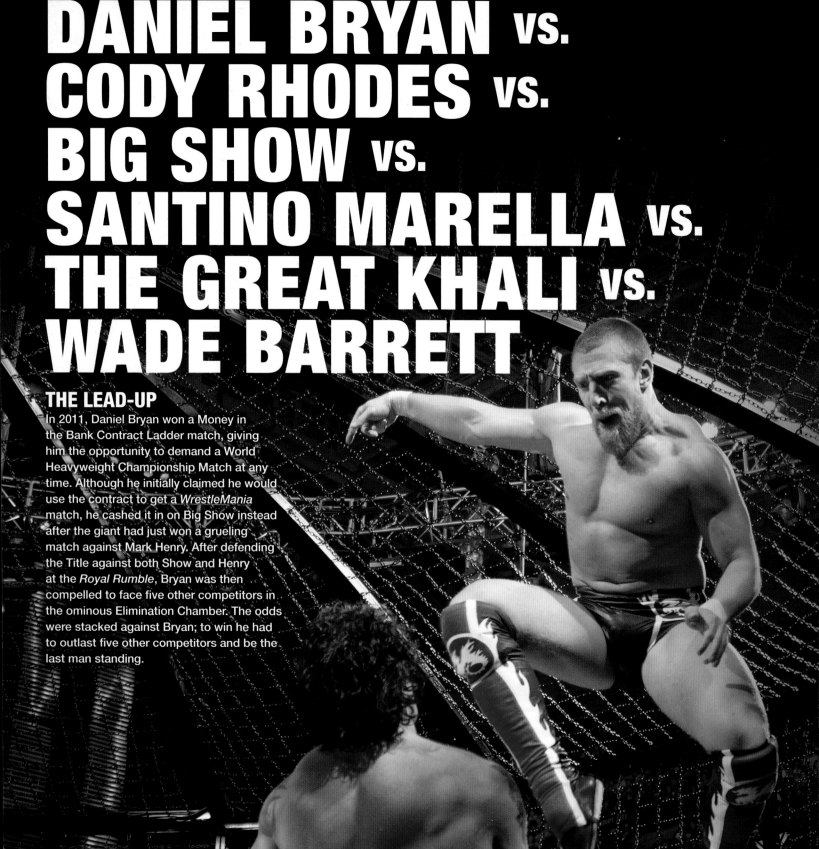

DANIEL BRYAN vs. CODY RHODES vs. BIG SHOW vs. SANTINO MARELLA vs. THE GREAT KHALI vs. WADE BARRETT

THE LEAD-UP

In 2011, Daniel Bryan won a Money in the Bank Contract Ladder match, giving him the opportunity to demand a World Heavyweight Championship Match at any time. Although he initially claimed he would use the contract to get a *WrestleMania* match, he cashed it in on Big Show instead after the giant had just won a grueling match against Mark Henry. After defending the Title against both Show and Henry at the *Royal Rumble*, Bryan was then compelled to face five other competitors in the ominous Elimination Chamber. The odds were stacked against Bryan; to win he had to outlast five other competitors and be the last man standing.

ELIMINATION CHAMBER MATCH

WWE ELIMINATION CHAMBER 2012

February 19, 2012

**Bradley Center
Milwaukee, Wisconsin**

THE MATCH

The first two men to start the match were Wade Barrett and Big Show. The two men exchanged moves with Show's power giving him the early advantage. Barrett finally took out Show's knee to chop the giant to the ground, and Barrett kept him down with a series of punches and kicks. Barrett focused his offense on Show's knee, trying to sap the giant's power. Show regained the advantage at the five-minute mark, and the third participant in the match, Cody Rhodes, entered the match.

Big Show continued to dominate, alternating his attention between Barrett and Rhodes. After launching Rhodes into the wall of the chamber like a dart, he tried to Chokeslam Barrett, but Barrett took out Show's knee again to get the giant off his feet. It briefly seemed like Rhodes and Barrett would work together, but Barrett instead turned on Rhodes and tossed Cody into the chamber wall repeatedly. Santino Marella soon entered as the fourth competitor. Marella got some offense on Barrett, but then Big Show grabbed Santino and tossed him around like a rag doll.

Show took over the match once again, but he made the mistake of trying to Chokeslam both Barrett and Rhodes at the same time. Instead, the two countered and delivered a double suplex to Show on the steel floor outside the ring. The fifth man to enter the ring, Great Khali, overwhelmed Rhodes, Barrett, and Santino, but the Punjabi Playboy found himself on the receiving end of a spear from Big Show, who pinned Khali, making him the first man eliminated. Big Show then decided he didn't want to wait for Bryan to enter the match, so he broke the chains on the top of the pod and entered Bryan's locked pod. Show choked Bryan until the Champion escaped the pod, although Show then tossed Bryan through the pod.

Show dominated Bryan until Wade Barrett took out Show's legs a third time. Rhodes landed two disaster kicks on the giant as well as a DDT. Barrett dropped a top-rope elbow on Show, and then Rhodes pinned him, making him the second man eliminated from the match. Before Rhodes could celebrate too much, Santino snuck up on Cody and rolled him up for a three-count. Barrett took over the match, knocking Santino and Bryan into the chamber walls. By focusing on Santino, however, Barrett lost track of Bryan, who launched a top-rope knee into Barrett. Bryan hit Barrett with a headbutt off the top rope and Marella pinned Barrett, leaving Santino and Bryan as the final two competitors. Bryan buffeted Santino with a series of wicked kicks, but he managed to kick out at two, and hit Bryan with a Cobra that got him a two-count. Bryan finally locked in the LaBell Lock and Santino had no choice but to submit, allowing Bryan to retain the World Heavyweight Championship.

THE AFTERMATH

Bryan continued to hold the Championship until *WrestleMania XXVIII*, where he had to face *Royal Rumble* winner Sheamus. Accompanied to the ring by his girlfriend AJ Lee, Bryan and Lee shared a kiss on the apron. Bryan should have been more focused on his opponent and less on his woman, as the Champion turned around right into a Brogue Kick from Sheamus, and the Celtic Warrior pinned Bryan in just 18 seconds to become the new World Heavyweight Champion. Bryan's LaBell Lock was later renamed the "Yes!" Lock, after Bryan's world-famous catch phrase.

UNDERTAKER VS.

SHAWN MICHAELS

IN YOUR HOUSE: BADD BLOOD

HELL IN A CELL

October 5, 1997

Kiel Center
St. Louis, Missouri

THE LEAD-UP

When Shawn Michaels served as the Special Guest Referee for Undertaker's WWE Title Match against Bret "Hit Man" Hart, most assumed he would cost Hit Man the match. However, an errant attempt at interference by HBK hit the Champion Undertaker instead of its intended target. Michaels effectively delivered the WWE Championship to his most hated rival. Undertaker looked to get his hands on Michaels for a measure of revenge, but with DX getting involved, a regular match would not do. Instead, WWE designed a new demonic structure that surrounded the ring and included a roof. Interference would be impossible once the two men were locked inside Hell in a Cell.

THE MATCH

As the cell lowered from the ceiling, with Michaels on the inside and his D-Generation X compatriots on the outside, the gravity of the situation became clear to the Heartbreak Kid. Undertaker quickly made his evil intentions clear. He deliberately stalked Michaels in and around the ring, knowing Michaels had nowhere to escape. Undertaker repeatedly used the cell to his advantage, throwing Michaels into the walls.

Michaels would also get in some offense, most notably when he delivered Undertaker onto the steel steps with a piledriver. With Undertaker on the floor outside the ring, Michaels followed with a double axe-handle from the top turnbuckle. He also introduced some steel of his own into the match, twice-hitting The Deadman on the back.

On several occasions during the match, Michaels found cameramen in his way. The third time occurred when Undertaker tossed the Heartbreak Kid out of the ring and onto a cameraman. Out of frustration, Michaels attacked the cameraman, beating him so savagely that other ringside officials called for someone to help the downed technician.

With the door opened so officials could assist the injured cameraman, the battle between Undertaker and Michaels spilled outside the cell. Twice Undertaker launched Michaels headfirst into the side of the cell. The Heartbreak Kid knew he had to get away from The Deadman, so he climbed the side of the cell to reach the roof. To Michaels' surprise, Undertaker followed him and slammed Michaels onto the top of the cell. Michaels realized his decision was not a wise one, so he started to climb down the cell, but Undertaker caught him and tossed him through the Spanish announcers' table.

With both men back in the cell, Undertaker looked to finish off the Heartbreak Kid. He executed a painful Chokeslam off the top turnbuckle and delivered his signature throat-slashing gesture, indicating to the arena that the Tombstone Piledriver was next. Suddenly, the lights went out in the arena and some eerie music began to play. When the lights came back on, Paul Bearer was making his way down the aisle, accompanied by a large masked man in red and black. The announcers speculated that after months of promising to deliver Undertaker's brother, the WWE Universe was getting its first look at Kane! The Big Red Monster made quite a first impression, ripping the cell door off its hinges and standing face to face with The Deadman. Distracted by Kane's pyrotechnics, Undertaker was then hit in the gut by his brother and subjected to a Tombstone Piledriver. Kane and Paul Bearer left the cell, but Michaels had enough ring presence to crawl to Undertaker and drape an arm across him, stealing a pinfall victory.

THE AFTERMATH

The win allowed Shawn Michaels to earn a shot at the WWE Championship at the following month's *Survivor Series*. There he faced his longtime nemesis Bret "Hit Man" Hart in what will forever be known as the "Montreal Screwjob." Undertaker got another crack at the Heartbreak Kid at the 1998 *Royal Rumble*, when he challenged Michaels for the WWE Championship in a Casket Match. Once again, Shawn Michaels defeated Undertaker, largely due to the outside interference of Undertaker's brother Kane. After initially refusing to fight him, Undertaker agreed to battle his brother at *WrestleMania XIV*, the same event where Michaels would lose the WWE Championship to Stone Cold Steve Austin.

THE TWO-MAN POWER TRIP vs. THE BROTHERS OF DESTRUCTION

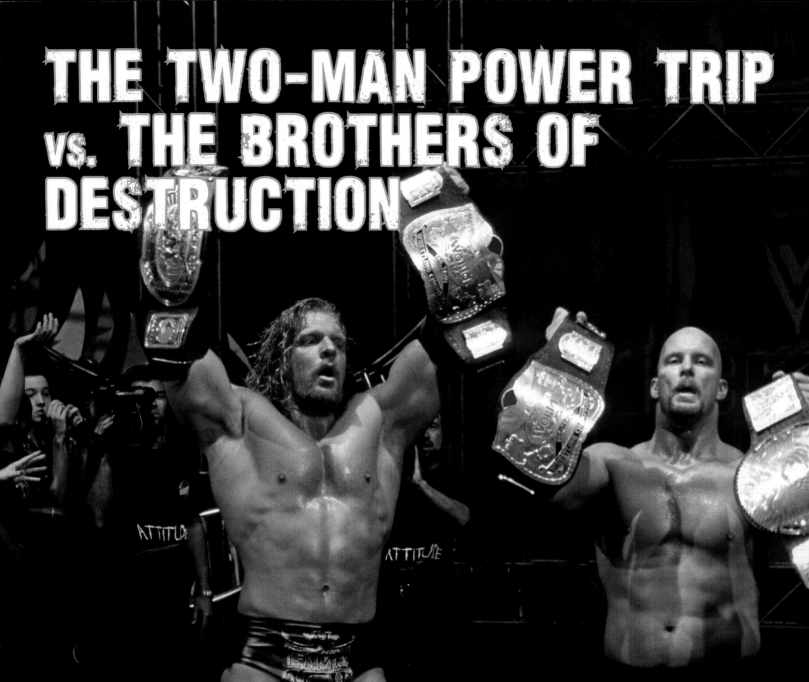

BACKLASH 2001

WINNER TAKE ALL MATCH FOR THE WWE CHAMPIONSHIP, INTERCONTINENTAL CHAMPIONSHIP, AND WWE TAG TEAM CHAMPIONSHIP

April 29, 2001

Allstate Arena
Chicago, Illinois

THE LEAD-UP

The WWE Universe thought they'd seen it all when Stone Cold Steve Austin turned his back on the fans and aligned himself with longtime nemesis, Mr. McMahon. But their shock deepened when The Texas Rattlesnake also partnered with another former rival, Triple H. As Stone Cold held the WWE Championship and Triple H was the Intercontinental Champion, the Two-Man Power Trip held dominion over WWE, and flaunted their position by decimating Superstars, Divas, Announcers, and anyone else that got in their way. Kane and Undertaker, the WWE Tag Team Champions, decided to stand up to the duo, and a unique match was set for *Backlash* in which all the Championships were on the line.

THE MATCH

Once Kane and Undertaker entered the ring, Austin and Triple H bailed and were reluctant to reenter. The two gathered themselves on the stage and Triple H was knocked back out of the ring the first time he tried to enter. Again, the two retreated up toward the stage, but this time the Brothers followed them and began assaulting both men. Kane and Undertaker dragged the two back to the ring, with Undertaker punching Austin while Kane and Triple H squared off. Kane nursed his left elbow, which had been injured by the Two-Man Power Trip a few weeks earlier. But the Big Red Monster demonstrated his willingness to fight through the pain by delivering devastating elevated Chokeslams to his two competitors.

Triple H finally managed to stem Kane's momentum, and Austin prepared to enter the match. But Kane tagged in his brother and Undertaker beat the WWE Champion from pillar to post. Triple H tried to illegally enter the ring and help Austin, but Undertaker beat on him as well. Austin tried to stop the violence by offering The Deadman a handshake, but Undertaker chose to level the WWE Champion with a kick instead, before hitting both Austin and Triple H with his Old School move.

Triple H and Austin isolated Undertaker in their corner and wore The Deadman down with double-team moves and effective quick tags. Undertaker finally managed to fight his way out of the corner, but he would not tag his brother in, apparently concerned about the injury to Kane's elbow. Kane finally decided to tag in himself and immediately caught both Austin and Triple H with kicks to their faces. He blasted Austin with a flying move off the top rope and slammed Triple H, but their superior numbers finally caught up to him. The Two-Man Power Trip focused their attacks on Kane's injured elbow, even slamming it with a foreign object when the official was distracted. Kane tried to reach his brother, but Austin and Triple H kept him from making it to the corner. The official was hit in the eye, so he missed Kane tagging in his brother and prevented Undertaker from pinning Triple H after performing a Last Ride. In the resulting chaos, all four men fought and Stephanie McMahon-Helmsley tried to get involved. She got a big boot to the face from Kane, which led to Mr. McMahon coming to the ring with a sledgehammer. The Chairman did not connect with the weapon, but Triple H did. He floored Kane to pin him and win the WWE Tag Team Championship for the Two-Man Power Trip.

At the next pay-per-view, Kane challenged Triple H for the Intercontinental Championship and Undertaker faced Stone Cold for the WWE Title. Kane pinned Triple H when Stone Cold's interference went wrong, but Undertaker fell short in his bid to capture the WWE Championship. Meanwhile, a new team emerged as challengers for the Two-Man Power Trip's Tag Team Championship—Chris Jericho and Chris Benoit. In the match for the Titles, the two defeated the Power Trip in a bout that saw Triple H tear his quad, an injury that put him on the shelf for more than half a year.

JOHN CENA VS. THE ROCK

THE LEAD-UP

Leading into *WrestleMania XXVII*, The Rock announced that he would be returning to WWE as special host of the event. The Great One then took verbal aim at John Cena, unhappy at some of the remarks Cena made about The Rock and his commitment to WWE. Tensions built until The Rock involved himself in Cena's main-event match at *WrestleMania XXVII*, costing John Cena the Title. The day after *WrestleMania XXVII*, Cena challenged The Rock to a match. They both agreed it should happen on the grandest stage, *WrestleMania XXVIII*. For one year, the WWE Universe eagerly anticipated this Once in a Lifetime Match.

WRESTLEMANIA XXVIII
ONCE IN A LIFETIME MATCH

April 1, 2012

**Sun Life Stadium
Miami, Florida**

THE MATCH

After acknowledging the fan's cheers, the two Superstars locked up in a test of strength, in which Cena caught The Rock off-guard by winning and tossing The Great One down. The two locked up again, and The Rock got the better of Cena. Cena may have expected some ring rust from The Rock, but The Great One surprised Cena and took early advantage, until Cena used some shoulder blocks and a clothesline to gain an offensive advantage.

Tossing The Rock outside the ring, Cena decided to focus on The Rock's ribs by dropping him over the guardrail and then on the announcers' table. Cena then attacked The Rock's midsection with kicks, a suplex, and a bear hug in order to further press his advantage. The Rock was finally able to get Cena to break the hold with a series of rights and a DDT. The Rock went for a People's Elbow, but Cena was able to counter with an attempted STF. Cena then delivered a Five Knuckle Shuffle, but The Rock was able to block an Attitude Adjustment.

The two Superstars traded power moves and The Rock seemed on his way to victory, even mocking Cena's "You Can't See Me" gesture. But Cena surprised The Rock with an Attitude Adjustment and a two-count. Cena may have been able to further press his advantage, but he spent too much time reacting to the crowd chants, which allowed The Rock to hit a Rock Bottom. However, Cena was able to kick out before the three-count. As both men saw the difficulty in keeping their opponent down, Cena went to the top rope for a high-risk leg drop, but, again, The Rock kicked out.

Cena decided to attempt a second Attitude Adjustment, but The Rock fought out of it and put Cena in the Sharpshooter. Cena was able to reach the rope and force a break. The Rock then put Cena in the Sharpshooter a second time. After that was unsuccessful in getting a submission, The Rock punished Cena outside the ring. But Cena is a resilient Superstar and he put Rock into the STF, almost gaining a submission. The Rock was finally able to then hit The People's Elbow on Cena, but the move would not deliver a three-count. Like Cena before him, The Rock decided to go for a high-risk move, but Cena rolled through the high-cross body and hit The Great One with another Attitude Adjustment. But Cena again could only get a two-count.

Cena decided to beat The Rock with his own move. Kicking at the Brahma Bull's shoulders, Cena looked to execute his own version of The People's Elbow. But after Cena crossed a prone Rock a second time, The Great One popped up and delivered a Rock Bottom, scoring the three-count and the victory.

THE AFTERMATH

The loss ate at John Cena, and it seemed like he'd never get a chance to even the score. But circumstances would bring the Superstars together the following year at *WrestleMania 29*. The Rock won the WWE Championship at the 2013 *Royal Rumble* and was set to defend the Title at *WrestleMania* against the #1 contender. John Cena earned the right to challenge the Champion of his choosing by winning the Royal Rumble Match, and he decided to face The Rock one more time. This time, Cena was able to overcome The Great One and win his eleventh WWE Championship in the process.

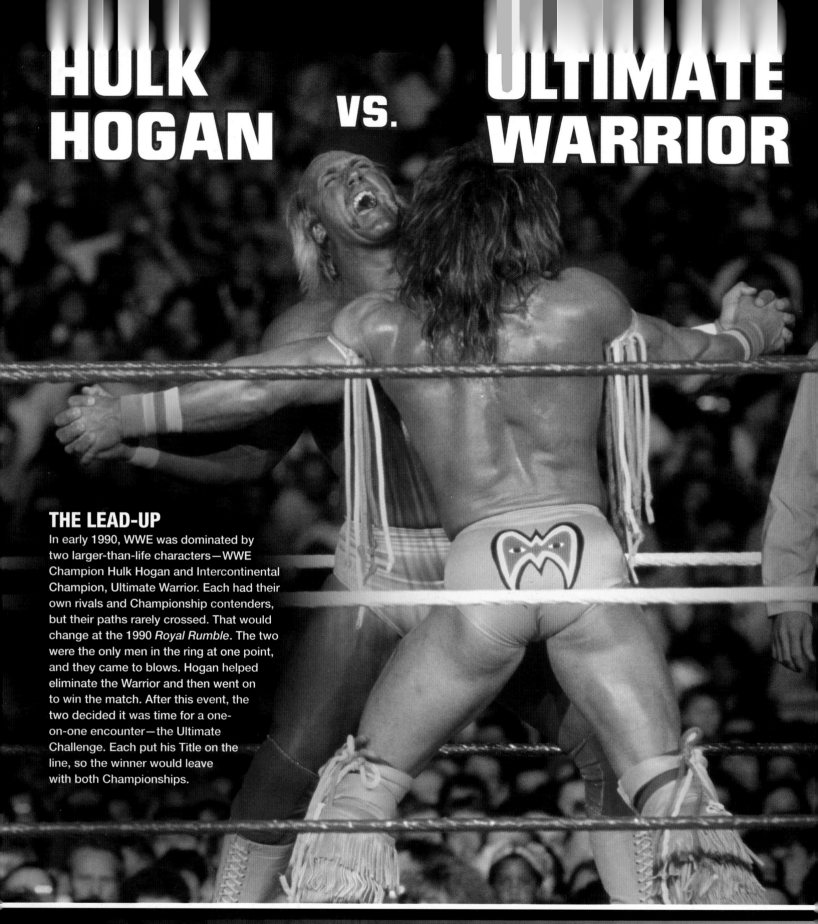

HULK HOGAN VS. ULTIMATE WARRIOR

THE LEAD-UP

In early 1990, WWE was dominated by two larger-than-life characters—WWE Champion Hulk Hogan and Intercontinental Champion, Ultimate Warrior. Each had their own rivals and Championship contenders, but their paths rarely crossed. That would change at the 1990 *Royal Rumble*. The two were the only men in the ring at one point, and they came to blows. Hogan helped eliminate the Warrior and then went on to win the match. After this event, the two decided it was time for a one-on-one encounter—the Ultimate Challenge. Each put his Title on the line, so the winner would leave with both Championships.

WRESTLEMANIA VI
TITLE VS. TITLE MATCH

April 1, 1990

SkyDome
Toronto, Ontario, Canada

THE MATCH

The SkyDome was packed, and it seemed like the audience allegiances were split almost equally down the middle. Each man appealed to the crowd during introductions, keeping a wary eye on his opponent. The two stood nose-to-nose during the official's match instructions. Then, Warrior surprised the Hulkster by giving him a shove, and Hogan returned the favor.

The two locked up for an extended show of strength. Warrior had the early advantage, forcing Hogan to his knees. But Hogan called on an impressive reservoir of strength and got back to his feet, forcing Warrior down. When Warrior started to make a comeback, Hogan knocked him to the mat, dropped an elbow on him, and attempted the first pinfall of the match. But Warrior could not be held down, and he was able to slam Hogan to the mat and then clothesline the Hulkster out of the ring onto the floor below. The fall seemed to injure Hogan's knee, as he was having trouble putting weight on one of his legs. Warrior knew he couldn't win the Title if Hogan was counted out, so he rolled Hulk back into the ring and began kicking Hogan's injured leg.

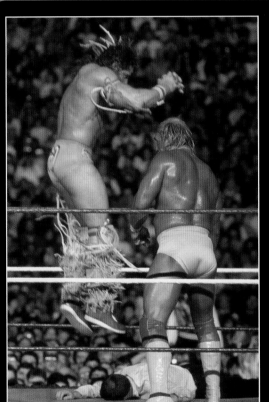

Luckily, Hogan's malady seemed short-lived. Hogan was soon able to walk on the leg and launch some offense at the Intercontinental Champion. Hogan made several attempts to pin Warrior, but Warrior kept kicking out before the three-count. Hogan then used a reverse chinlock to try and wear Warrior down. It seemed like it might be working, until Warrior hit Hogan in the chest with a few big elbows, breaking Hogan's hold. Then both Champions simultaneously clotheslined each other and crashed to the mat. When Warrior recovered, he went on the offensive—Hulk's blows seemed to have no effect on him, and he kept knocking Hogan down with clotheslines. Warrior then began squeezing the life out of Hogan with a crushing Bear Hug.

Hogan finally broke the Bear Hug, and in the aftermath Warrior accidentally knocked out the official. Hogan drove the Warrior into the mat, but there was no one to count the pinfall. Warrior then suplexed Hogan, but again no one was there to make the count. Once the official revived, each man got a near fall. Then, to the crowd's amazement, Ultimate Warrior Gorilla-Pressed Hulk. But it seemed like it was Hogan's match to win,

as he hit Warrior with the big boot to the face and was set to deliver the Leg Drop. At the last second, Warrior rolled out of the way, splashed Hogan, and covered him for the three-count. After the defeat, Hogan grabbed the WWE Championship and presented it to Warrior in an incredible show of sportsmanship.

Ultimate Warrior was required to surrender the Intercontinental Championship, as he was not allowed to hold both Championships. A tournament was held to crown a new Champion and Mr. Perfect won the Title. Ultimate Warrior held the WWE Championship for almost 10 months until he lost to Sgt. Slaughter at the 1991 *Royal Rumble*, thanks to the actions of "Macho King" Randy Savage. Hogan and Warrior would team together at *SummerSlam 1991*, but they would not face each other again in a one-on-one match until 1998 in WCW when Hogan would even their rivalry to one win each.

CM PUNK
VS.
CHRIS JERICHO

EXTREME RULES 2012
CHICAGO STREET FIGHT FOR THE WWE CHAMPIONSHIP

April 29, 2012

Allstate Arena
Rosemont, Illinois

THE LEAD-UP

In January 2012, Chris Jericho made a surprising return to WWE. He targeted CM Punk, feeling disrespected by the WWE Champion's claims of being "the best in the world." To settle matters, Jericho challenged Punk in a match for the WWE Championship at *WrestleMania XXVIII*. Punk won the match and retained the Title, but Jericho was not satisfied. He then tried to make his war with Punk personal, questioning the Champ's straight-edge lifestyle and mocking the life decisions Punk's family made. Punk agreed to face Jericho again, but this time it would be a Chicago Street Fight.

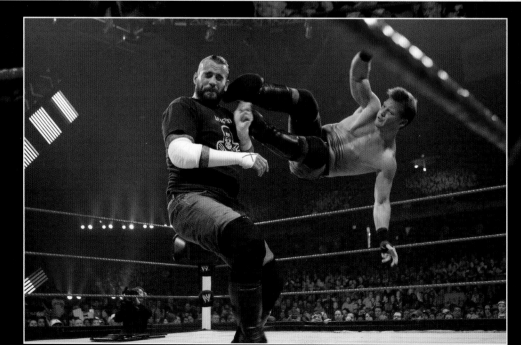

THE MATCH

While Jericho and Punk are two of the more skilled technical wrestlers of their generation, it was no surprise the match started as a brawl after all the things Jericho said about Punk and his family. The fight almost immediately spilled outside the ring and Punk tossed Jericho over a barricade. Punk then threw a few steel chairs into the ring and grabbed a kendo stick before joining Jericho back in the ring. With no disqualifications possible, Punk made liberal use of the kendo stick, hitting Jericho repeatedly on the back and midsection.

Jericho finally took control with an illegal thumb to Punk's eye. He then gave Punk some kendo stick shots of his own and tried to humiliate Punk by beating him up in front of Punk's sister. Jericho also taunted Punk's sister and she slapped him in the face. Jericho went to hit her, and that brazen act reenergized the Champion.

The two men battled back and forth, exchanging brutal moves and near falls. Jericho decided to press his psychological advantage by grabbing a can of beer from under the ring and pouring it on the downed champ. Jericho went for a second beer, but Punk rebounded and kicked Jericho in the gut, causing him to spit beer over the ring.

Jericho eventually locked Punk in The Walls of Jericho, and even though Punk reached the ring ropes, the rules of the match meant Jericho did not have to break the hold. It seemed like just a matter of time before Punk would have to tap out to the excruciating move, but, in an act of desperation, Punk grabbed a fire extinguisher from under the ring. He first blasted Jericho's face with the chemicals to break the hold, and then he used the canister as a weapon on his challenger. Once again, the battle spilled outside the ring and Jericho ended up lying across the Spanish announcers' table.

Punk shocked the crowd by leaping off the top turnbuckle onto a prone Jericho, breaking the Spanish announcers' table. Somehow Jericho managed to kick out of the pinfall, and then deliver a Codebreaker, enhanced with a foreign object. Jericho had one more indignity planned as he set up the Champion for a Go To Sleep, but Punk countered and sent Jericho into the exposed turnbuckle and his own Go To Sleep to pin Jericho and retain his Championship.

THE AFTERMATH

Punk continued to defend the WWE Championship, with Daniel Bryan becoming his next challenger. But Bryan would not be successful, and Punk wasn't even halfway through his historic Championship run. The Straight Edge Superstar would hold the Title for an incredible 434 days, the sixth-longest reign of all time, and the longest in more than 25 years. Finally, at the 2013 *Royal Rumble*, The Rock would defeat CM Punk, ending his lengthy Title reign. Jericho turned his sights on the World Heavyweight Championship, but he was unsuccessful in that pursuit.

BRET "HIT MAN" HART VS. THE BRITISH BULLDOG

THE LEAD-UP

Bret "Hit Man" Hart and "The British Bulldog" Davey Boy Smith had much in common. Each experienced significant success as members of Championship-winning tag teams in the 1980s. Hart teamed with Jim "the Anvil" Neidhart to form the Hart Foundation, two-time winners of the WWE's World Tag Team Championship. Smith and partner Dynamite Kid, a.k.a. The British Bulldogs, also reigned as WWE World Tag Team Champions. But each man had broken away from his respective team and was looking to make a mark as a singles competitor. Hart had already earned more gold as a two-time Intercontinental Champion, and Smith wanted his shot at the Title.

But a similar background was not the only thing Hart and Smith shared. Davey Boy married Bret's sister Diana, so the men were also brothers in law. Their family ties were sure to be strained when Smith was named the #1 contender for the Intercontinental Championship in a match that would serve as the main event of the first WWE pay-per-view held outside of North America.

THE MATCH

Before the match, Sean Mooney interviewed Diana Smith, trying to discover whether she was rooting for her brother or husband to win. Diana acknowledged the strain the match was putting on the Hart family before revealing that she just wanted neither man to get hurt. Smith came to the ring first, accompanied by countryman and boxing champion Lennox Lewis. The crowd roared their approval, but also cheered the entrance of the Champion Hart. Both men were fan favorites, but once the action started, fans made their allegiance clear, cheering Smith's moves while booing Hart's maneuvers.

The announcing duo of Vince McMahon and Bobby "The Brain" Heenan pointed out that the match would pit the strength of The Bulldog against the technical expertise of Hart. Pent-up emotion boiled over as the two shoved each other before engaging in a series of holds. Smith gave Hart a taste of his power by tossing Hit Man out of the ring, and Hart responded with a series of takedowns and pinning combinations. The 80,355 fans jammed into Wembley Stadium watched in awe as control of the match swung back and forth. Hart used a series of sleeper holds in order to wear down The British Bulldog. Then Smith hit Hart with an incredible assortment of power moves, including a Press Slam and a bone-jarring vertical suplex. Hart almost won the match when he hit a belly-to-back suplex into a bridge pin, but Smith escaped the pinning predicament.

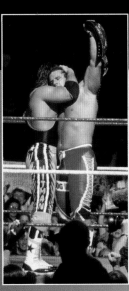

Each man thought he'd won the match by hitting their signature finishing move. Smith hoisted Hart into a Running Power Slam, but Hart was able to kick out before the referee counted three. Then Hart was able to kick out of a Superplex and put the Bulldog in the Sharpshooter, but Smith used his incredible strength to reach the ring ropes and force Hart to break the hold.

In a fitting twist, Smith used a technical move to finish off the Excellence of Execution. Smith whipped Hart into the ropes, and Hart prepared to hit Smith with a Sunset Flip. But mid-flip, Smith dropped his knees onto Hart's shoulders, leading to a Title-changing pinfall. The crowd exploded with delight for the new Champion, and Smith looked to bury the hatchet and shake the hand of the former Champion, his brother-in-law Bret. Twice Hart ignored the gesture, leading to loud disapproval from the fans. Eventually, Hart turned back and embraced Smith. Then Hart, his sister Diana, and the Bulldog all embraced, creating a lasting image to end an incredible match.

THE AFTERMATH

The British Bulldog held the Intercontinental Championship for two months before losing it to the "Heartbreak Kid" Shawn Michaels. Bret Hart sought a bigger prize, winning the WWE Championship for the first time just a few months later. While Hart's Title dreams became a beautiful reality, the family strife caused by his rivalry with Smith was just a minor blip compared to the eventual issues he had with his brother Owen.

SUMMERSLAM 2014
WWE WORLD HEAVYWEIGHT CHAMPIONSHIP MATCH

August 17, 2014

Staples Center
Los Angeles, California

THE LEAD-UP

After Daniel Bryan was forced to vacate his WWE World Heavyweight Championship, a Money in the Bank Match was set to crown a new Champion. John Cena was able to capture the Title, his 15th World Championship. At *SummerSlam*, Cena would defend his Title against Brock Lesnar. The challenger had some incredible momentum heading into the match—earlier in the year, he had done

JOHN CENA VS. BROCK LESNAR

THE MATCH

The two Superstars exchanged clubbing blows to start the match, and Lesnar managed to hit an early F-5 on the Champion. Cena kicked out of the pinfall attempt, which seemed to both amuse and anger The Beast. When Cena rose to his feet, Lesnar responded with two German Suplexes and then kneed Cena in the midsection. Cena managed to get in a flurry of punches, but Lesnar halted Cena's momentum with a series of knees to the ribs.

Again, Cena tried to take the offense with some punches, but Lesnar drove Cena to the mat with four consecutive German Suplexes. The challenger attempted a lazy cover, but Cena was able to kick out. Lesnar hit another German Suplex, and asked the official to see if Cena was ready to quit. When the Champion indicated he wanted to continue, Lesnar executed another German Suplex. He then set Cena up for another one, but Cena used a series of elbows and some flying punches off the ring ropes to stun the challenger. The Beast still attempted another F-5, but Cena reversed the move into an Attitude Adjustment. Lesnar kicked out after a two-count.

Lesnar sat up and began laughing at Cena. The Beast motioned for Cena to come at him. When Cena charged, the challenger took him down and began raining blows at the Champion's head. Once again, Lesnar ordered the official to ask if Cena was ready to quit. Cena honored his "Never Give Up" mantra, so Lesnar tried a new tact. The Beast delivered four rolling German Suplexes in succession, refusing to let go of Cena between each one. The announcers started openly wondering if it was time for the official to stop the match. Lesnar made the decision even more difficult when he delivered another set of three rolling German Suplexes. But Cena still refused to quit.

With Lesnar taunting the prone Champion, Cena demonstrated his incredible resiliency by pulling Lesnar down and putting the challenger in the STF. However, Lesnar was able to flip over and get Cena to release the hold. The challenger again rained down punches on Cena. Lesnar then picked up the Champion to deliver his second F-5 of the match. This time, Lesnar was able to keep Cena down for the three-count and capture his first WWE Championship in more than a decade. The announcers called the match the most dominant performance in a Championship Match in WWE history, with the final tally being 16 suplexes delivered by Lesnar.

THE AFTERMATH

John Cena got his Championship rematch the following month at *Night of Champions*. While the match was far more competitive, Cena did not regain the Championship. He did, however, win the match when Money in the Bank briefcase holder Seth Rollins interfered, attacking both competitors. Cena challenged Lesnar again at the *Royal Rumble*, but that attempt fell short as well. Lesnar held the WWE World Heavyweight Title through *WrestleMania 31*, but he lost the Title that night when Rollins used his Money in the Bank Title opportunity to turn the one-on-one Title Match into a Triple Threat Match. Rollins pinned challenger Roman Reigns to steal the Title from Lesnar.

TRIPLE H VS. THE ROCK

THE LEAD-UP

After years in the business, Triple H finally ascended the mountain, defeating Mankind for the WWE Championship (with a bit of assistance from Shane McMahon). Triple H and Chyna celebrated the Championship coronation with a speech to open the first-ever episode of *SmackDown* on UPN. The Rock interrupted the speech to challenge Triple H. When the WWE Champion claimed The Rock wasn't even in his league, WWE Commissioner Shawn Michaels came out to make the match official. Michaels didn't want any outside interference, so he made himself the Special Guest Referee for the match.

SMACKDOWN
WWE CHAMPIONSHIP MATCH

August 26, 1999

Kemper Arena
Kansas City, Missouri

THE MATCH

Triple H and Chyna came to the ring and The Game got in the face of the guest referee, his former D-Generation X running mate Shawn Michaels. Once The Rock came to the ring, he and Triple H started trading blows. The Rock tried to end things quickly with an early Rock Bottom, but Triple H countered the move with an elbow to the head. Triple H tried to then perform a Pedigree, but The Rock resisted it. When The Rock became tangled in the ropes, Chyna got in a shot of her own, but Michaels saw the action and warned her to not get involved.

As the two men battled up the ramp, Michaels followed them instead of starting a 10-count. The Commissioner knew the WWE Universe wanted to see a pinfall or submission decision. The two combatants worked their way back to the ring area, but just as The Rock was about to nail Triple H, Chyna hit the People's Champion with a low blow. Michaels decided he'd had enough and ejected Chyna from the match. While Michaels was arguing with Chyna on the ramp, The Rock hit Triple H with a DDT and looked to score a pin. Chyna's distraction gave the Champion enough time to recover and kick out of the pin.

Triple H may have lost one outside advantage, but another soon took its place. Shane McMahon came to the ring to argue that Michaels did not have the right to eject Chyna, and he then stayed at ringside. Shane cheered Triple H on as he kept The Rock down with knees and headlocks. The Rock dropped Triple H on the ropes and went for another pinfall, but Shane argued with Michaels, preventing the Commissioner from immediately starting to count the pin. When The Rock attempted to pin Triple H after a Swinging Neckbreaker, Shane again tried to distract Michaels, but this time The Rock took out Shane. He then executed the Rock Bottom and was about to hit the Champion with the People's Elbow, but the Heartbreak Kid stunned the WWE Universe by nailing The Rock with a Superkick. One Triple H Pedigree later, and Triple H had successfully defended his Championship. The WWE Universe was sickened by the sight of Triple H, Shane McMahon, Shawn Michaels, and Chyna embracing in the ring. They had to wonder who would dethrone the Champion when he had that type of support?

THE AFTERMATH

A number of Superstars came forward to challenge Triple H, including Mankind, The Rock, Kane, Undertaker, and Big Show. But Triple H chose Mr. McMahon as his Title challenger two weeks later. Vince tried to talk Triple H out of the match, but The Game continued to taunt the owner of WWE, challenging his manhood. Mr. McMahon took the bait, attacking the Champion and starting the match. His pride could have proven his undoing, as Triple H began to systematically dismantle Vince. But with Shane McMahon as the Special Guest Referee and an assist from Stone Cold Steve Austin, Vince McMahon pulled off the most shocking upset in WWE history, ending Triple H's first reign as the WWE Champion.

ROYAL RUMBLE MATCH

FOR THE VACANT

WWE CHAMPIONSHIP

THE LEAD-UP

Ric Flair entered the WWE in the fall of 1991 and immediately caused chaos. The self-proclaimed "Real World's Champion" aided Undertaker in his WWE Championship Match at *Survivor Series*, allowing The Phenom to win his first WWE Title. One week later, Hulk Hogan regained the Title in a controversial fashion. This lead to WWE President Jack Tunney's decision to vacate the Championship. In a historic first, he decided that whoever won the 1992 Royal Rumble Match would then become the new WWE Champion. Flair had boasted he was the real World Champion, and now he could prove it in the ring. Unfortunately, 29 other men looked to do the same, including four former WWE Champions.

It's a clear advantage to draw a higher number in the Rumble Match—the later one enters, the fewer competitors one needs to eliminate. Because of their roles in the vacated WWE Title situation, Jack Tunney stated that Hulk Hogan and Undertaker would draw numbers between 20 and 30. The third man in the controversy, Ric Flair, was considerably less lucky—he entered third. The British Bulldog, who had entered first, immediately began beating on the Nature Boy. Bobby "The Brain" Heenan lamented how unfair the situation was to Flair. Flair was able to hang on early, even though Gorilla Monsoon reminded Heenan that in the first four Royal Rumble Matches no one in the first five positions had ever made it to the end. In fact, the previous three winners had all entered 24th or later. Flair remained crafty, as he eliminated three competitors, including the Big Boss Man. This gave Flair a short period of rest when he was the only man in the ring.

The next man to enter the ring was Flair's long-time nemesis, "Rowdy" Roddy Piper. Piper attacked Flair and almost eliminated him until the next contestant, Jake "The Snake" Roberts, came to the ring. Initially it seemed Roberts was content to let Piper finish off Flair, but then the Snake showed his true colors and attacked the Rowdy one and Flair. Punishing Flair seemed to be a theme for the match, as every Superstar that entered the contest managed to get their licks in on the Nature Boy.

As the Rumble continued, the bout became more intense. Four former WWE Champions—Undertaker, "Macho Man" Randy Savage, Hulk Hogan, and Sgt. Slaughter—were among the last 10 entrants. The likelihood of Flair winning seemed remote, particularly with all the punishment he was taking, but the number of participants dwindled and Flair was still in it. After Flair helped the massive Sid Justice eliminate Savage, it was down to three men:

Flair, Justice, and Hulk Hogan. It looked like Flair's luck had finally run out and Hogan (the winner of the previous two *Royal Rumble* events) was poised to dump the Nature Boy from the ring. But Sid took the opportunity to eliminate the Hulkster, and as Hulk was angrily reacting to Sid, Flair dumped Sid, winning both the 1992 *Royal Rumble* and the vacant WWE Championship.

An emotional Ric Flair, surrounded by his advisors Mr. Perfect and Bobby "The Brain" Heenan, gave a heartfelt speech about the importance of the WWE Title in the sports-entertainment world. He knew, however, that he now had a target on his back, and Hogan, Justice, Savage, Piper, and Undertaker would all be coming after him and the Championship. Hogan was originally chosen to be Flair's challenger at *WrestleMania VIII*, but Savage received the nod after it was clear Hogan and Justice were going to have to settle their grudge at *WrestleMania*. Savage made the most of his opportunity, beating Flair at *WrestleMania* to win the WWE Championship for the second, and final, time in his career.

UNDERTAKER vs. SHAWN MICHAELS

THE LEAD-UP

As Undertaker's *WrestleMania* streak grew in stature, so did the number of Superstars seeking the immortality of facing The Deadman and ending the streak. Heading into *WrestleMania 25*, it was fitting that Mr. WrestleMania, Shawn Michaels, stepped up to face Undertaker. HBK had to defeat both JBL and Vladimir Kozlov to earn the *WrestleMania* match, but once he did, the mind games between the two iconic Superstars began. Michaels ambushed Undertaker, telling The Phenom that his light would overcome Undertaker's darkness. Undertaker warned the Showstopper that he might regret asking for the match as sometimes it was "hell trying to get to heaven."

WRESTLEMANIA 25
SINGLES MATCH

April 5, 2009

Reliant Stadium
Houston, Texas

THE MATCH

The two men danced around each other early, with Michaels using his quickness to dodge Undertaker's strikes, landing blows and kicks of his own. The Deadman grabbed HBK with a wristlock, and after several shoulder blocks, landed his Old School maneuver on Michaels. Undertaker went for a splash in the corner, but Michaels dodged it and wrapped The Phenom in a Figure-Four Leg Lock, but Undertaker managed to escape by clubbing Michaels with a series of punches. Undertaker dropped Michaels to the canvas with a Snake Eyes, a big boot, and a leg drop, but the Heartbreak Kid kicked out of the pinfall attempt at two. Undertaker attempted a Chokeslam, but Michaels countered it into a crossface submission hold. The Deadman broke the hold by getting to his feet and dropping Michaels with a side slam.

The two men regained their footing, and Mr. WrestleMania dodged Undertaker's strikes and countered them with chops of his own. HBK also landed a pair of atomic drops and flying forearms, and attempted a Sweet Chin Music, but Undertaker dropped to avoid the move. Michaels tried to lock The Deadman in a Figure-Four, but Undertaker countered into a submission move of his own, Hell's Gate. Michaels draped a leg over the bottom rope, which forced Undertaker to release the hold. Looking to get a break, Michaels rolled out of the ring, but The Deadman followed him, slamming HBK against the steel steps. Undertaker then went for a leg drop while Michaels lay on the apron, but the Showstopper moved out of the way. Michaels then dropped The Deadman with a baseball slide and tried to hit a moonsault, but The Phenom instead drove him into the floor.

Undertaker tried a running dive over the ropes onto Michaels, but HBK pulled a cameraman in front of The Deadman instead. Michaels made his way into the ring and demanded that the official start the 10-count on Undertaker so he could win the match. Undertaker barely made his way into the ring before the official could count to 10. Michaels attempted Sweet Chin Music, but Undertaker dodged it and caught Michaels with a Chokeslam instead. After a two-count, Undertaker lifted Michaels up, only to eat a Sweet Chin Music from HBK. Now it was Undertaker that kicked out of a pinfall attempt.

Michaels went to pick up Undertaker, but The Deadman grabbed HBK by the throat and set up a Last Ride. Michaels countered the move, but Undertaker countered the Showstopper's counter into a Last Ride. Amazingly, Michaels kicked out. Undertaker tried to toss Michaels out of the ring, but HBK skinned the cat and caught The Phenom in a leg scissors that The Deadman countered into a Tombstone and a near fall. Undertaker lifted Michaels for a second Tombstone, but HBK countered the move into a DDT. Michaels dropped an elbow off the top rope and a second Sweet Chin Music, but Undertaker kicked out again. After exchanging chops and punches, Michaels dropped The Deadman with another kick. He tried to follow up with another moonsault, but Undertaker caught him midair and performed another Tombstone Piledriver for a three-count, running his *WrestleMania* Streak to 17-0.

THE AFTERMATH

The universally acclaimed match won the 2009 Slammy for Match of the Year, but Michaels clearly wanted another shot at the Streak more than the honor, so he challenged Undertaker to a rematch at *WrestleMania XXVI* while accepting the award. Undertaker was more focused on defending his World Heavyweight Championship, so The Deadman declined. After failing to win the 2010 *Royal Rumble*, Michaels ended up costing Undertaker the World Heavyweight Championship at the 2010 *Elimination Chamber* event. Undertaker finally agreed to face Michaels, but only if HBK put his career on the line in the match. Michaels accepted and, after another brilliant combination, Undertaker continued his Streak to 18-0 and ended one of the greatest careers in WWE history.

ULTIMATE WARRIOR VS. "MACHO KING" RANDY SAVAGE

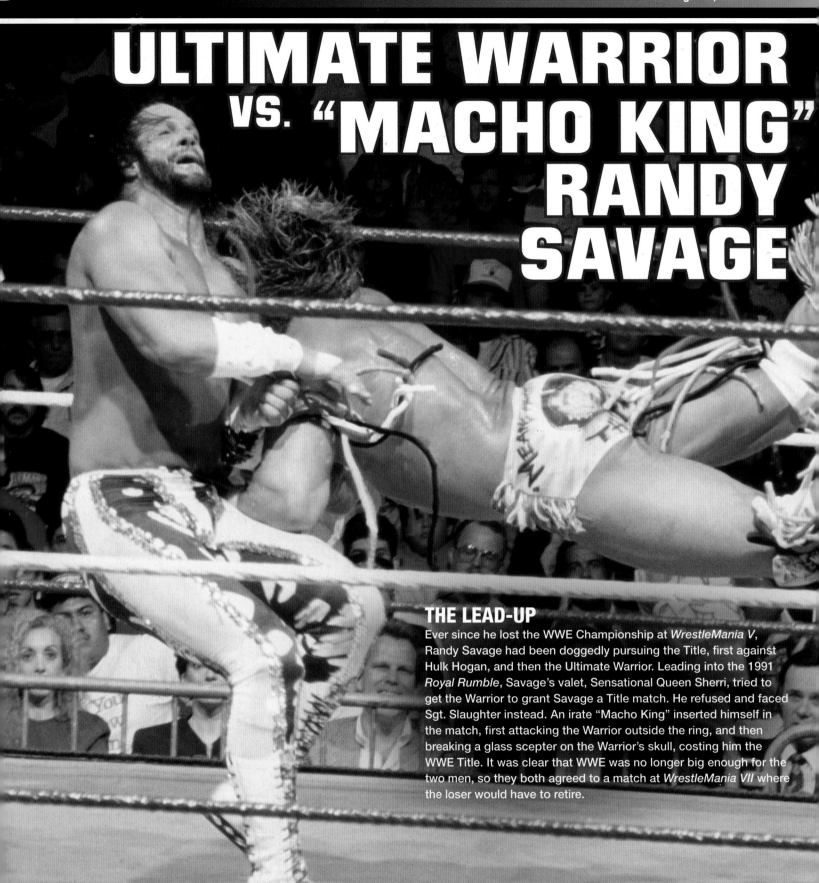

THE LEAD-UP

Ever since he lost the WWE Championship at *WrestleMania V*, Randy Savage had been doggedly pursuing the Title, first against Hulk Hogan, and then the Ultimate Warrior. Leading into the 1991 *Royal Rumble*, Savage's valet, Sensational Queen Sherri, tried to get the Warrior to grant Savage a Title match. He refused and faced Sgt. Slaughter instead. An irate "Macho King" inserted himself in the match, first attacking the Warrior outside the ring, and then breaking a glass scepter on the Warrior's skull, costing him the WWE Title. It was clear that WWE was no longer big enough for the two men, so they both agreed to a match at *WrestleMania VII* where the loser would have to retire.

THE MATCH

Both men started the match cautiously, perhaps afraid to make a mistake with their careers on the line. While Savage took an early advantage, the Warrior demonstrated his incredible power with a shoulder block that knocked the "Macho King" to the ground. Savage regrouped outside the ring, attacking the Warrior from behind while he was arguing with Sensational Queen Sherri. The advantage did not last, and the Warrior delivered a slam and an atomic drop to Savage. Warrior lifted Savage for another slam just as Sherri entered the ring to interfere. Warrior simply tossed the "Macho King" in her direction and they both went down.

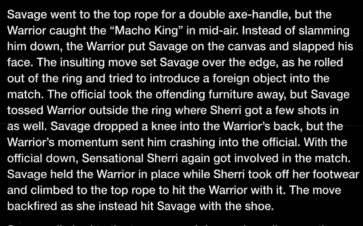

Savage went to the top rope for a double axe-handle, but the Warrior caught the "Macho King" in mid-air. Instead of slamming him down, the Warrior put Savage on the canvas and slapped his face. The insulting move set Savage over the edge, as he rolled out of the ring and tried to introduce a foreign object into the match. The official took the offending furniture away, but Savage tossed Warrior outside the ring where Sherri got a few shots in as well. Savage dropped a knee into the Warrior's back, but the Warrior's momentum sent him crashing into the official. With the official down, Sensational Sherri again got involved in the match. Savage held the Warrior in place while Sherri took off her footwear and climbed to the top rope to hit the Warrior with it. The move backfired as she instead hit Savage with the shoe.

Savage climbed to the top rope and dropped an elbow on the Warrior. Normally the "Macho King" would then go for the pin against his opponent, but instead Savage returned to the top rope four additional times for a total of five flying elbows. Everyone assumed the match was over, but the Warrior kicked out before the three-count. The Warrior dug deep and found the strength to deliver a series of clotheslines, a press slam, and his big Splash. But Savage surprised the Warrior as well when he managed to kick out.

The Warrior looked to the heavens, trying to figure out his next move. He seemed conflicted and stepped outside of the ring ropes and onto the apron, leading the announcers to speculate that he might be leaving. In the confusion, Savage recovered and knocked Warrior to the floor below. He draped the Warrior's neck on the guard rail and had Sherri hold the Warrior in place while Savage climbed to the top turnbuckle. His plan was to drop an elbow on the Warrior and drive his neck into the rail. But Warrior knocked Sherri away and moved in time for Savage to hit the rail instead. The Warrior brought Savage back into the ring and hit three flying shoulder blocks, pinning the "Macho King" with a single foot on his chest.

Furious that Savage lost the match, Sherri entered the ring and started assaulting Savage with a series of kicks. Savage's former manager, Miss Elizabeth, who was watching the match in the crowd, made her way to the ring and tossed Sherri out of the ring. Savage was initially wary of Miss Elizabeth's intentions, but eventually shared an emotional moment with her. The couple later married at *SummerSlam 1991*. When Jake Roberts attacked the newlyweds at their wedding reception, Savage began an extended campaign to be reinstated. His efforts finally bore fruit in November when Savage got his in-ring revenge on the Snake.

INDEX

NUMBERS

1-2-3 Kid, The, ... 102-103

A

Aksana, ... 73
Ali, Muhammad, ... 33
Alliance, The, ... 157
Ambrose, Dean, ... 28-29, 105, 132
Andre the Giant, ... 80-81, 116-117, 153
Angle, Kurt, ... 30-31, 39, 42-43, 62-63, 66-67, 79, 82, 84-85, 109, 112-113, 141, 153, 156-157, 160-161, 170-171, 177
Armageddon 2000, ... 160-161
Armageddon 2001, ... 171
Armageddon 2002, ... 119
A-Team, The, ... 33
Attitude Era, ... 94
Austin, "Stone Cold" Steve, ... 18-19, 25, 30-31, 41, 47, 50-51, 57, 66-67, 79, 106-107, 129, 131, 140-141, 148-149, 157, 160-161, 176-177, 185-187, 199
Authority, The, ... 29, 61, 105, 126-127, 180
AWA (American Wrestling Association), ... 36, 139

B

Backlash 2001, ... 186-187
Backlash 2002, ... 41
Backlash 2004, ... 134-135
Backlash 2005, ... 38, 101
Backlash 2007, ... 158-159
Backlash: In Your House, ... 149
Backlund, Bob, ... 22-23, 36-37, 69, 75, 121
Balor, Finn, ... 133
Banks, Sasha, ... 114-115, 172-173
Barbie, ... 135
Barrett, Wade, ... 65, 182-183
Bass, "Outlaw" Ron, ... 152-153
Batista, ... 21, 38-39, 100-101, 104-105, 122-123, 126-127, 134
Battleground 2014, ... 88-89
Battleground 2015, ... 133
Bayley, ... 114-115, 172-173
Bearer, Paul, ... 185
Beefcake, Brutus "The Barber" 92, 152-153, 167
Benjamin, Shelton, ... 38-39
Benoit, Chris, ... 38, 91, 95, 130-131, 187
Big Boss Man, ... 31, 201
Big Show, ... 16-17, 30-31, 43, 57, 65, 79, 84, 87, 141, 148-149, 153, 155, 182-183, 199
Bigelow, Bam Bam, ... 146-147
Bischoff, Eric, ... 38, 83-84, 118, 135
Black Demon, ... 46
Blackman, Steve, ... 141
Blassie, "Classy" Freddie, ... 22, 92
Bliss, Alexa, ... 173
Booker T, ... 31, 65, 67, 79, 118-119
Bradshaw, ... 31
Bragging Rights 2010, ... 44-45
British Bulldog. See Smith, "British Bulldog" Davey Boy
British Bulldogs, The, ... 92-93, 194
Brothers of Destruction, ... 79, 95, 109, 140, 186-187
Bryan, Daniel, ... 21, 44-45, 60-61, 65, 105, 126-127, 145, 182-183, 193, 196
Buchanan, Bull, ... 141

C

Cactus Jack, ... 86-87, 134-135
Carey, Drew, ... 141
Carlito, ... 39
Cena, John, ... 20-21, 26-27, 29, 53, 60-61, 65, 77, 84-85, 113, 122, 124-125, 132-133, 142-145, 154-155, 158-159, 164, 180-181, 188-189, 196-197
Cesaro, ... 48-49, 132
Charlotte, ... 73, 114-115, 172-173
Christian, ... 31, 52-53, 94-95
Chyna, ... 11, 19, 198-199
Corporation, The, ... 57, 148-149
Corre, The, ... 65
"Cult of Personality" 125
CWC (Capitol Wrestling Corporation), ... 14
Cyber Sunday 2007, ... 165

D

Daivari, ... 85
Dallas, Bo, ... 48-49
Davis, "Dangerous" Danny, ... 93, 153
Del Rio, Alberto, ... 27, 53, 65, 125, 133
D-Generation X (DX), ... 10-11, 16-18, 57, 98-99, 103, 108, 119, 165, 185, 199
DiBiase, "Million Dollar Man" Ted, ... 54-55, 80-81, 102, 166
DiBiase Jr., Ted, ... 65
Diesel, ... 59, 65, 128-129
Douglas, Buster, ... 167
Dream Team, The, ... 93
Dudley, Bubba Ray, ... 94-95
Dudley, Devon, ... 94-95
Dudley, Spike, ... 94-95
Dudley Boyz, ... 94-95
Duggan, "Hacksaw" Jim, ... 146, 153
Dynamite Kid, The, ... 92-93, 194

E

ECW (Extreme Championship Wrestling), ... 66, 78-79, 122, 135, 154-155, 157, 177
ECW Championship, ... 122, 155
ECW One Night Stand, ... 154-155
ECW World Championship, ... 154-155
Edge, ... 12-13, 38-39, 45, 65, 85, 91, 94-95, 123, 142-143, 155, 174
Elimination Chamber 2010, ... 203
Elimination Chamber 2012, ... 182-183
Elimination Chamber 2013, ... 144
Elimination Chamber 2014, ... 28-29
Elimination Chamber 2015, ... 132-133
Elizabeth, Miss, ... 7, 166-167, 205
Emma, ... 72-73
European Championship, ... 71, 130, 162-163, 170
Evolution, ... 29, 91, 100-101, 104-105, 127
Extreme Rules 2009, ... 174
Extreme Rules 2012, ... 192-193
Extreme Rules 2014, ... 105

F

Faarooq, ... 31, 141
Fabulous Moolah, The, ... 34
Flair, "Nature Boy" Ric, ... 4, 8-9, 15, 40, 54-55, 67, 79, 90-91, 96-97, 101, 134, 142-143, 179, 200-201
Foley, Mick, ... 25, 86-87, 134-135, 149, 160-161
Four Horsemen, ... 97
Fox, Alicia, ... 73

G

Gallows, Luke, ... 17
Garea, Tony, ... 139
Goldberg, Bill, ... 111
Goldust, ... 31, 50-51, 89
Goodfather, The, ... 141
Graham, "Superstar" Billy, ... 36, 68-69, 120-121
Grand Master Sexay, ... 141
Grand Wizard, ... 47, 121
Great American Bash 2004, The, ... 111
Guerrero, Eddie, ... 63, 110-111
Guerrero, Vickie, ... 45
Gunn, Billy, ... 31, 57, 141

H

Hall, Scott, ... 41
Hansen, Stan, ... 36-37, 68
Hardy, Jeff, ... 31, 70-71, 94-95, 141, 158, 174-175
Hardy, Matt, ... 31, 94-95, 141, 158
Hardy Boyz, ... 31, 70, 94-95, 141, 158
Harper, Luke, ... 28-29, 88-89
Harris, Husky, ... 65
Hart, Bret "The Hitman" 50-51, 54-55, 74-75, 93, 102-103, 106-107, 128-129, 146-147, 163, 178-179, 185, 194-195
Hart, Helen, ... 51, 75
Hart, Jimmy, ... 93
Hart, Owen, 50-51, 74-75, 103, 107, 162-163, 195
Hart, Stu, ... 51, 75
Hart Foundation, ... 50-51, 93, 107, 163, 179, 194
Heenan, Bobby "The Brain" 54, 80, 116, 195, 201
Hell in the Cell 2015, ... 133
Hennig, Curt, ... 97
Henry, Mark, ... 11, 182
Hercules, ... 153
Heyman, Paul, ... 76, 79, 83, 155
Hogan, Hulk, ... 4, 22-23, 32-33, 40-41, 47, 55, 80-81, 116-117, 146, 153, 166-167, 190-191, 200-201, 204
Honky Tonk Man, ... 7, 141, 152-153
Hornswoggle, ... 65
Hurricane, The, ... 31

I

In Your House: Badd Blood, ... 184-185
In Your House: Canadian Stampede, ... 50-51
Intercontinental Championship, 4, 6-7, 10-11, 38, 44-45, 51, 58-59, 89, 110, 130-135, 142, 153, 170, 178-179, 186-187, 190-191, 194-195
Iron Sheik, ... 22-23, 37, 92-93
IRS, ... 102

J

J&J Security, ... 181
Jackson, Ezekiel, ... 65
James, Mickie, ... 35, 150-151
JBL, ... 100, 111, 202
Jericho, "Y2J" Chris, ... 16-17, 31, 53, 66-67, 79, 95, 118-119, 130-131, 136-137, 187, 192-193
Jeri-Show, ... 16-17
Judgment Day 2007, ... 159
Justice, Sid, ... 201

K

Kane, ... 25, 30-31, 38-39, 65, 79, 84, 95, 105, 108-109, 118-119, 132, 140-141, 185-187, 199
Khali, The Great, ... 65, 182-183
Kidd, Tyson, ... 52-53
King of the Ring 1993, ... 146-147
King of the Ring 1994, ... 74
King of the Ring 1998, ... 24-25
King of the Ring 2000, ... 108, 170
King of the Ring 2001, ... 156-157
King of the Ring 2002, ... 42-43, 82-83
Kingston, Kofi, ... 45
Koloff, Ivan, ... 15
Kozlov, Vladimir, ... 202
Kruger, Leo, ... 48

L

Lashley, Bobby, ... 122
Lauper, Cyndi, ... 33
Laurinaitis, John, ... 27
Lawler, Jerry "The King" 147
Lee, AJ, ... 53, 73, 183
Legion of Doom, ... 50-51
Lesnar, Brock, ... 43, 62-63, 76-77, 82-83, 110-111, 169, 180-181, 196-197
Lewis, Lennox, ... 195
Lita, ... 34-35, 95, 142-143, 151
Living Colour, ... 125
Love, Dude, ... 25
Luger, Lex, ... 146
Lynch, Becky, ... 114-115, 172-173

M

Maddox, Brad, ... 60
Main Event, The, ... 80-81
Mankind, ... 24-25, 56-57, 129, 148-149, 163, 199
Marella, Santino, ... 52-53, 65, 182-183
Masters, Chris, ... 65
Maven, ... 31
McGillicutty, Michael, ... 65
McMahon, Linda, ... 87, 108
McMahon, Mr. 8, 18, 25-27, 31, 40, 42, 47, 57, 60, 67, 78-79, 87, 91, 97, 108-109, 124, 148-149, 160-161, 164, 177, 186, 199
McMahon, Shane, ... 57, 78-79, 97, 108-109, 156-157, 198-199
McMahon, Stephanie, ... 31, 61, 73, 78-79, 83, 97, 108, 157, 170-171
McMahon, Vince, ... 195
McMahon-Helmsley Faction, ... 108
Mega Powers, ... 166
Michaels, "The Heartbreak Kid" Shawn, ... 8-9, 16-19, 38-39, 51, 58-59, 84-85, 98-99, 107, 112-113, 118-119, 128-129, 136-137, 149, 158-159, 163, 165, 168-169, 184-185, 195, 198-199, 202-203
Miz, The, ... 17, 65, 125
Monday Night Raw. See Raw
Money in the Bank 2011, ... 26-27, 124
Money in the Bank 2012, ... 52-53
Money in the Bank 2013, ... 60
Money in the Bank 2014, ... 105
Money in the Bank 2015, ... 133
Monsoon, Gorilla, ... 23, 201
Montreal Screwjob, ... 27, 51, 185
Mooney, Sean, ... 195
Morrison, John, ... 65
Mountie, The, ... 54
MTV, ... 33
Mysterio, Rey, ... 27, 45, 65, 124-125

N

Nash, Kevin, ... 41
Nation of Domination, ... 10
Neidhart, Jim "The Anvil" 50, 74, 93, 103, 107, 179, 194
Neville, Adrian, ... 49, 132
New Age Outlaws, ... 88
New Year's Revolution 2006, ... 85, 142, 150
Nexus, ... 65
Night of Champions 2009, ... 174
Night of Champions 2014, ... 197
No Holds Barred, ... 167
No Mercy 2000, ... 109, 170
No Mercy 2007, ... 164-165, 170-171
No Mercy 2008, ... 137
No Way Out 2000, ... 86-87
No Way Out 2001, ... 141, 161, 171
No Way Out 2002, ... 31, 67
No Way Out 2004, ... 63, 110-111
No Way Out 2007, ... 122
NWA (National Wrestling Alliance), ... 14-15, 36, 139
nWo (New World Order), ... 40-41, 97, 103

NXT, ...48-49, 172-173
NXT Arrival, ...72-73
NXT Championship, ...48-49, 132-133
NXT TakeOver: Brooklyn, ...114-115, 173
NXT TakeOver: Respect, ... 115
NXT TakeOver: Rival, ...172-173
NXT Women's Championship, ...72-73, 114-115, 172-173

O

One Night Stand 2005, ... 135
Orndorff, "Mr. Wonderful" Paul, ...32-33
Orton, "Cowboy" Bob, ...32-33
Orton, "The Viper" Randy, ...20-21, 61, 65, 90-91, 104-105, 126-127, 134-135, 159, 164-165
Otunga, David, ... 65
Owens, Kevin, ...132-133

P

Paige, ...72-73, 172
Palumbo, Chuck, ... 31
Patrick, Nick, ... 67
Patterson, Pat, ...33, 46-47
Payback 2014, ...104-105
Perfect, Mr. 31, 96-97, 146, 178-179, 191, 201
Pillman, Brian, ... 50, 107
Piper, "Rowdy" Roddy, ...32-33, 54-55, 116, 201
Piper's Pit, ... 116
Punk, CM, ...17, 26-27, 65, 124-125, 144-145, 174-175, 192-193

R

Race, Harley, ... 153
Ramon, Razor, ...58-59, 96, 102, 146
Raven, ... 141
Raw, ...9, 26, 38-39, 44-45, 53, 56-57, 60, 65, 70-71, 73, 78-79, 83-84, 91, 96-97, 100, 102-103, 113, 124-125, 135, 142-145, 158-159, 162-163
Regal, William, ... 65, 71, 161, 172
Reigns, Roman, ...28-29, 105, 181, 197
Rhodes, Cody, ...52-53, 182-183
Rhodes, "The American Dream" Dusty, ...120-121
Rhyno, ... 95
Rikishi, ...31, 89, 140-141, 160-161, 171
Riley, Alex, ... 65
Roberts, Jake "The Snake" 4, 152-153, 201, 205
Rock, The, ...10-11, 40-43, 56-57, 66-67, 79, 82-83, 87, 108-109, 134, 140-141, 144, 148-149, 153, 160-161, 170-171, 176-177, 188-189, 193, 198-199
Rogers, "Nature Boy" Buddy, ...14-15
Rollins, Seth, ...28-29, 105, 127, 133, 180-181, 197
Ross, Jim, ... 19, 25
Rowan, Erick, ...28-29, 88-89
Royal Rumble 1988, ... 80
Royal Rumble 1990, ... 190, 201
Royal Rumble 1991, ... 191, 201, 204
Royal Rumble 1992, ...55, 200-201
Royal Rumble 1995, ... 128
Royal Rumble 1997, ... 106
Royal Rumble 1998, ... 18, 148, 185
Royal Rumble 1999, ... 57
Royal Rumble 2000, ... 86
Royal Rumble 2001, ...130-131, 140-141, 161, 171, 177
Royal Rumble 2002, ...30-31, 67, 70, 97
Royal Rumble 2004, ... 134
Royal Rumble 2005, ... 100, 112
Royal Rumble 2006, ... 85, 143
Royal Rumble 2007, ...122-123
Royal Rumble 2010, ... 203
Royal Rumble 2011, ...64-65
Royal Rumble 2012, ...182-183
Royal Rumble 2013, ... 144, 189, 193
Royal Rumble 2014, ... 21, 126, 197
Royal Rumble 2015, ...180-181
RVD. *See* Van Dam (Rob)
Ryan, Mason, ... 65

S

Sammartino, Bruno, ...14-15, 23, 36-37, 68-69, 138-139
Sandow, Damien, ...52-53
Saturday Night's Main Event, ... 92
Saturn, Perry, ... 31, 130, 141
Savage, "Macho Man" Randy, ...4, 6-7, 81, 96, 152-153, 166-167, 191, 201, 204-205
Sensational Sherri, ...55, 167, 204-205
Shamrock, Ken, ...11, 50-51, 57, 106-107
Sheamus, ... 45, 65, 183
Shield, The, ...28-29, 104-105, 127, 153
Showdown at Shea 1976, ... 68
Showdown at Shea 1980, ...138-139
Sin Cara, ...52-53
Skaaland, Arnold, ... 22, 37, 69
Slammy Awards 2009, ... 203
Slaughter, Sgt. 46-47, 201, 204
SmackDown, ...39, 42, 44-45, 53, 62-63, 78, 83, 100-101, 110, 118, 175, 198-199
Smith, "British Bulldog" Davey Boy, ...50, 54-55, 92-93, 107, 129, 162-163, 194-195, 201
Smith, Diana, ... 194
Snow, Al, ...31, 141
Snuka, "Superfly" Jimmy, ...32-33
Snuka, Tamina, ... 73
Socko, Mr. 57
St. Valentine's Massacre, ... 57
Stardust, ... 89
Steamboat, Ricky "The Dragon".......4-7, 152-153
Steele, George "The Animal" 7
Storm, Lance, ... 31
Stratus, Trish, ...34-35, 150-151
Strowman, Braun, ... 89
Summer Rae, ... 73
SummerSlam 1991, ...178-179, 191, 205
SummerSlam 1992, ...194-195
SummerSlam 1994, ...74-75, 103
SummerSlam 1995, ... 59
SummerSlam 1997, ... 51
SummerSlam 1998, ...10-11
SummerSlam 1999, ... 11
SummerSlam 2000, ... 94, 109
SummerSlam 2002, ...19, 43, 82-83, 98-99
SummerSlam 2003, ... 62
SummerSlam 2004, ... 91, 135
SummerSlam 2008, ...12-13
SummerSlam 2009, ...174-175
SummerSlam 2011, ... 27, 125
SummerSlam 2012, ... 53
SummerSlam 2013, ...60-61, 145
SummerSlam 2014, ...77, 180-181, 196-197
SummerSlam 2015, ... 77, 173
Super Bowl XXXIII, ... 57
Survivor Series 1987, ...117, 152-153
Survivor Series 1990, ... 153
Survivor Series 1991, ...54-55, 200
Survivor Series 1992, ... 96, 179
Survivor Series 1994, ... 75, 103
Survivor Series 1995, ... 128, 153
Survivor Series 1996, ... 129
Survivor Series 1997, ... 51, 185
Survivor Series 1998, ... 11, 57, 148
Survivor Series 1999, ... 140, 153, 170
Survivor Series 2000, ... 171
Survivor Series 2001, ... 78, 157
Survivor Series 2002, ...43, 99, 118-119, 153
Survivor Series 2003, ... 63
Survivor Series 2005, ... 85
Survivor Series 2006, ... 35
Survivor Series 2007, ... 165
Survivor Series 2012, ... 153
Survivor Series 2014, ... 180

T

T, Mr. 32-33
Taboo Tuesday 2004, ...90-91
Taboo Tuesday 2005, ...84-85, 113
Tag Team Championship (Unified), ...16-17
Tag Team Championship (World), ... 23, 25, 70, 92, 131, 139, 158, 163, 178-179, 194
Tag Team Championship (WWE), ...88-89, 94-95, 110, 186-187
Tatanka, ... 146
Tazz, ... 141
Team Alliance, ...78-79
Team Austin, ...50-51
Team Flair, ...54-55
Team Honky Tonk, ...152-153
Team Piper, ...54-55
Team Savage, ...152-153
Team WWE, ...78-79
Tensai, ...52-53
Test, ... 31
Thesz, Lou, ... 14, 151
This Tuesday in Texas, ... 55
TLC III, ... 95
TLC 2009, ...16-17
TLC 2013, ...20-21
Tough Enough, ... 31
Triple H, ... 10-11, 16-17, 19-20, 29-31, 38, 41-42, 60-61, 67, 86-87, 91, 98-101, 104-105, 108-109, 118-119, 124, 126-127, 131, 141, 160-161, 164-165, 168-171, 180-181, 186-187, 198-199
Tunney, Jack, ...55, 58, 81, 200-201
Two-Man Power Trip, ...186-187
Tyson, Mike, ...18-19

U

UFC (Ultimate Fighting Championship), ... 76
Ultimate Warrior, ...47, 190-191, 204-205
Umaga, ... 164
Undertaker, ... 12-13, 17, 24-25, 30-31, 42-43, 51, 55, 63, 70-71, 76-77, 79, 95, 108-109, 122-123, 140, 145, 149, 153, 160-161, 168-169, 171, 175, 184-187, 196, 199-203
Undisputed Championship, ...30-31, 41-43, 66-67, 70-71, 82-83
Unforgiven 2005, ... 84
Unforgiven 2006, ...34-35, 143
Unforgiven 2008, ... 137
United States Championship, ...44-45, 110, 132-133
UPN, ... 198
Uso, Jey, ...88-89
Uso, Jimmy, ...88-89
Usos, The, ...88-89

V

Vachon, Luna, ... 147
Vader, ... 163
Valentine, Greg "The Hammer" 92
Van Dam, Rob (RVD), ...79, 118-119, 154-155
Vengeance 2001, ...66-67
Vengeance 2002, ...41-43, 82
Vengeance 2005, ... 39, 101, 113
Vengeance 2006, ... 155
Venis, Val, ... 31
Virgil, ...54, 80-81
Volkoff, Nikolai, ...23, 92-93, 102

W

Warlord, ...54-55
WCW (World Championship Wrestling), ...78-79, 96-97, 103, 139, 156-157, 177, 191
WCW Championship, ...66-67, 131
World Heavyweight Championship, ...20-21, 29, 38-39, 45, 52-53, 65, 76-77, 83, 91, 99-101, 105, 118-119, 122-123, 126-127, 133, 135, 137, 174-175, 180-183, 193, 196-197, 203
WrestleMania I, ...23, 32-33, 92, 139
WrestleMania II, ... 92, 139
WrestleMania III, ...4, 6-7, 33, 80-81, 116-117, 153
WrestleMania IV, ...7, 81, 166-167
WrestleMania V, ...166-167
WrestleMania VII, ...47, 190-191, 204-205
WrestleMania VIII, ... 201
WrestleMania IX, ... 146
WrestleMania X, ... 74, 102
WrestleMania XII, ...106, 128-129
WrestleMania 13, ...106-107
WrestleMania XIV, ...18-19, 98, 107, 185
WrestleMania XV, ...57, 148-149, 177
WrestleMania 2000, ... 87, 130
WrestleMania X-Seven, ...94-95, 141, 176-177
WrestleMania X8, ... 31, 40-41, 58-59, 67, 109, 131
WrestleMania XIX, ...30, 62, 136-137, 177
WrestleMania XX, ... 63
WrestleMania 21, ... 38-39, 53, 100-101, 112-113
WrestleMania 22, ...85, 150-151, 154
WrestleMania 23, ...122-123, 158
WrestleMania XXIV, ...8-9
WrestleMania 25, ...202-203
WrestleMania XXVI, ... 17, 203
WrestleMania XXVII, ...64-65, 111, 168, 188
WrestleMania XXVIII, ... 168-169, 183, 188-189, 192
WrestleMania 29, ...53, 144-145, 189
WrestleMania 30, ...21, 61, 76-77, 126-127, 169, 196
WrestleMania 31, ... 77, 105, 132, 181, 197
WWE Championship, ...7, 11, 14-15, 18-23, 25-27, 30, 33, 36-37, 41, 47, 51, 55-57, 60-63, 65-69, 74-75, 79-87, 96, 100, 102-103, 106-111, 113, 116-117, 120-122, 124-125, 128-129, 131, 139, 141-143, 145-146, 148-149, 153-155, 158-161, 164-167, 170-171, 176-179, 185-187, 189-193, 195, 197-201, 204
WWE Divas Championship, ... 73, 172
WWE Draft 2005, ... 101
WWE Hall of Fame, ... 15, 23, 35, 37, 47, 139
WWE Women's Championship, ...34-35, 150-151
Wyatt, Bray, ...21, 28-29, 77
Wyatt Family, ...21, 28-29, 88-89

X

X-Pac, ... 11, 103

Y

Yokozuna, ... 146

Z

Zayn, Sami, ...48-49, 132
Zbyszko, Larry, ...138-139
Zeus, ... 167
Ziggler, Dolph, ...44-45, 52-53

Development Editor
Matt Buchanan

Senior Development Editor
Jennifer Sims

Senior Book Designer
Dan Caparo

Senior Production Designers
Areva
Wil Cruz

VP & Publisher
Mike Degler

Editorial Manager
Tim Fitzpatrick

Design and Layout Manager
Tracy Wehmeyer

Licensing
Christian Sumner
Paul Giacomotto

Marketing
Katie Hemlock

Digital Publishing
Julie Asbury
Tim Cox
Shaida Boroumand

Operations Manager
Stacey Beheler

CONSUMER PRODUCTS

Global Publishing Manager
Steve Pantaleo

**Vice President,
Licensing North America**
Jess Richardson

**Executive Vice President,
Consumer Products**
Casey Collins

PHOTO DEPARTMENT

Josh Tottenham, Frank Vitucci,
Jamie Nelson, Melissa Halladay,
Mike Moran, Georgiana Dallas,
and JD Sestito

ARCHIVES
Archivist
Ben Brown

CREATIVE SERVICES

**Senior Vice President,
Creative Services**
Stan Stanski

Creative Director
John Jones

Project Manager
Sara Vazquez

Cover Design
Adam McGinnis

LEGAL
**Vice President, Intellectual
Property**
Lauren Dienes-Middlen

DK/Prima Games, a division of Penguin Random House LLC
6081 East 82nd Street, Suite #400
Indianapolis, IN 46250

ISBN: 978-1-4654-5158-3

Printing Code: The rightmost double-digit number is the year of the
book's printing; the rightmost single-digit number is the number of the
book's printing. For example, 16-1 shows that the first printing of the book
occurred in 2016.

19 18 17 16   4 3 2 1

Printed in China.

WWE'S SPECIAL THANKS: Tom Casiello, Dave Kapoor, Alex Reznik, Kieran
Bent, and Craig Tello.

ABOUT THE AUTHOR

Dean Miller has written or co-written seven books on sports entertainment,
programming, and sports. He has edited books for more than two decades,
and currently serves as the Managing Editor at Ripley's Believe It or Not! He
currently resides in Orlando, Florida, with his wife Fran Hatton, and his three
children, John, Alice, and Margaret.

Dean Miller would like to thank the Prima and WWE teams for giving him
such an incredible opportunity to revisit the rich history of WWE. The
match suggestions and lists from fellow authors, WWE.com, and fans
were invaluable in picking these 100 matches—a list that could have easily
been 500 or more. He'd also like to apologize to his family for hogging the
television over several months all in the name of "research." Finally, he'd
like to dedicate the book to his mother for being such a pillar of support
throughout his professional and personal life.